D1152336

Pascal and Delphi
Programming

61069

MACMILLAN MASTER SERIES

Accounting
Advanced English Language
Advanced Pure Mathematics
Arabic
Banking
Basic Management
Biology
British Politics
Business Administration
Business Communication
Business Law
C Programming
C++ Programming
Catering Theory
Chemistry
COBOL Programming
Communication
Databases
Economic and Social History
Economics
Electrical Engineering
Electronic and Electrical Calculations
Electronics
English as a Foreign Language
English Grammar
English Language
English Literature
French
French 2
German
German 2

Global Information Systems
Human Biology
Internet
Italian
Italian 2
Java
Manufacturing
Marketing
Mathematics
Mathematics for Electrical and
    Electronic Engineering
Microsoft Office
Modern British History
Modern European History
Modern World History
Pascal and Delphi Programming
Philosophy
Photography
Physics
Psychology
Science
Shakespeare
Social Welfare
Sociology
Spanish
Spanish 2
Statistics
Study Skills
Visual Basic
World Religions

Macmillan Master Series
Series Standing Order ISBN 0–333–69343–4
(outside North America only)

You can receive future titles in this series as they are published by placing a standing order.
Please contact your bookseller or, in case of difficulty, write to us at the address below with
your name and address, the title of the series and the ISBN quoted above.

Customer Services Department, Macmillan Distribution Ltd
Houndmills, Basingstoke, Hampshire RG21 6XS, England

Mastering

Pascal and Delphi Programming

William Buchanan, BSc, CEng, PhD
Senior Lecturer
Department of Electrical and Electronic Engineering
Napier University
Edinburgh

Series Editor
William Buchanan

MACMILLAN

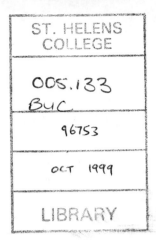
© William Buchanan 1998

Published 1998 by
MACMILLAN PRESS LTD
Houndmills, Basingstoke, Hampshire RG21 6XS
and London
Companies and representatives
throughout the world

ISBN 0–333–73007–0

A catalogue record for this book is available
from the British Library.

This book is printed on paper suitable for recycling and
made from fully managed and sustained forest sources.

10   9   8   7   6   5   4   3   2   1
07   06   05   04   03   02   01   00   99   98

Printed and bound in Great Britain by
Biddles Ltd, Guildford and King's Lynn

Contents

Preface

Pascal is one of the most widely used PC-based programming languages. It is also one of the best programming languages to teach good software development techniques. This book provides an introduction to programming with Pascal and extends this to show how Borland Delphi, which uses Pascal, is used to develop Microsoft Windows programs.

After many years of teaching software development to undergraduates I have found that C and C++ suffer from several pitfalls, especially in parameter passing, pointers and the lack of strong data type checking. These areas may provide flexibility for experienced programmers, but for novices they add to the complexity of the program.

I have also been involved with extensive consultancy work and book writing over the years and I have used C, C++ (Borland C++ and Visual C++), HTML/JavaScript, Java, Visual Basic, Turbo Pascal and Borland Delphi. From this, I can say, without doubt, that Delphi is the easiest and most powerful development system I have found. It provides a great deal of flexibility in that it doesn't try to write all the code for the programmer, and basically it provides a framework for the user to add code to.

The best way to learn a programming language is to write real applications. For this reason the book includes many real-life applications. Chapters 13 to 20 cover some practical applications, such as: software interrupts, hardware interrupts, graphics, date and time, system commands, RS-232 and parallel ports.

The book thus covers three main areas:

- Pascal programming (Chapters 1 to 12).
- Pascal applications (Chapters 13 to 20).
- Delphi programming (Chapters 21 to 26).

Further information and source code can be found on the WWW page:

```
http://www.eece.napier.ac.uk/~bill_b/pascal.html
```

Help from myself can be sought using the email address:

```
w.buchanan@napier.ac.uk
```

Dr. William Buchanan.

1 | Introduction

1.1 Introduction

Software development has grown over the years from simple BASIC programs written on small hobby computers to large software systems that control factories. Many applications that at one time used dedicated hardware are now implemented using software and programmable hardware. This shift in emphasis has meant that, as a percentage, an increasing amount of time is spent on software and less on hardware development.

The software that runs on a system must be flexible in its structure as the developer could require to interrogate memory addresses for their contents or to model a part of the system as an algorithm. For this purpose the programming languages C and Pascal are excellent in that they allow a high level of abstraction (such as algorithm specification) and allow low-level operations (such as operations on binary digits). They have a wide range of applications, from commerce and business to industry and research, which is a distinct advantage as many software languages have facilities that make them useful only in a particular environment. For example, in the past, business and commercial applications used COBOL extensively, whereas engineering and science used FORTRAN.

1.2 Hardware, software and firmware

A system consists of hardware, software and firmware, all of which interconnect. Hardware is 'the bits that can be touched', that is, the components, the screws and nuts, the case, the electrical wires, and so on. Software is the programs that run on programmable hardware and change their operation depending on the inputs to the system. These inputs could be taken from a keyboard, interface hardware or from an external device. The program itself cannot exist without some form of programmable hardware such as a microprocessor or controller. Firmware is a hardware device that is programmed using software. Typical firmware devices are EEPROMs (Electrically Erasable Read Only Memories), and interface devices that are programmed using registers.

1

In most applications, dedicated hardware is faster than hardware that is running software, although systems running software programs tend to be easier to modify and require less development time.

1.3 Basic computer architecture

The main elements of a basic computer system are a central processing unit (or microprocessor), memory, and input/output (I/O) interfacing circuitry. These are interconnected by three main buses: the address bus; the control bus; and the data bus, as illustrated in Figure 1.1. External devices such as a keyboard, display, disk drives, and so on, can connect directly onto the data, address and control buses, or connect through I/O interfacing circuitry.

Memory normally consists of RAM (random access memory) and ROM (read only memory). ROM stores permanent binary information, whereas RAM is a non-permanent memory and loses its contents when the power is taken away. RAM memory is used to run application programs and to store information temporarily.

The microprocessor is the main controller of the computer. It fetches binary instructions (known as machine code) from memory, it then decodes these into a series of simple actions and carries out the actions in a sequence of steps. These steps are synchronized by a system clock.

The microprocessor accesses a memory location by putting its address on the address bus. The contents at this address are placed on the data bus and the microprocessor reads the data from the data bus. To store data in memory the microprocessor places the data on the data bus. The address of the location in memory is then put on the address bus and the data is then read from the data bus into the required memory address location.

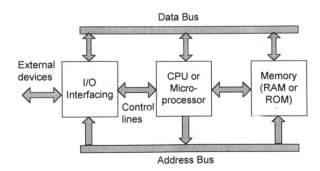

Figure 1.1   Block diagram of a simple computer system

1.4 Compiling, linking and producing an executable program

A microprocessor only understands binary information and operates on a series of binary commands known as machine code. It is extremely difficult to write large programs in machine code, so that high-level languages are used instead. A low-level language is one which is similar to machine code and normally involves the usage of keyword macros to replace machine code instructions. A high-level language has a syntax that is almost like written English and thus makes a program easy to read and to modify. In most programs the actual operation of the hardware is invisible to the programmer.

A compiler changes the high-level language into machine code. High-level languages include C, BASIC, COBOL, FORTRAN and Pascal; an example of a low-level language is 80386 Assembly Language.

Figure 1.2 shows the sequence of events that occur to generate an executable program from a Pascal source code file (the filenames used in this example relate to a PC-based system). An editor creates and modifies the source code file; a compiler then converts this source code into a form which the microprocessor can understand, that is, machine code. The file produced by the compiler is named an object code file (note that Turbo Pascal does not produce an object code file). This file cannot be executed as it does not have all the required information to run the program. The final stage of the process is linking, which involves adding extra machine code into the program so that it can use devices such as a keyboard, a monitor, and so on. A linker links the object code file with other object code files and with libraries to produce an executable program. These libraries contain other object code modules that are compiled source code.

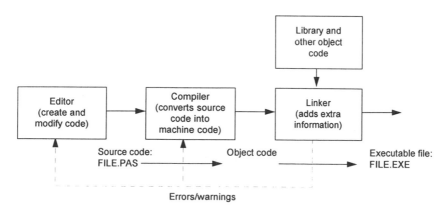

Figure **1.2**   Edit, compile and link processes

If compilation or linking steps generate errors or warnings then the source code must be modified to eliminate them and the process of compilation/linking begins again. Warnings in the compile/link process do not stop the compiler or linker from producing an output, but errors will. All errors in the compilation or linking stage must be eliminated, whereas it is only advisable to eliminate warnings.

1.5 Compilation

Turbo Pascal Version 5.0 is an integrated development package available for PC-based systems. It contains an editor, compiler, linker and debugger (used to test programs). The editor creates and modifies source code files and is initiated by running TURBO.EXE. Figure 1.3 shows a main screen with a source code file PROG1_1.PAS.

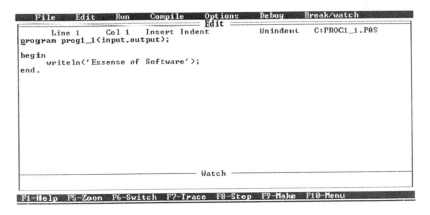

Figure 1.3 Turbo Pascal Version 5.0 main screen

Figure 1.4 shows the compile menu options within this package. A source code file is compiled by selecting Compile. If there are no errors then an executable program is produced. If the destination is given as Memory then it does not save the executable file to the disk but runs it from memory. If the destination is to the Disk then an executable file will be produced (producing the file PROG_1.EXE). The destination can be toggled by pressing the ENTER key while the line cursor is on the Destination option. A program is run from the Run menu option.

1.6 Introduction to Pascal

This section gives a brief introduction to Turbo Pascal.

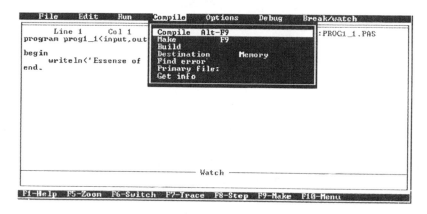

Figure 1.4 Turbo Pascal Version 5.0 compile menu options

1.6.1 Constant declarations

Pascal uses the `const` keyword to defined constant numeric values. The following examples show constant declarations for π and the speed of light (which is 3×10^8).

```
const      PI=3.14;
           SPEED_OF_LIGHT=3e8;
```

In Pascal the case of the characters is ignored but, as a matter of programming style, the definition of constants, such as π, is given in uppercase characters.

1.6.2 Structure

Normally programs are split into a number of sub-tasks named procedures or functions. These are clearly distinctive pieces of code that perform particular operations. The main program is the basic routine to control the flow of a program and calls other sub-functions.

Pascal Program 1.1 is a simple program which uses the `writeln` procedure to display the text 'Mastering Pascal'. The `writeln` procedure is a standard procedure which is used to output text to the display.

The statement terminator (;) is used to end a line of code (or statement) and the keywords `begin` and `end` define the beginning and end of a block of code. Comments are inserted into the program between a start comment identifier ((*) and an end identifier (*)).

All Pascal programs have a main program which defines the entry point into the program and, by means of calling functions and procedures, controls general program flow. In most cases it is located at the end of the source code file.

Program 1.1

```
program prog1_1(input,output);
(* Simple program *)
begin
    writeln('Mastering Pascal');
end.
```

Figure 1.5 shows the basic structure of a simple Pascal program. Each program has a program header which is defined with the `program` keyword. After this the program variables are declared. In this case the variables declared are *var1*, *var2* (which are integers) and *var3*, *var4* (which are real values). The main program is defined after the variable declaration and can be identified between the `begin` and `end` keywords. The final `end` keyword has a full-stop after it.

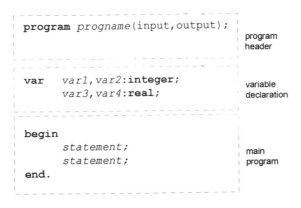

Figure 1.5 Pascal program structure

1.6.3 Data types

Variables within a program can be stored as either numbers or characters. For example, the resistance of a copper wire would be stored as a number (a real value) and the name of a component (such as 'R1') would be stored as characters. Table 1.1 gives the four basic data types which define the format of variables.

Table 1.1 Basic Pascal data types

Type	Usage	Range
char	single character 'a', '1', and so on	Character range
integer	signed integer	−32768 to 32767
real	single-precision floating point	2.9×19^{-39} to 1.7×10^{38}
boolean	boolean type	true or false

Other data types used in Turbo Pascal include:

shortint, longint, byte, word and double

An integer is any value without a decimal point; its range depends on the number of bytes used to store it. A floating point value is any number and can include a decimal point; this value is always in a signed format. Again, the range depends on the number of bytes used.

The integer type uses 2 bytes in memory. This gives ranges of −32 768 to 32 767 (a 2-byte integer) and −2 147 483 648 to 2 147 483 647 (a 4-byte longint), respectively.

1.6.4 Declaration of variables

A program uses variables to store data. Before the program can use a variable, its name and its data type must first be declared. A comma groups variables of the same data type. For example, if a program requires integer variables num_steps and bit_mask, floating point variables resistor1 and resistor2, and two character variables char1 and char2, then the following declarations can be made:

```
var       num_steps,bit_mask:integer;
var       resistor1,resistor2:float;
var       char1,char2:char;
```

Pascal Program 1.2 is a simple program that determines the equivalent resistance of two resistors of $1000\,\Omega$ and $500\,\Omega$ connected in parallel. It contains three floating point declarations for the variables resistor1, resistor2 and equ_resistance.

📋 **Program 1.2**
```
program prog1_2(input,output);
(* Program to determine the parallel equivalent        *)
(* resistance of two resistors of 1000 and 500 Ohms    *)

var     resistor1,resistor2,equ_resistance:real;

begin
     resistor1:=1000;
     resistor2:=500;

     equ_resistance:=1/(1/resistor1+1/resistor2);
     writeln('Equivalent resistance is ',equ_resistance);
end.
```

1.6.5 Keywords

Turbo Pascal has 52 reserved keywords; these cannot be used as program identifiers and can be in upper or lower case. Large programs can be built from these simple building blocks. The following gives a list of the keywords.

absolute	and	array	begin	case
const	constructor	destructor	div	do
downto	else	end	external	file
for	forward	function	goto	if
implementation	in	inline	interface	interrupt
label	mod	nil	not	object
of	or	packed	procedure	program
record	repeat	set	shl	shr
string	then	to	type	unit
until	uses	var	virtual	while
with	xor			

1.6.6 Modular programming

Functions and procedures are sections of code that perform a specified operation. They receive some input and produce an output in a way dictated by their functionality. These can be standardized functions which are inserted into libraries or are written by the programmer. Turbo Pascal defines some standard functions which provide basic input/output to/from the keyboard and display, mathematical functions, character handling, and so on. They are grouped together into library files and are not an intrinsic part of the language. These libraries link into a program to produce an executable program. Appendix A lists the functions and procedures available with Turbo Pascal.

1.7 Exercises

1.7.1   Determine the errors in Pascal Programs 1.3 to 1.5. Each program has a single error. Enter them into the compiler and after the error has been corrected, run them.

📋 **Program 1.3**
```
program prog1_3(input,output)
(*      Simple program      *)
begin
   writeln('This is sample program');
end.
```

📋 **Program 1.4**
```
program prog1_4(input,output);
(*      Simple program      *)
begin

   writeln('This is sample program');
```

Program 1.5

```
program prog1_5(input,output);
(*      Simple program
begin

   writeln('This is sample program');

end.
```

1.7.2 Enter Pascal Program 1.1 and save this to a file on a floppy disk as PROG1_1.PAS (for the Pascal file). Compile the program and note any messages that the compiler gives. If there are errors in the program then compare the entered file with the program listing and try to identify how they differ. The compiler should identify the location of the error (note look also at the line before). Then recompile. After the program has been successfully compiled, run the program and determine its output.

1.7.3 Enter Pascal Program 1.2 and save this to a file on a floppy disk as PROG1_2.PAS (for the Pascal file).

1.7.4 Using Pascal Program 1.2 determine the equivalent resistance for two parallel resistors. Use this program and by changing the resistor values complete Table 1.2.

Table 1.2 Equivalent resistance

Resistor1 (Ω)	Resistor2 (Ω)	Equivalent resistance (Ω)
1000	1000	
25	100	
1e6 (1MΩ)	1e6	
150	50	

2 Input/Output

2.1 Introduction

Every useful program has some form of output and normally an input. Figure 2.1 shows some examples of input and output devices. The input could be from a keyboard, a file, input/output ports, a mouse, and so on. Output can be sent to devices such as displays, printers, hard disks, and so on. Typically, computers can also communicate with devices such as external devices, such as lights, motors, and so on.

The default input device is normally from a keyboard and the default output from a display. Most programs prompt the user to enter data from the keyboard. This data is then processed and the results displayed to the screen. The user can then enter new data and so the cycle continues.

Most operating systems also allows redirection of the input or output. For example, a text file can act as an input to a program and the printer as the output.

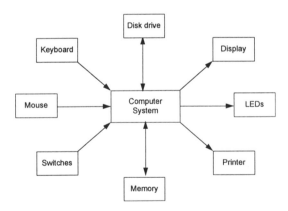

Figure 2.1 Input/output devices

2.2 Pascal input/output

Pascal has a very limited set of input/output statements. Pascal uses the keyboard as the standard input and the display as the standard output. The two statements which are used to control this input and output are `read`, `readln`, `readkey`, `writeln` and `write`.

2.2.1 *writeln*

The statements used to output data from a program to the screen are `writeln` and `write`. The `write` statement does not move the cursor to a new line once the data has been printed, whereas the `writeln` will. The standard format is:

`writeln` (*'text'*, *arg1*, *arg2* ... *argn*);	outputs a text string defined by *'text'* and values given by arguments *arg1..argn*. The output is appended with a new line.
`write` (*'text'*, *argn1*, *arg2* ... *argn*);	outputs a text string defined by *'text'* and values given by arguments *arg1..argn*. The output is not appended with a new line.

A text string is enclosed within quotes (' ') and can be printed at any place in the `write` statement. Values will be printed in a format defined by their type. For example an integer will be displayed without a decimal point, a very large or small real value will be displayed in exponent form. The actual format of the value to be printed can be modified using the colon modifier, the standard format is:

`value:n`	prints `value` with n spaces used to print the variable
`value:n:m`	prints `value` with n spaces and m places after the decimal point

Note that all printed values are right justified.

2.2.2 *readln*

The statements used to input data into a program from the keyboard are `read` and `readln`. The `read` statement ignores extra data at the end of line while the `readln` does not. The standard format is:

`readln`(*arg1, arg2...argn*)	reads values from the keyboard and loads them into the arguments *arg1*, *arg2*, and so on.
`read`(*arg1, arg2...argn*)	reads values from the keyboard and loads them into the arguments *arg1*, *arg2*, and so on.
ch= `readkey`()	reads a single character from the keyboard into *ch*

Pascal Program 2.1 shows a simple example of a program which uses input/output statements.

📋 **Program 2.1**

```
program prog2_1(input,output);
var     voltage,current,resistance:real;
begin
    writeln('Enter voltage and current');
    readln(voltage,current);
    resistance:=voltage/current;
    writeln('Resistance is ' ,resistance:8:3,  ' Ohms');
end.
```

2.3 Examples

This section contains some practical examples of Pascal programs.

2.3.1 Fahrenheit to centigrade conversion

Temperature is typically measured in either centigrade or Fahrenheit. The conversion from Fahrenheit to centigrade is:

$$C = \frac{5}{9}(F - 32) \ \ °C$$

Program 2.2 converts from an entered value of Fahrenheit (faren) into centigrade (cent) and Test run 2.1 shows a sample run for an entered value of 80°F. The resultant value is displayed with 8 places reserved for the answer and 2 decimal places. This is specified in Pascal with $:8:2$ after the variable.

📋 **Program 2.2**

```
program prog2_2(input,output);

var     faren,cent:real;

begin
    writeln('Program to convert Fahrenheit to centigrade');
    writeln('Enter a temperature (in Fahrenheit)');

    readln(faren);
    cent:=5/9*(faren-32);
    writeln('Temperature is ',cent:8:2,' deg C');

end.
```

🖥 **Test run 2.1**

```
Program to convert Fahrenheit to centigrade
Enter a temperature (in Fahrenheit)   80
Temperature is     26.67 deg C
```

2.3.2 Gradient of a straight line

The equation of a straight line is:

$$y = mx + c$$

where m is the gradient of the line and c is the point at which the line cuts the y-axis. If two points on the line are known, (x_1, y_1) and (x_2, y_2) then m can be calculated by:

$$m = \frac{y_2 - y_1}{x_2 - x_1}$$

and the c value can be calculated from:

$$c = y - mx$$
$$= y_1 - mx_1$$

Program 2.3 determines the gradient of a straight line for entered values of x_1, y_1 and x_2, y_2 (note that the solution of the value for c will be left as an exercise). Test run 2.2 is a sample test run.

Program 2.3

```
program   prog2_3(input,output);

var       x1,x2,y1,y2,m:real;
begin

   writeln('Program to determine the gradient');
   writeln('of a straight line');

   write('Enter x1, y1 >> ');
   readln(x1,y1);
   write('Enter x2, y2 >> ');
   readln(x2,y2);

   m:=(y2-y1)/(x2-x1);

   writeln('Gradient is ',m:8:2);
end.
```

Test run 2.2

```
Program to determine the gradient
of a straight line
Enter x1, y1 >> 3 4
Enter x2, y2 >> 5 6
Gradient is     1.00
```

2.3.3 Force of attraction

The gravitational force between two objects of mass m_1 and m_2 of a distance d apart is given by:

$$F = \frac{G m_1 m_2}{d^2} \ \text{N}$$

where G is a gravitation constant and is equal to 6.67×10^{-11} $\text{m}^3\text{kg}^{-1}\text{sec}^{-2}$. Program 2.4 determines the gravitation force and Test run 2.3 shows a test run for the gravitation force between an apple and the earth. The parameters used are:

$$m_{earth} = 6 \times 10^{24} \ \text{kg}$$
$$m_{apple} = 0.1 \ \text{kg}$$
$$r_{earth} = 6\,370\,000 \ \text{m}$$

The resultant gravitation force is 0.99 N, which is similar to the calculation using:

$$F = ma$$
$$= 0.1 \times 9.81\,\text{N}$$
$$= 0.981\,\text{N}$$

The gravitation force constant (G) has been defined with a `const`.

📋 **Program 2.4**

```
program prog2_4(input,output);
const    G=6.67e-11;

var      force,m1,m2,distance:real;

begin
    writeln('Program to calculate force between two objects');

    writeln('Enter mass of first object (kg)');
    readln(m1);

    writeln('Enter mass of second object (kg)');
    readln(m2);

    writeln('Enter distance between objects (m)');
    readln(distance);

    force:=G*m1*m2/(distance*distance);

    writeln('Force is ',force:8:2,' N');

end.
```

```
Program to calculate force between two objects
Enter mass of first object (kg)   6e24
Enter mass of second object (kg) 0.1
Enter distance between objects (m) 6.37e6
Force is      0.99 N
```

2.3.4 Capacitive reactance

The reactance of a capacitor depends upon the applied frequency. At low frequencies the reactance is extremely high and at high frequencies it is low. The reactance (X_C) of a capacitor, of capacitance C (Farads), at an applied frequency f (Hertz) is be given by:

$$X_C = \frac{1}{2\pi fC} \ \Omega$$

Figure 2.2 shows a schematic of this arrangement. There is one output variable (X_C), two input variables (f and C) and a single constant (π). Program 2.5 shows a sample program and Test run 2.4 is a sample run. In C a constant is declared with the #define pre-processor option and Pascal uses the const keyword.

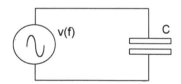

Figure 2.2 Capacitor connected to sinusoidal voltage source

📋 **Program 2.5**

```
program    prog2_5(input,output);

const    PI=3.14157;   (* PI is normally already defined,    *)
                       (* thus there is no need for this line *)

var      freq,cap,X_c:real;

begin
     writeln('Enter frequency and capacitance');

     readln(freq,cap);

     X_c:=1/(2*PI*freq*cap);

     writeln('Capacitive reactance is ',X_c:8:3,' ohms');
end.
```

```
Enter frequency and capacitance
10e3 1e-6
Capacitive reactance is 15.916 ohms
```

2.3.5 Right-angled triangle

Figure 2.3 shows a right angled triangle with sides of length x, y and z. If the values of x and y are known then the value of z will be:

$$z = \sqrt{x^2 + y^2}$$

and the angle θ will be:

$$\theta = \tan^{-1}\left(\frac{y}{x}\right)$$

Program 2.6 determines these values for entered values of x and y. In Pascal the inverse tangent function is named `arctan()` and it returns a value in radians. The program converts the returned value into degrees by scaling it by $\pi/180$. In Pascal the square root function is `sqrt()`.

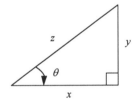

Figure 2.3   Right-angled triangle

Test run 2.5 is a sample output using entered values $x = 3$, $y = 4$. In this case z has a value of 5 and the angle is 53.13°.

📖 **Program 2.6**
```
program  prog2_6(input,output);

var        x,y,z,angle:real;

begin
   write('Enter x and y >>');
   readln(x,y);
   z := sqrt(x*x+y*y);
   angle := arctan(y/x)*180.0/PI;
      (* arctan is arc tan and returns radians   *)
      (* 180/PI converts to degrees              *)
   writeln('z= ', z:8:2, ' angle ',angle:8:2,' deg');
end.
```

Test run 2.5
```
Enter x and y >> 3 4
z=      5.00 angle      53.13 deg
```

2.3.6 *Resistors in parallel*

Program 2.7 determines the equivalent resistance of three resistors connected in parallel. Figure 2.4 gives a schematic diagram of this set-up. The resistors connected are R_1, R_2 and R_3 and the equivalent input resistance is R_{equ}. Test run 2.6 shows a run with values of 250, 500 and 1000 Ω.

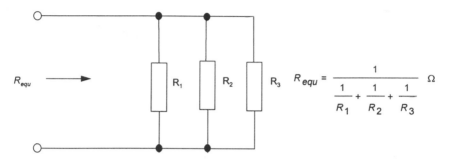

$$R_{equ} = \cfrac{1}{\cfrac{1}{R_1} + \cfrac{1}{R_2} + \cfrac{1}{R_3}} \ \Omega$$

Figure 2.4   Three resistors connected in parallel

Program 2.7
```
program  prog2_7(input,output);

var      R1,R2,R3,R_equ:real;

begin
   writeln('Program to determine equivalent resistance');
   writeln('of three resistors connected in parallel');
   write('Enter three values of resistance >>');

   readln(R1,R2,R3);

   R_equ:=1.0/(1/R1+1/R2+1/R3);

   writeln('R1=',R1,'R2=',R2,' and R3=',R3, ' ohms');
   writeln('Equivalent resistance is ',R_equ,' ohms');
end.
```

Test run 2.6
```
Program to determine equivalent resistance
of three resistors connected in parallel
Enter three values of resistance >>   1000 500 250
R1=1000.000, R2= 500.000, R3= 250.000 ohms
Equivalent resistance is 142.857 ohms
```

2.4.1 Enter two programs from the chapter and verify that their output conforms with the sample test runs.

2.4.2 Modify Program 2.3 so that it also calculates the value of c. Use this program to complete Table 2.1.

Table 2.1 Straight lines calculations

x_1	y_1	x_2	y_2	m	c
3	3	6	5	0.67	
7	1	−1	4		4.375
1000	500	10	40		
−100	3	−5	−9		
5	−10	−10	10		

2.4.3 Write a program which calculates the magnitude of a complex number of x+jy (or in another form x+iy) and complete Table 2.2 (note that the first row has been completed). The magnitude is given by:

$$Mag = \sqrt{x^2 + y^2}$$

Table 2.2 Magnitude

x	y	Mag
3	4	5
50	70	
−9	−9	
100	100	
0.1	0.5	
30	−10	

2.4.4 Write a program which calculates the angle of a complex number of x+jy (or in another form x+iy) and complete Table 2.3. The angle is given by:

$$Angle = \tan^{-1}\left(\frac{y}{x}\right) \text{ radians}$$

Table 2.3   Angle

x	y	Angle (radians)
3	4	0.9273
−9	−9	
100	100	
0.1	0.5	
30	−10	

2.4.5   Modify the program written in 2.4.4 so that it converts the angle to degrees and complete Table 2.4. An angle converted from radians to degrees using:

$$Angle(\text{degrees}) = \frac{180}{\pi} Angle(\text{radians})$$

Table 2.4   Angle

x	y	Angle (degrees)
3	4	53.13
−9	−9	
100	100	
30	−10	

2.4.6   Write a program which determines the equivalent resistance of three parallel resistors (refer to Program 2.7). Use this program to complete Table 2.5.

Table 2.5   Equivalent parallel resistance

R1 (Ω)	R2 (Ω)	R3 (Ω)	R_equ (Ω)
1000	1000	1000	
200	100	50	
1.2K	1K	800	
1M	0.5M	250K	

3 | If Statement

A decision is made with the `if` statement. It logically determines whether a conditional expression is TRUE or FALSE. For a TRUE, the program executes one block of code; a FALSE causes the execution of another (if any). The keyword `else` identifies the FALSE block. In Pascal, the `begin` and `end` keywords are used.

Relationship operators include:

- Greater than (>).
- Less than (<).
- Greater than or equal to (>=).
- Less than or equal to (<=).
- Equal to (=).
- Not equal to (<>).

These operations yield a TRUE or FALSE from their operation. Logical statements can then group these together to give the required functionality. These are:

- AND.
- OR.
- NOT.

The result of these operations is given in Appendix C.

The following is an example syntax of the `if` statement. If the statement block has only one statement then the `begin` and `end` can be excluded.

⎘ Syntax

```
if (expression) then
begin
    statement block
end;
```

The following is an example format with an `else` extension.

Syntax

```
if (expression) then
begin
   statement block1
end
else
begin
   statement block2
end;
```

It is possible to nest `if..else` statements to give a required functionality. In the next example, *statement block1* is executed if `expression1` is TRUE. If it is FALSE then the program checks the next expression. If this is TRUE the program executes *statement block2*, else it checks the next expression, and so on. If all expressions are FALSE then the program executes the final `else` statement block, in this case, *statement block4*:

📋 **Syntax**

```
if (expression1) then
begin
   statement block1
end
else if (expression2) then
begin
   statement block2
end
else if (expression3) then
begin
   statement block3
end
else
begin
   statement block4
end;
```

Figure 3.1 shows a diagrammatic represention of this example statement.

3.2 Examples

This section contains some Pascal example programs.

3.2.1 *Quadratic equations*

Some problems require the solution of a quadratic equation. The standard form is:

If statement   21

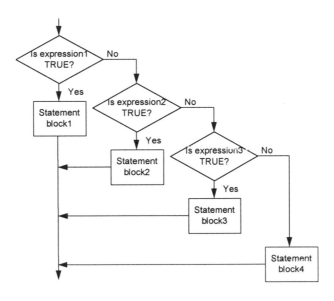

Figure 3.1 Structure of the compound `if` statement

$$ax^2 + bx + c = 0$$

The solution of x in this equation is given by:

$$x_{1,2} = \frac{-b \pm \sqrt{b^2 - 4ac}}{2a}$$

This can yield three possible types of results:

1. if `b`^{2}`=4ac`, there will be a single real root (`x=-b/2a`)
2. else, if `b`^{2}`>4ac`, there will be two real roots:

$$x_1 = \frac{-b + \sqrt{b^2 - 4ac}}{2a}, \qquad x_2 = \frac{-b - \sqrt{b^2 - 4ac}}{2a}$$

3. else, the roots will be complex:

$$x_1 = \frac{-b}{2a} + j\frac{\sqrt{4ac - b^2}}{2a}, \qquad x_2 = \frac{-b}{2a} - j\frac{\sqrt{4ac - b^2}}{2a}$$

Program 3.1 determines the roots of a quadratic equation. In this program the `if..else` statement is used to determine if the roots are real, complex or singular. The value passed to the square-root function (`sqrt()`) should be tested to determine if it is negative. If it is, it may cause the program to terminate as the square root of a negative number cannot be calculated (it is numerically invalid). The program may also terminate if a is zero as this causes a divide by zero error (the trap for this error is left as a tutorial question).

Three test runs 3.1, 3.2 and 3.3 test each of the three types of roots that occur. In Test run 3.1 the roots of the equation are real. In Test run 3.2 the roots are complex, i.e. in the form x+jy. In Test run 3.3 the result is a singular root.

Program 3.1

```
program prog3_1(input,output);
(* Program to determine roots of a quadratic equation *)
var a,b,c,real1,real2,imag:real;

begin
    writeln('Program to determine roots of a quadratic equation');
    write('Enter a, b and c >>');
    readln(a,b,c);

    writeln('Equation is ',a:6:2,'x*x+',b:6:2,'x+',c:6:2);

    if ((b*b)=(4*a*c)) then
    begin
        real1:=-b/(2*a);
        writeln('Root is ',real1:6:2);
    end
    else if ((b*b)>=(4*a*c)) then
    begin
        real1:=(-b+sqrt( (b*b)-4*a*c))/(2*a);
        real2:=(-b-sqrt( (b*b)-4*a*c))/(2*a);
        writeln('Roots are ',real1:6:2,real2:6:2);
    end
    else
    begin
        real1:=-b/(2*a);
        imag:=sqrt(4*a*c-b*b)/(2*a);
        writeln('Roots are ',real1:6:2,'+/-j',imag:6:2);
    end;
end.
```

Test run 3.1
```
Program to determine roots of a quadratic equation
Enter a,b and c >> 1 1 -2
Equation is 1.00x*x + 1.00x + -2.00
Roots are 1.00, -2.00
```

Test run 3.2
```
Program to determine roots of a quadratic equation
Enter a,b and c >> 2 2 4
Equation is 2.00x*x + 2.00x + 4.00
Roots are -0.50 +/- j1.32
```

```
Program to determine roots of a quadratic equation
Enter a,b and c >>> 1 2 1
Equation is 1.00x*x + 2.00x + 1.00
Root is -1
```

3.2.2 Electromagnetic (EM) waves

Program 3.2 uses the if statement to determine the classification of an EM wave given its wavelength. Figure 3.2 illustrates the EM spectrum spanning different wavelengths. The classification of the wave is determined either by the frequency or the wavelength (normally radio and microwaves are defined by their frequency, whereas other types by their wavelength). For example, an EM wave with a wavelength of 10 m is classified as a radio wave, a wavelength of 500 nm as visible light and a wavelength of 50 cm is in the microwave region. Test run 3.4 shows a sample run.

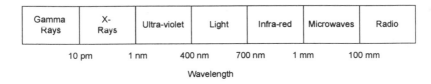

Figure 3.2 EM spectrum

📋 **Program 3.2**

```
program if2(input,output);
(*    Program to determine type of EM wave for a given wavelength *)
var    lambda:real;

begin

   write('Enter wavelength (metres) >>>');
   readln(lambda);

   write('Electomagnetic wave is ');

   if (lambda<1e-11) then writeln('Gamma Ray !!!')
   else if (lambda<1e-9) then writeln('X-ray')
   else if (lambda<400e-9) then writeln('Ultra-violet')
   else if (lambda<700e-9) then writeln('LIGHT')
   else if (lambda<1e-3) then writeln('Infrared')
   else if (lambda<1e-1) then writeln('Microwave')
   else writeln('Radio wave');
end.
```

⌨ **Test run 3.4**

```
Enter wavelength>>> 1e-10
Electromagnetic wave is X-ray
```

EM waves can also be specified by their frequency. Program 3.3 allows the user to enter the frequency of the wave, and the program then determines the wavelength using the formula:

$$\lambda = \frac{c}{f}$$

where c is the speed of light and f the frequency of the wave.

📋 **Program 3.3**

```
program prog3_3(input,output);
(* Program to determine type of wave for an entered frequency *)
const SPEED_OF_LIGHT=3e8;

var lambda,freq:real;

begin

    write('Enter frequency >>>');
    readln(freq);

    lambda:=SPEED_OF_LIGHT/freq;

    write('Wavelength is ',lambda:6:2,' EM wave is ');

    if (lambda<1e-11) then writeln('Gamma Ray !!!')
    else if (lambda<1e-9) then writeln('X-ray')
    else if (lambda<400e-9) then writeln('Ultra-violet')
    else if (lambda<700e-9) then writeln('LIGHT')
    else if (lambda<1e-3) then writeln('Infrared')
    else if (lambda<1e-1) then writeln('Microwave')
    else writeln('Radio wave');

end.
```

Test run 3.5 shows a sample run.

⌨ **Test run 3.5**

```
Enter frequency >>> 10e9
Wavelength is 3.0e-02 m. EM wave is Microwave
```

3.2.3 Series/parallel resistances

Program 3.4 determines the equivalent resistance of two resistors connected either in series or parallel. The user enters either an 's' for series connection or a 'p' for a parallel connection. A function named upcase() converts the entered character into upper case. The if statement is used to determine if the entered character is an 's' or a 'p'. If it is any other character then the program displays the message 'Invalid entry'.

□ **Program 3.4**

```
program if4(input,output);

(* Program to determine the equivalent resistance of two   *)
(* resistors either connected in series or parallel        *)

var    R1,R2,R_equ:real;
       ch:char;
begin
   writeln('Enter two resistor values >>');
   readln(R1,R2);

   writeln('Do you require (s)eries or (p)arallel >>');
   readln(ch);

   if (upcase(ch)='S') then (* convert character to uppercase *)
   begin
      R_equ:=R1+R2;
      writeln('Equivalent series resistance is ',R_equ,' Ohms');
   end
   else if (upcase(ch)='P') then
   begin
      R_equ:=(R1*R2)/(R1+R2);
      writeln('Equivalent parallel resistance is ',R_equ,' Ohms');
   end
   else writeln('Invalid entry');
end.
```

3.3 Exercises

3.3.1   Write a program in which the user enters an integer value. The program will then display one of the following messages:

'Less than zero'   If the value is less than zero.
'Greater than zero'   If the value is greater than zero.
'Equal to zero'   If the value is equal to zero.

3.3.2   Write a program which determines if an entered integer value is exactly divisible by 4. For example, the following outline code can be used to determine if a value is exactly divisible by 2:

```
program test(input,output);
var value:integer;
begin
   writeln('Enter an integer value');
   readln(value);
   if ((value mod 2)=0) then
      writeln('Value is even')
   else writeln('Value is odd');
end.
```

3.3.3   Modify the program developed in Exercise 3.3.2 so that it determines if the entered value is exactly divisible by 10.

3.3.4   Write a program which determines if an entered integer value is exactly divisible by 3 and 4. The following outline code can be used to determine if a value is exactly divisible by 2 and 3:

```
if (((value mod 2)=0) and ((value mod 3)=0))) then
   writeln('Value is divisible by 2 and 3')
else writeln('Value is not divisible by 2 and 3');
```

3.3.5   Modify the program developed in Exercise 3.3.4 (using the or operator) so that it displays if the value is exactly divisible by 3 or 4.

3.3.6   Write a program that displays if an entered character is in upper case. The following program can be used to determine if an entered character is in lower case:

```
program test(input,output);

var ch:char;

begin
   write('Enter a character >>');
   readln(ch);
   if ((ch>='a') and (ch<='z')) then
      writeln('Letter is in lower case')
   else writeln('Letter is not in lower case');
end.
```

3.3.7   Modify the program developed in Exercise 3.3.6 so that it displays if an entered character is in upper case or lower case (that is, it is an alphabet letter). The message should be either 'Character is a letter' or 'Character is not a letter'.

3.3.8   Modify the program developed in Exercise 3.3.6 so that it displays if an entered character is in upper case, in lower case or is a numerical value. The message should be 'Character is a letter', 'Character is numerical' or 'Other character'.

3.3.9   Enter Program 3.1 and use it to complete Table 3.1.

3.3.10   Modify Program 3.1 so that it cannot generate a divide by zero error, that is, when a is 0 (zero). Use it to complete Table 3.2. Note that if a is 0 then the root will be $-c/b$.

Table 3.1   Roots of a quadratic equation

Equation	Root(s)
$x^2 + 21x - 72 = 0$	
$5x^2 + 2x + 1 = 0$	
$25x^2 - 30x + 9 = 0$	
$6x^2 + 9x - 20 = 0$	

Table 3.2   Root of a quadratic equation

Equation	Root
$0x^2 + 4x - 2 = 0$	
$0x^2 + 6x + 6 = 0$	

3.3.11   Write a program in which the user enters a value of resistance and the program displays the resistance value in the best possible units. A possible implementation could be:

If the resistance is less than $1000\,\Omega$ (1e3) then it is printed as the value in ohms;
else, if it is between 1000 (1e3) and $1\,000\,000\,\Omega$ (1e6) then the value is printed as kΩ;
else, if it is greater than $1\,000\,000$ (1e6) then it is printed in MΩ.

Test run 3.6 shows some sample runs.

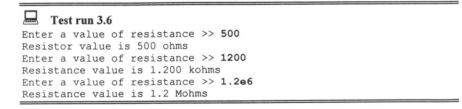

Test run 3.6

```
Enter a value of resistance >> 500
Resistor value is 500 ohms
Enter a value of resistance >> 1200
Resistance value is 1.200 kohms
Enter a value of resistance >> 1.2e6
Resistance value is 1.2 Mohms
```

3.3.12   Modify Program 3.2 so that the user can enter the EM wave as a frequency or a wavelength. A sample run is shown in test run 3.7.

Test run 3.7

```
Do you wish to enter
(f)requency or
(w)avelength  >>> f
Enter frequency >>> 10e9
Wavelength is 3.0e-02 Electromagnetic wave is Microwave
```

4 | Case Statement

4.1 `case statement`

The `case` statement is used when there are multiple decisions to be made. It is normally used to replace the `if` statement when there are many routes of execution the program execution can take. The syntax of `case` is as follows.

📋 **Syntax**

```
case (constant) of
  const1: statement(s);
  const2: statement(s);
  :        :
  else statements(s);
end;
```

In Pascal, the `case` statement simply selects which one of the constants (`const1`, `const2`, and so on) matches the `constant` value. If none of the constants matches the `case` statement a set of statements associated with the default condition (`else`) is executed.

Several constant values can be included in the `case` statement. These can either be separated by a comma (to indicate several options) or by double dot (to indicate a sequence of options). For example the following code determines if a character is a letter, a digit or an operator:

```
case ch of
   'A'..'Z', 'a'..'z':  writeln('Character is a letter');
   '0'..'9':            writeln('Character is a digit');
   '+', '-', '*', '/':  writeln('Character is an operator');
   else  writeln('Other character');
end;
```

4.2 Examples

4.2.1 Resistor colour code

Resistors are normally identified by means of a colour code system, as outlined in Table 4.1. Program 4.1 uses a `case` statement to determine the colour of a resistor band for an entered value.

29

Table 4.1 Resistor colour coding system

Digit	Colour	Multiplier	Digit	Colour	Multiplier
	SILVER	0.01	4	YELLOW	10K
	GOLD	0.1	5	GREEN	100K
0	BLACK	1	6	BLUE	1M
1	BROWN	10	7	VIOLET	10M
2	RED	100	8	GREY	
3	ORANGE	1 K	9	WHITE	

Program 4.1

```
program prog4_1(input,output);
(*     Program to determine colour code for a single   *)
(*     resistor band digit                             *)

var colour:integer;

begin
     write('Enter value of colour band (0-9) >>');
     readln(colour);

     write('Resistor colour band is ');

     case (colour) of
     0: write('BLACK');
     1: write('BROWN');
     2: write('RED');
     3: write('ORANGE');
     4: write('YELLOW');
     5: write('GREEN');
     6: write('BLUE');
     7: write('VIOLET');
     8: write('GREY');
     9: write('WHITE');
     end;
end.
```

Test run 4.1 shows a sample run.

Test run 4.1
```
Enter value of colour band(0-9)>> 3
Resistor colour band is ORANGE
```

Program 4.2 uses const to define each of the resistor colour bands. There may be a clash with these defines if other header files contain these definitions. If this occurs change the defines to RES_BLACK, RES_BROWN, and so on.

An else has been added to catch any invalid input (such as less than 0 or greater than 9).

📋 **Program 4.2**

```
program prog4_2(input,output);
(* Program to determine colour code for resistor band digit *)

const RES_BLACK=0;   RES_BROWN=1;   RES_RED=2;    RES_ORANGE=3;
      RES_YELLOW=4;  RES_GREEN=5;   RES_BLUE=6;   RES_VIOLET=7;
      RES_GREY=8;    RES_WHITE=9;

var colour:integer;

begin
    write('Enter value >>');
    readln(colour);
    write('Resistor colour band is ');

    case (colour) of
    RES_BLACK:   write('BLACK');
    RES_BROWN:   write('BROWN');
    RES_RED:     write('RED');
    RES_ORANGE:  write('ORANGE');
    RES_YELLOW:  write('YELLOW');
    RES_GREEN:   write('GREEN');
    RES_BLUE:    write('BLUE');
    RES_VIOLET:  write('VIOLET');
    RES_GREY:    write('GREY');
    RES_WHITE:   write('WHITE');
    else write('INVALID');
    end;
end.
```

4.2.2 Resistance of a conductor

The resistance of a cylindrical conductor is a function of its resistivity, cross-sectional area and length. These parameters are illustrated in Figure 4.1. The resistance is given by:

$$R = \frac{\rho l}{A} \ \Omega$$

where

ρ = resistivity of the conductor (Ωm);
l = length of the conductor (m);
A = cross-sectional area of the conductor (m^2).

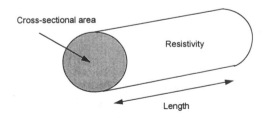

Figure 4.1 Cylindrical conductor

Program 4.3 determines the resistance of a cylindrical conductor made from either copper, aluminium, silver or manganese. The resistivities of these materials have been defined using const.

The user enters the conductor type as a character ('c', 'a', 's' or 'm') which can either be in upper or lower case format as the case statement test for both upper and lower case characters. When an invalid character is entered the default condition of the case statement is executed, and the text Invalid option is displayed. The program then calls the exit function; the argument passed to this function is the termination status. A value of 0 describes a normal termination; any other value signals an abnormal program termination.

Program 4.3

```
program prog4_3(input,output);
(*    Program to determine the resistance          *)
(*    of a cylindrical conductor                   *)
const RHO_COPPER=17e-9;
      RHO_AL=25.4e-9;
      RHO_SILVER=16e 9;
      RHO_MANGANESE=1400e-9;
var radius,length, area, rho, resistance:real;
    ch:char;

begin
    writeln('Type of conductor >>');
    writeln(' (c)opper');
    writeln(' (a)luminum');
    writeln(' (s)ilver');
    writeln(' (m)anganese');
    readln(ch);

    writeln('Enter radius and length of conductor >>');
    readln(radius,length);
    area:=Pi*(radius*radius);
    case (ch) of
    'c','C': rho:=RHO_COPPER;
    'a','A': rho:=RHO_AL;
    's','S': rho:=RHO_SILVER;
    'm','M': rho:=RHO_MANGANESE;
    else
         begin
             writeln('Invalid option');
             exit;
         end;
    end; (* end of case statement *)
    resistance:=rho*length/area;
    writeln('Resistance of conductor is ',resistance:6:2, ' ohms');
end.
```

Test run 4.2 uses an aluminium conductor with a radius of 1 mm and length 1000 m. The resistance is found to be 8.08 Ω.

```
Type of conductor >>
(c)opper
(a)luminium
(s)ilver
(m)anganese
a
Enter radius and length of conductor >> 1e-3 1000
Resistance of conductor is 8.08e+00 ohms
```

4.3 Exercises

4.3.1   Enter Program 4.1 and test the results.

4.3.2   Write a program in which the user enters two real values. The program will then prompt the user to enter an arithmetic operator (such as '+', '−', '/' or '*'). After this the program determines the result of the operator on the two values.

The following program is an outline of the final program with the '+' and '−' operators:

```
program test(input,output);

var   ch:char;
      val1,val2:real;

begin
   write('Enter two values >>');
   readln(val1,val2);
   write('Enter operator >>');
   readln(ch);

   case (ch) of
   '+': begin
          result:=val1+val2;
          writeln('Result is ',result);
        end;
   '-': begin
          result:=val1-val2;
          writeln('Result is ',result);
        end;
   (* **** Put the other operators in here *** *)
   else writeln('INVALID OPERATOR');
   end; (* end of case statement *)
end.
```

4.3.3   The textbackground function allows the colour of the background to be changed to BLACK, BROWN, RED, ... and clrscr clears the screen. Program 4.4 shows an example program of their use. Write a program which allows the user to enter a colour and the program then changes the background colour. Table 4.2 shows the colour definitions.

Table 4.2

Colour	Value	Colour	Value
BLACK	0	CYAN	3
BLUE	1	RED	4
GREEN	2	MAGENTA	5

 Program 4.4

```
program temp;
uses crt;
begin
      textbackground(RED);
      clrscr;
end.
```

Test run 4.3

```
Select a background colour >>
(0)BLACK
(1)BLUE
(2)GREEN
(3)CYAN
(4)RED
(5)MAGNETA

Option >> 2
```

4.3.4   Modify the program 3.4, using the `case` statement, so that the user enters an 's' for series resistance and a 'p' for parallel. Test run 4.4 shows a sample test run. Note that the program should accept the input characters in upper case or lower case.

The calculation of series and parallel resistance is as follows:

$$R_{series} = R_1 + R_2 \ \Omega \qquad R_{parallel} = \frac{R_1 R_2}{R_1 + R_2} \ \Omega$$

Test run 4.4

```
Enter R1 >> 100
Enter R2 >> 100

Select an option
(S)eries resistance
(P)arallel resistance
Option >> p
Equivalent resistance is 50.00 ohms
```

4.3.5   Write a program using the `case` statement that allows the user to select from a menu of options. These options allow the user to select either the calculation of the equivalent resistance of two series or two parallel resistors. The user should enter a 1 if the series equivalent is required or a 2 if parallel required. Test run 4.5 shows a sample test run.

⌨ **Test run 4.5**

```
Enter R1 >> 100
Enter R2 >> 100
Select an option
(1) Series resistance
(2) Parallel resistance
Option >> 2
Equivalent resistance is 50.00 ohms
```

---

5 For Loop

5.1 Introduction

Iterative, or repetition, allows the looping of a set of statements. There are three forms of iteration:

	🗐 **Syntax**

for loop	`for val:=startval to endval do`
	`begin`
	    `statement block;`
	`end;`

repeat...until	`repeat`
	    `statement block;`
	`until (condition);`

while	`while (condition) do`
	`begin`
	    `statement block;`
	`end;`

5.2 `for`

Many tasks within a program are repetitive, such as prompting for data, counting values, and so on. The `for` loop allows the execution of a block of code for a given control function or a given number of times. In Pascal the format is:

🗐 **Syntax**

```
for value:=startval to endval do
begin
      statement block
end;
```

In this case, `value` starts at `startval` and ends at `endval`. Each time round the loop, value will be incremented by 1. If there is only one statement in the block then the `begin` and `end` reserved words can be omitted.

5.3.1 ASCII characters

Program 5.1 displays ASCII characters for entered start and end decimal values. Test run 5.1 displays the ASCII characters from decimal 40 (' (') to 50 ('2').

Program 5.1

```
program for1(input,output);
(* Program to display ASCII characters *)
var i,startloop,endloop:integer;

begin
     write('Enter start and end for ASCII characters >> ');
     readln(startloop,endloop);

     writeln('INTEGER   CHARACTER');
     (* The function chr() is used to determine the character  *)
     (* associated with the ASCII integer value                *)
     for i:=startloop to endloop do
          writeln(i:5,chr(i):10);
end.
```

Test run 5.1

```
Enter start and end for ASCII characters >> 40 50
INTEGER   HEX      ASCII
   40      28        (
   41      29        )
   42      2a        *
   43      2b        +
   44      2c        '
   45      2d        -
   46      2e        .
   47      2f        /
   48      30        0
   49      31        1
   50      32        2
```

5.3.2 Simulation of a mathematical equation

The program in this section will simulate the results of the equation:

$$y = 3x^2 - 12x - 1$$

for values of x from 0 to 100 in steps of 10. Unfortunately, the for loop can only increment a variable by 1. It is also limited in that it can only operate on an integer variable. Thus in Program 5.1 the variable i is used to give the number of times round the loop and this is scaled to give the required x value.

Program 5.2

```
program prog5_2(input,output);

var x,y:real;
    i:integer;

begin
        writeln('          X              Y');

        for i:=0 to 10 do
        begin
                x:=10*i;
                y:=3*sqr(x)-12*x-1;
                writeln(x:10:2,y:10:2);
        end
end.
```

Test run 5.2 shows a sample run of the program. It can be seen that the value of x varies from 0 to 100, in steps of 10.

Test run 5.2

X	Y
0.00	-1.00
10.00	179.00
20.00	959.00
30.00	2339.00
40.00	4319.00
50.00	6899.00
60.00	10079.00
70.00	13859.00
80.00	18239.00
90.00	23219.00
100.00	28799.00

5.3.3 Boolean logic

Program 5.3 is an example of how a Boolean logic function can be analysed and a truth table generated. The `for` loop generates all the required binary permutations for a truth table. The Boolean function used is:

$$Z = \overline{(A.B) + C}$$

A schematic of this equation is given in Figure 5.1. Test run 5.3 shows a sample run.

38   *Mastering Pascal*

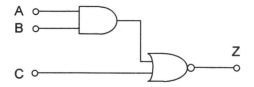

Figure 5.1 Digital circuit

📋 **Program 5.3**

```
program for3(input,output);

(* Program to generate truth table for Boolean function      *)

var   A,B,C,Z:boolean;

begin
    writeln('Boolean function NOR(AND(A,B),C)');
    writeln('    A       B       C       Z');

    for A:=FALSE to TRUE do
       for B:=FALSE to TRUE do
          for C:=FALSE to TRUE do
          begin
             Z:=not( (A and B) or C);
             writeln(A:8,B:8,C:8,Z:8);
          end;
end.
```

🖥 **Test run 5.3**

```
Boolean function NOR(AND(A,B),C)
    A       B       C       Z
    FALSE   FALSE   FALSE   TRUE
    FALSE   FALSE   TRUE    FALSE
    FALSE   TRUE    FALSE   TRUE
    FALSE   TRUE    TRUE    FALSE
    TRUE    FALSE   FALSE   TRUE
    TRUE    FALSE   TRUE    FALSE
    TRUE    TRUE    FALSE   FALSE
    TRUE    TRUE    TRUE    FALSE
```

5.4 Exercises

5.4.1   Write a program which prints all the characters from '0' (zero) to 'z' in sequence using a `for` loop.

5.4.2   Enter Program 5.1 and use it to complete Table 5.1.

Table 5.1   ASCII characters

Value	Character
34	
35	
36	
37	
38	
64	
65	
66	
67	
68	
69	
70	

5.4.3   Write a program which lists the square of the values from 1 to 10. A sample run in shown next.

```
Value    Square
1        1
2        4
3        9
4        16
5        25
6        36
7        49
8        64
9        81
10       100
```

5.4.4   Write a program in which the user enters the number of real values that will be entered and the program then prompts for each of these values and calculates the summation of all the entered numbers. An outline of the program is given next:

```
writeln('How many numbers are to be entered >>')
readln(num_vals);

for i:=1 to num_vals do
begin
   writeln('Enter value >> ');
   readln(value);
   total:=total+value;
end;
writeln('Total is ',total:8:2);
```

5.4.5   Write a program which displays the squares, cubes and fourth powers of the first 10 integers. A sample output is given next.

```
Number   Square   Cube   Fourth
---------------------------------
1        1        1      1
2        4        8      16
3        9        27     81
    etc
```

5.4.6 Write a program which displays the y values in the formulas given below and with the given x steps.

Equation	Range of x
(i) $y = 4x + 1$	0 to 50 in steps of 5
(ii) $y = \sqrt{x} - 1$	1 to 10 in steps of 0.5
(iii) $y = 5x^2 + 3x - 2$	-5 to 5 in steps of 0.5

A sample run of the first equation is given next.

```
EQUATION y=4x+1, x goes from 0 to 50 in steps of 5
 x      y
 0      1
 5      21
10      41
15      61
   etc
```

5.4.7 Write a program which displays the sine of a number from $0°$ degrees to $90°$ in steps of $10°$.

5.4.8 Modify Program 5.3 so that it determines the truth table for the following Boolean equation:

$$Z = \overline{(A + B).C}$$

Table 5.2   Truth table

A	B	C	Z
FALSE	FALSE	FALSE	
FALSE	FALSE	TRUE	
FALSE	TRUE	FALSE	
FALSE	TRUE	TRUE	
TRUE	FALSE	FALSE	
TRUE	FALSE	TRUE	
TRUE	TRUE	FALSE	
TRUE	TRUE	TRUE	

6 | While/Repeat Loops

6.1 while

The `while` statement allows a block of code to be executed while a specified condition is TRUE. It checks the condition at the start of the block; if this is TRUE the block is executed, else it will exit the loop. The syntax is

while

📋 **Syntax**
```
while (condition) do
begin
    statement block;
end;
```

If the statement block contains a single statement then the braces may be omitted (although it does no harm to keep them). A few examples are:

📋 **Syntax**

`while (i>10) do`	this will repeat the associated *statement block* while `i` is greater than 10.
`while (letter <> 'q') do`	this will repeat the associated *statement block* while `letter` is not equal to the character 'q'.
`while ((index <= 10) and (value ==3)) do`	this will repeat the associated *statement block* while `index` is less than or equal to 10 and `value` is equal to 3.

6.2 Repeat...until

The `repeat...until` statement is similar in its operation to `while` except that it tests the condition at the bottom of the loop and that the loop continues until the loop condition is TRUE (which is opposite to the while statement). This type of loop forces a *statement block* to be executed at least once. The syntax is:

📋 **Syntax**
```
repeat
    statement block;
until (condition);
```

6.3 Examples

6.3.1 Repeating program

Often a user is asked to repeat the program once it has finished calculating values. This is sometimes done by asking the user if they want to repeat (or continue) the program. If the user enters a 'y' character then the program is repeated, else an 'n' character will exit the program. Program 6.1 implements this with a repeat...until loop.

📋 **Program 6.1**
```
program prog6_1(input,output);

var   R1,R2,R_equ:real;
      ch:char;

begin
    repeat
          writeln('Enter R1 and R2 >>');
          readln(R1,R2);
          R_equ:=(R1*R2)/(R1+R2);
          writeln('Parallel resistance is ',R_equ:8:2,' ohms');

          writeln('Do you wish to continue (y/n)');
          readln(ch);
    until (ch='n');

end.
```

6.3.2 Limiting ranges of inputs

Most of the values that are entered into a program have a certain range. For example if a user is asked to enter their age then the value will always be:

- An integer.
- A positive value.
- Less than 130.

If a user enters an invalid value then the program could either:

- Crash, which typically happens when a program tries to divide by zero or determines the square root of a negative number.
- Give invalid results.

Thus it is important that the user is stopped from entering values which are invalid. Program 6.2 allows the user to determine the equivalent parallel resistance for two resistors in parallel. The range of values of entered resistance is between $0\,\Omega$ and $1\,M\Omega$. The repeat...until loop is placed around the user entry of each of the values. These loops continue until a user enters a valid value. Test run 6.1 shows a sample run.

Program 6.2

```
program prog6_2(input,output);

var R1,R2,R_equ:real;

begin
    repeat
            writeln('Enter R1 >>');
            readln(R1);
            if ((R1<0) or (R1>1e6)) then
                writeln('Invalid value: re-enter');
    until ( (R1>0) and (R1<1e6) );
    repeat
            writeln('Enter R2 >>');
            readln(R2);
            if ((R2<0) or (R2>1e6)) then
                writeln('Invalid value: re-enter');
    until ((R2>0) and (R1<1e6) );

    R_equ:=(R1*R2)/(R1+R2);

    writeln('Parallel resistance is ',R_equ:8:2,' ohms');
end.
```

Test run 6.1

```
Enter R1 >> 1e7
Invalid value: re-enter
Enter R1 >> -100
Invalid value: re-enter
Enter R1 >>   100
Enter R2 >>   100
Parallel resistance is      50.00 ohms
```

Program 6.3 gives an example of the determination of acceleration giving the initial and end velocity, and the time difference. The range of velocity values is between 0 and 1000 m/s, and the range of time difference values is between 0 and 60 s. Test run 6.2 shows a sample run.

```
program prog6_3(input,output);

var v1,v2,t,accel:real;

begin
    repeat
        writeln('Enter initial velocity (m/s)>>');
        readln(v1);
        if ( (v1<0) or (v1>1e3)) then
            writeln('Invalid value: re-enter');
    until ( (v1>0) and (v1<1e3) );

    repeat
        writeln('Enter final velocity (m/s)>>');
        readln(v2);
        if ( (v2<0) or (v2>1e3)) then
            writeln('Invalid value: re-enter');
    until ( (v2>0) and (v2<1e3) );

    repeat
        writeln('Enter time (secs)>>');
        readln(t);
        if ( (t<0) or (t>60)) then
            writeln('Invalid value: re-enter');
    until ( (t>0) and (t<60) );

    accel:=(v2-v1)/t;

    writeln('Acceleration is ',accel:8:2,' m/s2');
end.
```

□ **Test run 6.2**
```
Enter initial velocity (m/s)>> -100
Invalid value: re-enter
Enter initial velocity (m/s)>>  1e7
Invalid value: re-enter
Enter initial velocity (m/s)>> 20
Enter final velocity (m/s)>>  10
Enter time (secs)>> 2
Acceleration is    -5.00 m/s2
```

6.3.3 Conversion from decimal to octal

Octal numbers uses base eight. To convert a decimal value to an octal number the decimal value is divided by 8 recursively and each remainder noted. The first remainder gives the least significant digit and the final remainder the most significant digit. For example, the following shows the octal equivalent of the decimal number 55:

$$
\begin{array}{r|l}
8 & 55 \\
  & 6 \quad \text{r } 7 \quad <<< \text{LSD (least significant digit)} \\
  & 0 \quad \text{r } 6 \quad <<< \text{MSD (most significant digit)}
\end{array}
$$

Thus the decimal value 55 is equivalent to 68o (where the o represents octal). Program 6.4 shows a program which determines an octal value for an entered decimal value. Unfortunately it displays the least significant digit first and the most significant digit last, thus the displayed value must be read in reverse. Test run 6.3 shows a sample run.

Program 6.4

```
program prog6_4(input,output);

var    value,remainder:integer;

begin
      write('Enter a decimal value >>');
      readln(value);
      write('The value in octal is (in reverse) ');

      repeat
            remainder:=value mod 8;
            write(remainder);
            value:=value div 8;
      until (value=0);
      writeln;
end.
```

Test run 6.3

```
Enter a decimal value >> 55
The value in octal is (in reverse) 76
```

6.4 Exercises

6.4.1   Correct the errors in the following program:

```
Program tut1a(input,output)
(* This Program should calculate the current   *)
(* flowing in a resistor but has two syntax     *)
(* errors and one functional error              *)
var    resistance,voltage,ch:real;

begin
    writeln('Program to determine current flowing in');
    writeln('a resistor');

    repeat
       writeln('Enter voltage and resistance');
       readln(Voltage,Resistance);

       (* always catch divide by zero errors ! *)
```

```
      if (resistance=0) then  writeln('INFINITE CURRENT !!!')
      else writeln('Current is ',voltage/resistance:8:3,' Amps');

      write('Do you wish to continue (y/n)>>');
      readln(ch);
   until (ch='y');
end.
```

6.4.2   What will the following sections of code output to the screen.

(i)
```
i:=1;
while (i<10) do
begin
   i:=i+2;
   writeln('i = ',i);
end;
```

(ii)
```
i:=8;
while (i<10) do
begin
   i:=i+2;
   writeln('i = ',i);
end;
```

(iii)
```
i:=1;
repeat
   i:=i+2;
   writeln('i = ',i);
until (i<10);
```

(iv)
```
i:=10;
repeat
   i:=i-2;
   writeln('i = ',i);
until (i<10);
```

(v)
```
i:=1;
repeat
   i:=2*i;
   writeln('i = ',i);
until (i<10);
```

(vi)
```
i:=1;
repeat
   i:=2*i;
   writeln('i = ',i);
until not(i=10);
```

(vii)
```
i:=1;
repeat
   i:=2*i;
   writeln('i = ',i);
until (i>10);
```

6.4.3 Replace the following `for` loop with a `repeat...until` and with a `while` in the examples below.

(i)
```
for i:=1 to 20 do
begin
end;
```

(ii)
```
for j:=-10 to 10 do
begin
end;
```

(iii)
```
for k:= 4 to 100 do
begin
   j:= 4*k;
end;
```

6.4.4 Write a program to convert from decimal to binary (base 2). A sample run is shown in Test run 6.4 (see Appendix C and Program 6.4 for background theory). Program 6.5 shows a sample outline of the program (where the value of **x** is still to be added).

🖳 **Test run 6.4**
```
Enter a decimal value >> 42
The value in hexadecimal is (in reverse) 0100001
```

📋 **Program 6.5**
```
program prog6_5(input,output);

var   value,remainder:integer;

begin
      write('Enter a decimal value >>');
      readln(value);
      write('The value in binary is (in reverse) ');

      repeat
            remainder:=value mod x; (* add value of x *)
```

```
            write(remainder);
            value:=value div x;  (* add value of x *)
    until (value=0);
    writeln;
end.
```

6.4.5   Write a program to convert from decimal to hexadecimal (base 16). A sample run is shown in Test run 6.5 (see Appendix C and Program 6.4 for background theory). Program 6.6 shows a sample outline of the program.

🖥 **Test run 6.5**

```
Enter a decimal value >> 42
The value in hexadecimal is (in reverse) A2
```

📋 **Program 6.6**

```
program prog6_4(input,output);

var   value,remainder:integer;

begin
    write('Enter a decimal value >>');
    readln(value);
    write('The value in hexadecimal is (in reverse) ');

    repeat
        remainder:=value mod 16;
        if (remainder<10) then write(remainder);
        else if (remainder=10) then write('A');
        else if (remainder=11) then write('B');
        (* *** Put additional code in here *** *)
        value:=value div 16;
    until (value=0);
    writeln;
end.
```

6.4.6   Write a program to convert hexadecimal to decimal. A sample run is shown in Test run 6.5.

🖥 **Test run 6.6**

```
Number of hex characters> 2
Enter 1 > A
Enter 2 > 1
The hex. equivalent is 31
```

---

7 Functions

7.1 Introduction

Functions are identifiable pieces of code with a defined interface. They are called from any part of a program and allow large programs to be split into more manageable tasks, each of which can be independently tested. Functions are also useful in building libraries of routines that other programs use. Several standard libraries exist, such as maths and input/output libraries.

A function can be thought of as a 'black box' with a set of inputs and outputs. It processes the inputs in a way dictated by its function and provides some output. In most cases the actual operation of the 'black box' is invisible to the rest of the program. A modular program consists of a number of 'black boxes' working independently of all others, of which each uses variables declared within it (local variables) and any parameters sent to it. Figure 7.1 illustrates a function represented by an ideal 'black box' with inputs and outputs, and Figure 7.2 shows a main function calling several sub-functions (or modules).

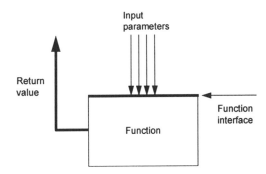

Figure 7.1 An ideal 'black-box' representation of a function

7.2 Arguments and parameters

The data types and names of parameters passed into a function are declared in the function header (its interface) and the actual values sent are referred to as arguments. They can be passed either as values (known as 'passing by value') or as pointers (known as 'passing by reference'). Passing by value involves sending a copy of it into the function. It is not possible to change the value of a variable using this method. Variables can only be modified if they are passed by reference (this will be covered in the next chapter). This chapter looks at how parameters pass into a function and how a single value is returned.

An argument and a parameter are defined as follows:

An 'argument' is the actual value passed to a function.
A 'parameter' is the variable defined in the function header.

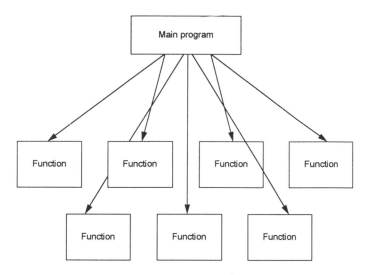

Figure 7.2 Hierarchical decomposition of a program

7.3 Pascal functions

In Pascal a function returns a single value. It is identified by the function header, which is in the form:

```
FUNCTION  function_name(formal_parameter_list) : result_type;
```

where the parameters are passed through the `formal_parameter_list` and the result type is defined by `result_type`.

Program 7.1 contains two functions named `addition` and `multiply`. In calling the `addition` function and variables a and b are passed into the parameters c and d, respectively; c and d are local parameters and only exist within `addition()`. The values of c and d can be changed with no effect on the values of a and b. This function returns a value back to the main program by setting a value which is the same name as the function.

Program 7.1 also uses a procedure which, in this case, is similar to a function but does not return any values back to the calling program (procedures will be covered in the next chapter).

Program 7.1

```pascal
program prog7_1(input,output);
var     a,b,summation,multi:integer;

function addition(c,d:integer):integer;
begin
   addition:=c+d;
end;

function multiply(c,d:integer):integer;
begin
   multiply:=c*d;
end;

procedure print_values(c,d,sum,mult:integer);
begin
   writeln(c,' plus ',d,' is ', sum);
   writeln(c,' multiplied by ',d, ' is ',mult);
end;

begin
   a:=5;
   b:=6;
   summation:=addition(a,b);
   multi := multiply(a,b);
   print_values(a,b,summation,multi);
end.
```

Figure 7.3 shows a simple structure chart of this program. The function addition() is called first; the variables sent are a and b and the return value is put into the variable summation. Next, the multiply() is called; the variables sent are also a and b and the value returned goes into multi. Finally, the function print_values() is called; the values sent are a, b, multi and summation.

Program 7.1 contains functions that return integer data types. It is possible to return any other of Pascal's data types, including float, double and char, by inserting the data type after the function name.

A function can have several return points, although it is normally better to have only one return point. This is normally achieved by restructuring the code. An example of a function with two return values is shown next. In this example a decision is made as to whether the value passed into the function is positive or negative. If it is greater than or equal to zero it returns the same value, else it returns a negative value (mag=-val).

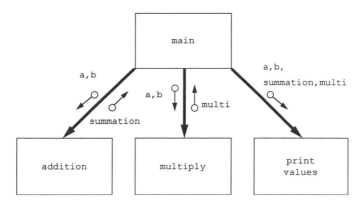

Figure 7.3 Basic structure chart for Program 7.1

```
program test(input,output);

var a:integer;

function mag(val:integer):integer;
begin

    if (val<0) then mag:=-val
    else mag:=val;

end;

begin

    a:=-5;
    writeln('Mag(a)  =  ',mag(a));

end.
```

Program 7.2 contains a function power() which has a return data type of double; the first argument is double and the second is integer. This function uses logarithms to determine the value of x raised to the power of n. The formula used is derived next; the ln() function is the natural logarithm and the exp() the exponential function.

$$y = x^n$$
$$\ln(y) = \ln(x^n)$$
$$\ln(y) = n\ln(x)$$
$$y = \exp(n\ln(x))$$

📋 **Program 7.2**

```
program prog7_2(input,output);

var    x,val:double;
       n:integer;

function power(x:double;n:integer):double;
begin
     power :=exp(n*ln(x));
end;

begin

   writeln('Program to determine the result of a value');
   writeln('raised to the power of an integer');

   writeln('Enter x to the power of n >>');
   readln(x,n);

   val:=power(x,n);
   writeln(x,' to power of ',n,' is ',val);
end.
```

7.4 Local variables

Typically variables are required within a function which are not used in the main program. These variables are called local variables and they only exist within the function. A local variable is declared directly after the function header and before the starting begin keyword. The following example shows a function called fact which is passed a single integer value (n) and returns a longint data type. It has two local variables, these are val and i.

```
function   fact(n:integer):longint;
var        val,i:longint;   (* LOCAL VARIABLES *)
begin
     val:=1;
     for i:=2 to n do
     begin
          val:=val*i;
     end;
     fact:=val;
end;
```

The outline rules of variable declarations are:

• Variables that are declared in the main declaration area of the program are known as global variables and they can be accessed by all parts of the program. It is advisable that functions should not use any of the global vari-

ables directly, but should depend on their values to be passed to them through the function header.
- Local variables only exist within the function they are declared in, whereas global variables exist throughout the program.
- A function cannot access another function's local variables.
- A local variable can have the same name as a global variable.
- A global variable which has the same name as a local variable will be treated as a different variable.

For example, the global variables i, j and k are declared in the following outline program. Within the function test the local variable i is declared. This will be a different variable to the i global variable.

```
program prog(input,output);

var i,j,k: integer;   (* GLOBAL VARIABLES *)

function test(val1:integer):integer;
var i:integer;   (* LOCAL VARIABLE  which is different to *)
                 (* the global variable i                 *)

end;

begin
   i:=1;
   k:=5;
   j:=test(k);
end.
```

7.5 Examples

This section contains a few sample Pascal programs which use functions.

7.5.1 Tan function

There is no tan function in Pascal; thus to overcome this Pascal Program 7.3 contains a tan function and Test run 7.1 shows a sample run.

Program 7.3
```
Program prog7_3(input,output);
(* Program that uses a function to calculate the  *)
(* tan of a number                                *)
var   answer,number:  real;

function tan(a:real):real;
begin
   tan:= sin(a)/cos(a);       (* tan is sin over cos *)
end;
```

```
begin
   write('Enter number >> ');
   readln(number);
   answer:=tan(number);
   writeln('The tan of ',number:8:3,' is ',answer:8:3);
end.
```

```
Enter number >> 1.23
The tan of    1.230 is    2.820
```

7.5.2 Centigrade to Fahrenheit conversion

Pascal Program 7.4 uses two functions to convert from Fahrenheit to centigrade, and vice versa. Test run 7.2 shows a sample test run.

📋 **Program 7.4**
```
Program prog7_4(input,output);
(* Program that uses a function to convert Fahrenheit to centigrade*)

var   fahrenheit,centigrade:real;

function convert_to_centigrade(f:real ):real;
begin
   convert_to_centigrade:=5/9* (f-32);
end;

function convert_to_fahrenheit(c:real ) :real;
begin
   convert_to_fahrenheit:=9/5*c+32;
end;

begin
   write('Enter value in Fahrenheit >> ');
   readln(Fahrenheit);

   centigrade:=convert_to_centigrade(Fahrenheit);

   writeln(Fahrenheit:6:3,'deg F is ',  centigrade:6:3,' deg C');

   write('Enter value in centigrade');
   readln(centigrade);

   Fahrenheit:=convert_to_fahrenheit(centigrade);
   writeln(centigrade:6:3,' deg C is ',Fahrenheit:6:3,' deg F');
end.
```

💻 **Test run 7.2**
```
Enter value in Fahrenheit >> 12
12.000 deg F is -11.111 deg C
Enter value in centigrade >> 60
60.000 deg C is 140.000 deg F
```

Pascal Program 7.5 uses the two functions developed in the previous programs to display a table of values from 0°C to 100°C in steps of 10°C. Test run 7.3 shows a sample run.

📋 **Program 7.5**

```
Program prog7_5(input,output);
(* Program that uses a function to convert centigrade to    *)
(* Fahrenheit. Centigrade goes from 0 to 100 in steps of 10. *)

var   fahrenheit,centigrade:real;
      i: integer;

function convert_to_fahrenheit(c:real ):real;
begin
   convert_to_fahrenheit:=9/5*c+32;
end;

begin
   writeln('Centigrade Fahrenheit');

   for i:=0 to 10 do
   begin
     centigrade:=10*i;
      fahrenheit:=convert_to_fahrenheit(centigrade);
     writeln(centigrade:8:3,Fahrenheit:8:3);
   end;
end.
```

💻 **Test run 7.3**
```
Centigrade Fahrenheit
    0.000    32.000
   10.000    50.000
   20.000    68.000
   30.000    86.000
   40.000   104.000
   50.000   122.000
   60.000   140.000
   70.000   158.000
   80.000   176.000
   90.000   194.000
  100.000   212.000
```

7.5.3 Combinational logic

In this example, the following Boolean equation is processed to determine its truth table.

$$Z = \overline{(A + B + (A.C))}.C$$

Figure 7.4 gives a schematic representation of this Boolean function. The four nodes numbered on this schematic are:

$(1)\ \overline{A+B}$
$(2)\ A.C$
$(3)\ \overline{A+B}+(A.C)$
$(4)\ \overline{(\overline{A+B}+(A.C)).C}$

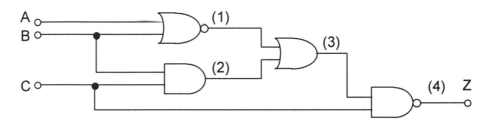

Figure 7.4   Schematic representation of the function $Z=\overline{(\overline{A+B}+(A.C)).C}$

Table 7.1 gives a truth table showing the logical level at each point in the schematic. This table is necessary to check the program results against expected results. Table 7.2 gives the resulting truth table.

Table 7.1   Truth table

A	B	C	$\overline{A+B}$ (1)	$A.C$ (2)	$\overline{A+B}+(A.C)$ (3)	$\overline{(\overline{A+B}+(A.C)).C}$ (4)
0	0	0	1	0	1	1
0	0	1	1	0	1	0
0	1	0	0	0	0	1
0	1	1	0	0	0	1
1	0	0	0	0	0	1
1	0	1	0	1	1	0
1	1	0	0	0	0	1
1	1	1	0	1	1	0

Table 7.2   Truth table

A	B	C	Z
0	0	0	1
0	0	1	0
0	1	0	1
0	1	1	1
1	0	0	1
1	0	1	0
1	1	0	1
1	1	1	0

Pascal Program 7.6 shows how this Boolean equation is simulated. The permutations of the truth table input variables (that is, `000`, `001`, `010`, `011`, ..., `111`) are generated using 3 nested `for` loops. The inner loop toggles C from a 0 to a 1, the next loop toggles B and the outer loop toggles A. The Boolean functions use the logical operators `and` and `or`. As Pascal has reserved keywords for AND, OR and NOT the function names have been changed to reflect the number of inputs they have, such as OR3 for a 3-input OR gate and AND2 for a 2-input AND gate. Test run 7.4 shows a sample run of the program. Notice that the results are identical to the truth table generated by analyzing the schematic (apart from 0/1 begin indicated with a FALSE/TRUE).

Test run 7.4

A	B	C	Result
FALSE	FALSE	FALSE	TRUE
FALSE	FALSE	TRUE	FALSE
FALSE	TRUE	FALSE	TRUE
FALSE	TRUE	TRUE	TRUE
TRUE	FALSE	FALSE	TRUE
TRUE	FALSE	TRUE	FALSE
TRUE	TRUE	FALSE	TRUE
TRUE	TRUE	TRUE	FALSE

Program 7.6

```pascal
program prog7_6(input,output);
var a,b,c,z:boolean;

function NOR2(x, y:boolean):boolean;
begin
   if ( x or y ) then nor2:=FALSE
   else nor2:=TRUE;
end;

function OR2(x, y:boolean):boolean;
begin
   if ( x or y) then or2:=TRUE
   else or2:=FALSE;
end;

function AND2(x, y:boolean):boolean;
begin
   if ( x and y) then and2:=TRUE
   else and2:=FALSE;
end;

function NAND2(x, y:boolean):boolean;
begin
   if ( x and y ) then nand2:=FALSE
   else nand2:=TRUE;
end;
```

```
begin
   writeln('      A      B      C      Result');
   writeln('      ****************************');

   for a:=FALSE to TRUE do
      for b:=FALSE to TRUE do
         for c:=FALSE to TRUE do
         begin
            z:=NAND2(OR2(NOR2(a,b),AND2(a,c)),c);
            writeln(a:6,b:6,c:6,z:6);
         end;
end.
```

7.5.4 Sine of a value

The sine of a value can be determined, from first principles, using the formula:

$$\sin(x) = x - \frac{x^3}{3!} + \frac{x^5}{5!} - \frac{x^7}{7!} + \frac{x^9}{9!} - \ldots$$

where $n! = n \times (n-1) \times (n-2) \times \ldots \times 2 \times 1$

and the value of x is in radians. Pascal Program 7.7 gives a Pascal program which has a function called sine(). This function calculates the sine of a value using the formula given above. It uses a repeat...until loop which calculates each term of the equation and adds it to a running total for the loop. The loop continues until the calculated term is less than 10^{-6}.

The program also includes the following functions:

- fact(n) which is used to determine the factorial of an integer value, the result is a longint as it may be a large value.
- pow(x,n) which is used to determine the value of x to the power of n.
- to_radians(x) which is used to convert the value of x into radians (by multiplying by π and dividing by 180).

Test run 7.5 gives a sample run of this program. It can be seen that the function sine() returns the same value as the Pascal sin() function.

⌨ **Test run 7.5**
```
Enter value (in degrees) >>   23
Sine is  0.391
Sin is   0.391
```

Program 7.7

```pascal
program prog7_7(input,output);
(* Program to determine the sine of a value from first principles *)

var invalue:real;

function pow(x:real;n:real):real;
begin
     pow:=exp(n*ln(x));
end;

function fact(n:integer):longint;
var val,i:longint;
begin
     val:=1;
     for i:=2 to n do
     begin
          val:=val*i;
     end;
     fact:=val;
end;

function sine(x:real):real;
var n,sign:integer;
    val,term:real;
begin
     sign:=1;
     val:=x;
     n:=3;
     repeat
            term:=pow(x,n)/fact(n);
            n:=n+2;
            sign:=-sign;
            val:=val+sign*term;
     until (term<1e-6);   (* repeat until term is less than 1e-6 *)

     sine:=val;
end;

function to_radians(val:real):real;
begin
     to_radians:=PI*val/180;
end;

begin

     writeln('Enter value (in degrees) >>');
     readln(invalue);

     invalue:=to_radians(invalue);

     writeln('Sine is ',sine(invalue):8:3);
     writeln('Sin is ',sin(invalue):8:3);

end.
```

7.5.1 Write a program which determines the magnitude of an entered value. The program should use a function to determine this.

7.5.2 Write a program with a function which is passed an arithmetic operator character and two real values. The function will then return the result of the operator on the two values. Program 7.8 shows an outline of the program.

📋 **Program 7.8**

```
program prog7_8(input,output);

var operator:char;
    value1,value2,result:real;

function math_function(ch:char;val1,val2:real):real;
var result:real;
begin
    case ch of
    '+': result:=val1+val2;
    '-': result:=val1-val2;
    (* *** Add extra code here *** *)
    end;
    math_function:=result;
end;

begin
    writeln('Enter operator >>');
    readln(operator);
    writeln('Enter two values >>');
    readln(value1,value2);
    result:=math_function(operator,value1,value2);
    writeln('Result is ',result);
end.
```

7.5.3 Write a program with separate functions which determine the gradient of a straight line (m) and the point at which a straight line cuts the y-axis (c). The entered parameters are two points on the line, that is, (x_1, y_1) and (x_2, y_2). From this program complete Table 7.3 (the first row has already been completed).

Table 7.3 Straight line calculations

x_1	y_1	x_2	y_2	m	c
3	3	4	5	2	−3
−1	5	0	−1		
100	50	−10	−10		
−1	−1	1	3		

Formulas to calculate these values are:

$$m = \frac{y_2 - y_1}{x_2 - x_1} \qquad c = y_1 - mx_1$$

7.5.4 Write a program which determines the magnitude and angle of a complex number (in the form $x+iy$, or $x+jy$). The program should use functions to determine each of the values. Complete Table 7.4 using the program (the first row has already been completed), where:

$$mag = \sqrt{x^2 + y^2} \qquad angle = \tan^{-1}\left(\frac{y}{x}\right)$$

Table 7.4 Complex number calculation

x	y	*Mag.*	*Angle(°)*
10	10	14.142	45
−10	5		
100	50		
−1	−1		

7.5.5 Referring to Program 7.7, write a function for a cosine function. It can be calculated, from first principles, with:

$$\cos(x) = 1 - \frac{x^2}{2!} + \frac{x^4}{4!} - \frac{x^6}{6!} + \frac{x^8}{8!} - \ldots$$

The error in the function should be less than 1×10^{-6}.

7.5.6 Using the functions developed in Exercise 7.5.5 and Program 7.7 and the standard sine and cosine library functions, write a program which determines the error between the standard library functions and the developed functions. From this, complete Table 7.5.

Table 7.5 Sine and cosine results

Value	Standard cosine function	Developed cosine function	Standard sine function	Developed sine function
2	−0.41614683		0.9092974	
−0.5				
1				
−1				

7.5.7 Write a mathematical function which determines the exponential of a value using the first principles formula:

$$e^x = 1 + \frac{x}{1!} + \frac{x^2}{2!} + \frac{x^3}{3!} + \frac{x^4}{4!} + \ldots$$

Compare the result with the standard `exp()` library function.

7.5.8 Write Boolean logic functions for the following four digital gates:

```
AND3 (A, B, C)
OR3 (A, B, C)
NAND3 (A, B, C)
NOR3 (A, B, C)
```

7.5.9 Write a program which has a function which will only return a real value when the entered value is within a specified range. Examples of calls to this function (which, in this case, is named `get_real`) are given next.

```
inval:=get_real(0,100);
```

which will only return a value from the function when the entered value is between 0 and 100. A sample run follows.

⌨ **Test run 7.6**
```
Enter a value > -1
INVALID INPUT PLEASE RE-ENTER
Enter a value > 6
Success. Bye.
```
---

8 Procedures

8.1 Introduction

Parameter passing involves passing input parameters into a module (a procedure in Pascal) and receiving output parameters back from the module. For example a quadratic equation module requires three parameters to be passed to it, these would be a, b and c. These are defined as the input parameters. The output parameters would be the two roots of the equation, such as `root1` and `root2`. Another parameter could also be passed back to indicate the type of root (such as singular, real or complex). This indication is normally known as a flag. Figure 8.1 illustrates the passing of parameters into and out of a module.

In Pascal the module would be defined as:

```
procedure calc_quadratic(a,b,c:integer; var root1,root2:real;
                         var type:integer)
```

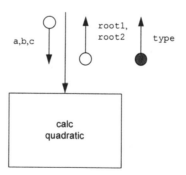

Figure 8.1 Parameter passing

8.2 Pascal parameter passing

Procedures are used in Pascal when parameters need to be passed back to the calling routine (they are also used when no parameters are to be passed back).

Functions are normally used when there is only one value passed back, whereas a procedure can return any number (or even none). The first part of defining a procedure is to define the input parameters and the output parameters. The input parameters are declared in the parameter list and output parameters are defined with a preceding `var` keyword. For example, if the input parameters are x and y, and the output parameters are w and z then the following procedure would be defined:

```
procedure   proc1(x,y:real; var w,z:real);
begin

end;
```

In this case only values will be passed into the variables x and y, whereas the values of w and z will be passed back to the calling module. If a procedure requires local variables then these are declared after the procedure header. For example, if the procedure in the last example has two local variables named `temp1` and `temp2` then it will have the form:

```
procedure   proc1(x,y:real; var w,z:real);
var   temp1,temp2:real;
begin

end;
```

Local variables only exist within the procedure and their contents are lost when the procedure quits.

Program 8.1 shows an example program with a procedure which swaps the values of two variables. In this case a temporary local value (`temp`) holds one of the values (`temp:=x`) so that the contents of the other value can be placed in it (`x:=y`). The temporary value is then put into the other variable (`y:=temp`). This operation performs a swap.

☐ **Program 8.1**
```
program prog8_1(input,output);

var a,b: integer;

procedure swap(var x,y: integer);
var temp: integer;
begin
   temp := x;
   x     := y;
   y     := temp
end;

begin
   write('Enter two integer values >> ');
```

```
   readln(a,b);

   writeln('Values are ',a,' and ',b);
   swap(a,b);
   writeln('Values swapped are ',a,' and ',b);
end.
```

Program 8.2 calculates the gradient of a straight line given two co-ordinates (*x1,y1*) and (*x2,y2*).

Program 8.2
```
program prog8_2(input,output);

var x1,y1,x2,y2:real;

procedure get_coord(var x,y:real);
begin
   writeln('Enter x and y coordinate');
   readln(x,y);
end;

function gradient(xstart,ystart,xend,yend:real):real;
begin
   gradient:=(yend-ystart)/(xend-xstart);
end;

begin
   writeln('Start co-ordinate');
   get_coord(x1,y1);
   writeln('End co-ordinate');
   get_coord(x2,y2);
   writeln('The gradient is ',gradient(x1,y1,x2,y2):6:2 );
end.
```

8.3 Examples

8.3.1 Quadratic equations

Program 8.3 determines the roots of a quadratic equation. The function get_values() gets variables a, b and c; these variables are passed as pointers.

The function to determine the root(s) of a quadratic equation is quadratic_equ(). This returns the root type (such as singular, real or complex) through the function header and passes the equation root(s) through the argument list using pointers. The root type is a value passed back that identifies the type of root, valid values are: SINGULAR (a value of 0), REAL_ROOTS (a value of 1) and COMPLEX_ROOTS (a value of 2). This value allows the program to determine how the root(s) are to be displayed. If the root is singular then `print_results()` prints a single value of `root1`; else, if the roots are real, then two values `root1` and `root2` are printed; and if the roots are complex the function will print the roots in the form `root1 +/-j root2`.

The flag for the quadratic equation is passed as one of the variables in the parameter of `quadratic_equ (rtype)`. The quadratic equation root types are defined as constants using `const`.

Figure 8.2 gives a basic structure chart of this program. The return flag from the `quadratic_equ()` function is represented by an arrow with a circle on the end.

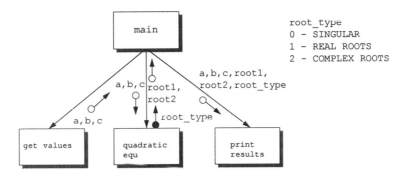

Figure 8.2 Structure chart for Program 8.3

📋 **Program 8.3**

```
program prog8_3(input,output);

const SINGULAR=0;  REAL_ROOTS=1; COMPLEX_ROOTS=2;

var     a,b,c,root1,root2:real;
        root_type:integer;

procedure get_values(var ain,bin,cin:real);
begin
   write('Enter a, b and c >>');
   readln(ain,bin,cin);
end;

procedure quadratic_equ(a,b,c:real; var r1,r2:real; var
rtype:integer);
begin
   if (a=0) then
   begin
      r1:=-c/b;
      rtype:=SINGULAR;
   end
   else if ((b*b)>(4*a*c)) then
   begin
      r1:=(-b+sqrt(b*b-4*a*c))/(2*a);
      r2:=(-b-sqrt(b*b-4*a*c))/(2*a);
      rtype:=REAL_ROOTS;
```

```
      end
   else if ((b*b)<(4*a*c)) then
   begin
      r1:=-b/(2*a);
      r2:=sqrt(4*a*c-b*b)/(2*a);
      rtype:=COMPLEX_ROOTS;
   end
   else
   begin
      r1:=-b/(2*a);
      rtype:=SINGULAR;
   end;
end;

procedure print_results(r_type:integer; a,b,c,r1,r2:real);
begin
   writeln('Quadratic equation ',a:8:3, ' x^2 + ',
                              b:8:3, ' x + ',c:8:3);
   if (r_type=SINGULAR) then
      writeln('Singular root of ',r1)
   else if (r_type=REAL_ROOTS)  then
      writeln('Real roots of ', r1:8:3, ' and ',r2:8:3)
   else
      writeln('Complex root of ',r1:8:3,' +/-j ',r2:8:3);
end;

begin
   get_values(a,b,c);
   quadratic_equ(a,b,c,root1,root2,root_type);
   print_results(root_type,a,b,c,root1,root2);
end.
```

Test run 8.1 shows tests for each of the root types.

🖳 Test run 8.1

```
Enter a, b and c >>  2 1 1

Quadratic equation    2.000 x^2 +    1.000 x +    1.000
Complex root of   -0.250 +/-j    0.661

Enter a, b and c >>  1 -2 -3

Quadratic equation    1.000 x^2 +   -2.000 x +   -3.000
Real roots of    3.000 and   -1.000

Enter a, b and c >>  1 2 1

Quadratic equation    1.000 x^2 +    2.000 x +    1.000
Singular root of   -1.000
```

8.3.2 Equivalent parallel resistance

Pascal Program 8.4 uses pointers to determine the equivalent parallel resistance of two resistors. A basic structure chart, given in Figure 8.3, shows that get_values() returns the variables R1 and R2; in order to change their values they are sent as pointers. It also shows that the variables sent to `calc_parallel_res()` are R1, R2 and R_equ is returned. Variables R1, R2 and R_equ are then passed into `print_results()`.Test run 8.2 shows a sample run.

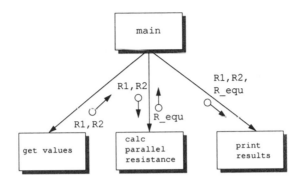

Figure 8.3 Structure chart for Program 8.4

Program 8.4

```
program prog8_4(input,output);

var      R1,R2,R_equ:real;

procedure get_values(var r1,r2:real);
begin
   repeat
      write('Enter R1 >>');
      readln(r1);
      if (r1<=0) then writeln('INVALID: re-enter');
   until (r1>0);

   repeat
      write('Enter R2 >>');
      readln(r2);
      if (r2<=0) then writeln('INVALID: re-enter');
   until (r2>0);
end;

procedure get_parallel_res(r1,r2:real;var r_e:real);
begin
   r_e:=1/(1/r1+1/r2);
end;

procedure print_results(r1,r2,r_e:real);
begin
      writeln('Parallel resistors ', r1:8:3, ' and ',r2:8:3, 'ohm');
      writeln('Equivalent resistance is ',r_e:8:3, ' ohm');
end;

begin
   get_values(R1,R2);
   get_parallel_res(R1,R2,R_equ);
   print_results(R1,R2,R_equ);
end.
```

```
Enter R1 >> 1000
Enter R2 >> 800
Parallel resistors 1000.000 and   800.000 ohm
Equivalent resistance is   444.444 ohm
```

8.4 Exercises

8.4.1   Write a program with a single procedure that returns the values of m and c for a straight line, given passed values of (x_1, y_1) and (x_2, y_2). The equation of the straight line is given by:

$$y = mx + c \qquad \text{where } m = \frac{y_2 - y_1}{x_2 - x_1} \text{ and } c = y_1 - mx_1$$

An example call for Pascal is:

```
calc_line(x1,y1,x2,y2,m,c);
```

where x1, y1, x2, y2 are the co-ordinates, m is the return gradient and c is the returned value for the point at which the line cuts the y-axis. The following is an outline of the program:

```
program prog(input,output);

var gradient, c_val, x1, x2, y1, y2: real;

procedure calc_line(x1,y1,x2,y2:real; var m,c:real);
begin
   (*  *** to be completed *** *)
end;

begin
   writeln('Enter x1 and y1 >>'); readln(x1,y1);
   writeln('Enter x2 and y2 >>'); readln(x2,y2);

   calc_line(x1,y1,x2,y2,gradient,c_val);

   writeln('Gradient is ', gradient:8:2);
   writeln('C value is ',c_val:8:2);
end.
```

8.4.2   Write a program which contains a module which is passed two parameters. The module should arrange the values of the parameters so that the first parameter is the largest. The following is an outline of the program:

```
program prog(input,output);

var value1, value2: real;

procedure find_largest(var val1,val2:real);
begin
   (*   *** to be completed *** *)
end;

begin
   writeln('Enter two values'); readln(value1,value2);
   find_largest(value1,value2);
   writeln('Largest is ', value1:8:2);
   writeln('Smallest is ',value2:8:2);
end.
```

8.4.3   Modify the program in Exercise 8.4.2 so that it orders the values in
the opposite way (that is, the smallest as the first parameter and the
largest as the second).

8.4.4   Write a module, with parameter passing, in which a minimum and
maximum value are passed to it and the module returns back an entered value which is between the minimum and maximum value.
Example call is:

```
get_value(min,max,val);
```

where min is the minimum value, max is the maximum value and
val is the return value. An outline program which uses this procedure is given next:

```
program prog(input,output);

var value: integer;

procedure get_value(min,max:integer; var val:integer);
begin

   repeat
      (*   *** to be completed *** *)
   until ((val>=min) and (val<=max));

end;

begin
   writeln('Enter a value >>');
   get_value(0,100,value);
            (* get value between 0 and 100 *)

   writeln('Entered value is ', value);
end.
```

8.4.5   Resistors are normally identified by means of a colour-coding system, which is given in Table 8.1. Figure 8.4 shows a four-band resistor, where the first two bands give a digit, the third a multiplier and the fourth the tolerance. Write a program, with parameter passing, in which the user enters the first three values of the code and the program determines the resistor value. The value range of inputs is between 0 and 9 and a sample run is shown in Test run 8.3.

⌨ **Test run 8.3**

```
Enter band 1 value >> 100
INVALID: re-enter
Enter band 1 value >> 3
Enter band 2 value >> 4
Enter band 3 value >> 2
Resistor value is 3400 ohms
```

An outline program is given next:

```
program prog(input,output);

var band1, band2, band3, multiplier, resistance: integer;

procedure get_value(min,max:integer; var val:integer);
begin

   repeat
      (*   *** to be completed *** *)
   until ((val>=min) and (val<=max));

end;

function pow(x,n:integer):integer;
begin
      (*   *** to be completed *** *)
end;

begin
   writeln('Enter band 1 value >>');
   get_value(0,9,band1);

   writeln('Enter band 2 value >>');
   get_value(0,9,band2);

   writeln('Enter band 3 value >>');
   get_value(0,7,band3);

   multiplier:=pow(10,band3);
   resistance:=band1*10*band1*multiplier;

   writeln(' Resistor value is ', resistance, ' ohms');

end.
```

Table 8.1 Resistor colour coding

Digit	Colour	Multiplier	No. of zeros
0	Black	1	0
1	Brown	10	1
2	Red	100	2
3	Orange	1K	3
4	Yellow	10K	4
5	Green	100K	5
6	Blue	1M	6
7	Violet	10M	7
8	Grey		
9	White		

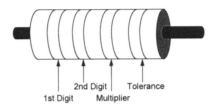

Figure 8.4 Four-band resistor colour code

8.4.6   Write a program which has a module which converts a complex number in rectangular form into polar form (magnitude and angle). The module should have two values passed to it (x and y) and return two values for the magnitude and angle of the complex number (*mag* and *angle*). These values are determined using:

if $z = |Z|\langle\theta\rangle = x + \mathrm{i}y$

then

$$|Z| = \sqrt{x^2 + y^2}$$
$$\theta = \tan^{-1}\left(\frac{y}{x}\right) \quad \text{radians}$$

Example call is:

```
convert_polar(x,y,mag,angle);
```

8.4.7 Write a program which has a module which converts a complex number in polar form into rectangular form (real and imaginary). The module should have two values passed to it (*mag* and *angle*) and return two values for the real and imaginary parts of the complex number (*x* and *y*). These values are determined using:

$$\text{if } z = |Z|\langle\theta\rangle = x + iy$$

then

$$x = |Z|\cos\theta$$
$$y = |Z|\sin\theta$$

Example call is:

```
convert_rect(mag,angle,x,y);
```

9 | Arrays

9.1 Introduction

An array stores more than one value, of a common data type, under a collective name. Each value has a unique slot and is referenced using an indexing technique. Figure 9.1 shows a circuit with five resistors, which could be declared with a program with five real declarations. If these resistor variables were required to be passed into a function all five would have to be passed through the parameter list. A neater method uses arrays to store all of the values under a common name (in this case R). Thus a single array variable can then be passed into any function that uses it.

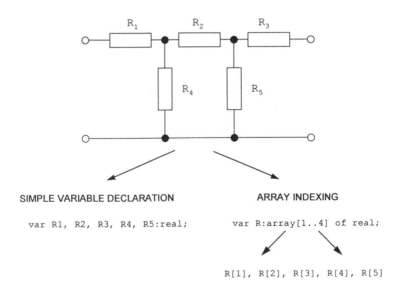

SIMPLE VARIABLE DECLARATION

```
var R1, R2, R3, R4, R5:real;
```

ARRAY INDEXING

```
var R:array[1..4] of real;
```

```
R[1], R[2], R[3], R[4], R[5]
```

Figure 9.1   Simple variables against array indexing

9.2 Pascal arrays

In Pascal, the declaration of an array specifies the data type, the array name and the number of elements in the array in brackets ([ ]). The following gives the standard format for an array declaration.

```
var arr_name : array[startval..endval] of datatype;
```

This declares an array of type *datatype* with the first element of *array_name* [*startval*] to the last array element *array_name* [*endval*]. The following gives some example array declarations and assignments.

```
var circuit:array[1..10] of integer;
var impedance:array[1..50] of real;

  circuit[1]:=42;
  impedance[20]:=3.14;
```

9.2.1 Passing arrays to functions

In order to pass an array into a Pascal function or a procedure the array type must first be defined. This is achieved with the `type` keyword and an array definition is normally done before any of the procedures or functions. For example to define an array type with 100 elements of real values:

```
type arrtype:array[1..100] of real;
```

and an example array is declared with:

```
var   myarr: arrtype;
```

When an array is passed into a function or a procedure, the type definition must be used to define the array type. The following section of code gives an example of array passing into a function. In this case the array type has been defined as `arrtype` and the name of the array in the main program is `arr1`. In the function the array name is `arrayin`.

```
program maxprog(input,output);

type arrtype=array[1..100] of real;
var   arr1:arrtype;
      x:real;

function maximum(n:integer; arrayin:arrtype):real;
var max:real;
    i:integer;
begin
(* n is the number of elements in the array            *)
(* This function determines maximum value in an array  *)

  max:=arrayin[1];
  for i:=2 to n do
    if (max<arrayname[i]) then max:=arrayin[i];
  maximum:=max;
```

```
end;

begin
    :   :   :
        x:=maximum(10,arr1);
    :   :   :
end.
```

If an array is passed to a procedure, the only way that the procedure can modify the contents of an array so that when its contents are changed when the
procedure has completed is to put the `var` keyword in front of its declaration
in the parameter list. The following shows an example of two procedures
which can modify the contents of an array. In the first, `fill_arr`, the function modifies the array passed to it as there is a `var` in front of it in the parameter list. If there was no var in front of the array name then the contents of
the passed array could be modified within this function but when the function
was complete then the array which is passed to the `fill_arr` function
(`array1`) would not have been modified. In the `copy_arr` procedure, the
first array passed (`arr1`) does not have its contents changed as there is no
`var` keyword in front of it in the parameter list, whereas the second array
passed (`arr2`) has the `var` keyword in front of it. The section of the code
should fill an array with entered values (`arr1`) and then copy this array into
another (`arr2`).

```
program arrprog(input,output);

type arrtype=array[1..100] of real;
var  array1, array2:arrtype;

procedure copy_arr(n:integer; arr1:arrtype; var arr2:arrtype);
var        i:integer;
begin
    for i:=1 to n do
        arr2[i]:=arr1[i];
end;

procedure fill_arr(n:integer;var arr:arrtype);
var        i:integer;
begin
    for i:=1 to n do
    begin
        write('Enter value >>');
        readln(arr[i]);
    end;
end;

begin
    fill_arr(10,array1);
    copy_arr(10,array1,array2);
    :   :   :
end.
```

9.3 Examples

9.3.1 *Running average program*

Program 9.1 is a three-point running average program. This type of program has a low-pass filter response and can filter data samples. Figure 9.2 illustrates how the output is a function of the average of three elements in the input array; this is achieved by generating a running average.

The first and last values of the processed array will take on the same values as the input array as there are not three values over which to take an average. Test run 9.1 shows a sample run with 10 entered values.

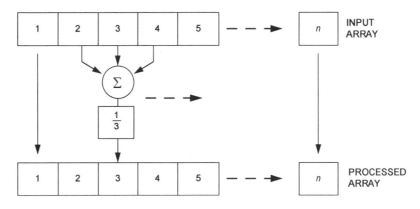

Figure 9.2 Array elements

📋 **Program 9.1**

```pascal
program prog9_1(input,output);

const ARRAYSIZE=150;

type arrtype = array[1..ARRAYSIZE] of real;

var   input,output:arrtype;
      nvalues:integer;

procedure filter(n:integer;array_in:arrtype;var array_out:arrtype);
var       i:integer;
begin

   array_out[1]:=array_in[1];
   array_out[n]:=array_in[n];

   for i:=2 to n-1 do
      array_out[i]:=(array_in[i-1]+array_in[i]+array_in[i+1])/3;
end;

procedure get_values(var n:integer;var arr:arrtype);
var   i:integer;
```

```
            okay:boolean;
begin
   repeat
      writeln('Enter number of values to be processed >>');
      readln(n);
      if ((n<0) or (n>ARRAYSIZE)) then
      begin
         writeln('Max elements are ',ARRAYSIZE);
         okay:=FALSE;
      end
      else okay:=TRUE;
   until (okay=TRUE);

   for i:=1 to n do
   begin
      write('Enter value >> ');
      readln(arr[i]);
   end;
end;

procedure print_values(n:integer; array_in,array_out:arrtype);
var        i:integer;
begin

   writeln('Input    Output');
   for i:=1 to n do
      writeln(array_in[i]:6:3,array_out[i]:6:3);
end;

begin
   get_values(nvalues,input);
   filter(nvalues,input,output);
   print_values(nvalues,input,output);
end.
```

🖳 **Test run 9.1**

```
Enter number of values to be processed >> 10
Enter value >> 3
Enter value >> -2
Enter value >> 4
Enter value >> 10

Enter value >> 3

Enter value >> 2
Enter value >> 1
Enter value >> 0
Enter value >> 19
Enter value >> 14
Input    Output
  3.000   3.000
 -2.000   1.667
  4.000   4.000
 10.000   5.667
  3.000   5.000
  2.000   2.000
  1.000   1.000
  0.000   6.667
 19.000  11.000
 14.000  14.000
```

9.3.2 Sorting program

Program 9.2 is an example of a sorting program where an array is passed to the `sort` function, which then orders the values from smallest to largest. The algorithm initially checks the first value in an array with all the other values. If the value in the first position is greater than the sampled array value then the two values are swapped.

Figure 9.3 shows an example of how a six-element array can be sorted to determine the smallest value. In the first iteration the value of 20 is compared with 22. Since 20 is smaller than 22 the values are not swapped. Next, the value of 20 is compared with 12 (the third element), as this is smaller the values are swapped. This now makes 12 the first element. This continues until the last value (15) is tested. At the end of these iterations the smallest value (3) will be the first element in the array. As the first element now contains the smallest value the operation can now continue onto the second element. This is tested against the third, fourth, fifth and sixth elements and so on. The number of iterations required to complete this process will therefore be 15 (5+4+3+2+1).

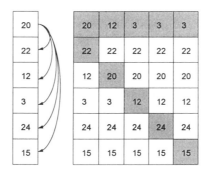

Figure 9.3 Array elements

Program 9.2

```
program prog9_2(input,output);
const ARRAYSIZE=150;

type arrtype = array[1..ARRAYSIZE] of real;

var  arr:arrtype;
     nvalues:integer;

procedure get_values(var n:integer;var arr:arrtype);
var  i:integer;
     okay:boolean;
begin
   repeat
     writeln('Enter number of values to be processed >>');
     readln(n);
     if ((n<0) or (n>ARRAYSIZE)) then
     begin
```

```
              writeln('Max elements are ',ARRAYSIZE);
              okay:=FALSE;
          end
          else okay:=TRUE;
      until (okay=TRUE);

      for i:=1 to n do
      begin
          write('Enter value >> ');
          readln(arr[i]);
      end;
  end;

  procedure print_values(n:integer; array_in:arrtype);
  var       i:integer;
  begin

      writeln('Ordered values');
      for i:=1 to n do
          writeln(array_in[i]:8:3);
  end;

  procedure order(var val1,val2:real);
  (* val1 is the smallest    *)
  var temp:real;
  begin
      if (val1 > val2) then
      begin
          temp := val1;
          val1 := val2;
          val2 := temp;
      end;
  end;

  procedure sort(n:integer; var inarr:arrtype);
  var i,j:integer;
  begin
      for i:=1 to n-1 do
          for j:=n downto i+1 do
              order(inarr[i],inarr[j]);
  end;

  begin
      get_values(nvalues,arr);
      sort(nvalues,arr);
      print_values(nvalues,arr);
  end.
```

Test run 9.2 shows a sample run with 10 entered values.

9.3.3 Preferred values

Program 9.3 determines the nearest preferred resistor value in the range 10
to 100 Ω. An initialized array pref_values[] contains normalized preferred values of 10, 12, 15, 18, 22, 27, 33, 39, 47, 56, 68, 82 and 100 Ω. The
set_pref procedure is used to fill up the pref_values array.

```
Enter number of values be processed >> 10
Enter value >> 3
Enter value >> -2
Enter value >> 4
Enter value >> 10
Enter value >> 3
Enter value >> 2
Enter value >> 1
Enter value >> 0
Enter value >> 19
Enter value >> 14
Ordered values
  -2.000     0.000    1.000    2.000    3.000    3.000    4.000   10.000
 14.000    19.000
```

The find_nearest_pref function determines the nearest preferred value. Its operation uses the difference between the entered value and an index value in the preferred value array. If the difference is less than the difference between the previous nearest value and the entered value then the current preferred value will take on the current indexed array value. Figure 9.4 shows a basic structure chart for this program (note the set_pref function has been included for the Pascal equivalent program). Test run 9.3 shows a sample run.

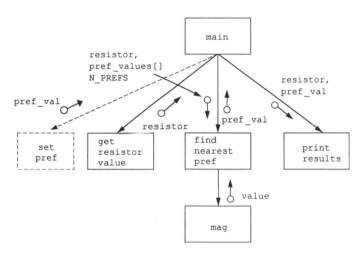

Figure 9.4   Structure chart for Program 9.3

```
Enter a resistance (10-100 ohm) >> 3
Invalid value, re-enter
Enter a resistance (10-100 ohm) >> 45
Value entered   45.000 ohm, pref value is   47.000 ohm
```

Program 9.3

```
program prog9_3(input,output);
const N_PREF=13;

type arrtype = array[1..N_PREF] of integer;

var   pref_values:arrtype;
      resistor,pref_val:integer;

procedure set_pref(var arr:arrtype);
begin
      arr[1]:=10;   arr[2]:=12;   arr[3]:=15;   arr[4]:=18;
      arr[5]:=22;   arr[6]:=27;   arr[7]:=33;   arr[8]:=39;
      arr[9]:=47;   arr[10]:=56;  arr[11]:=68;  arr[12]:=82;
      arr[13]:=100;
end;

procedure get_resistor_value(var r:integer);
var   okay:boolean;
begin
   (* get a value between 10 and 100 ohms *)
   repeat
      write('Enter a resistance (10-100 ohm) >> ');
      readln(r);
      if ( (r<10) or (r>100)) then
      begin
         writeln('Invalid value, re-enter');
         okay:=FALSE;
      end
      else okay:=TRUE;
   until (okay=TRUE);
end;

function mag(val:integer):integer;
begin
   (* Determine the magnitude of val    *)
   if (val<0.0) then mag:=-val
   else mag:=val;
end;

procedure find_nearest_pref(r:integer;pref_arr:arrtype;
                           n_prf:integer; var p_val:integer);
var   i:integer;
begin
   p_val:=pref_arr[1];

   for i:=2 to n_prf do
   begin
      if (mag(r-pref_arr[i])<mag(p_val-r)) then
         p_val:=pref_arr[i];
   end;
end;

procedure print_results(r,pref_r:real);
begin
   writeln('Value entered ', r:8:3, ', pref value is ',
                                    pref_r:8:3,' ohm');
```

```
end;

begin
    set_pref(pref_values);
    get_resistor_value(resistor);
    find_nearest_pref(resistor,pref_values,N_PREF,pref_val);
    print_results(resistor,pref_val);
end.
```

9.4 Multidimensional arrays

Multidimensional arrays are declared in a similar way to one dimensional arrays. In the array type declaration the dimensions of the arrays are seperated by commas. For example an array with 4 rows and 3 columns would be declared with:

```
type arrtype=array[1..4,1..3] of integer;

var arr1:arrtype;
```

The members of this array will thus be:

```
arr1[1,1]    arr1[1,2]    arr1[1,3]
arr1[2,1]    arr1[2,2]    arr1[2,3]
arr1[3,1]    arr1[3,2]    arr1[3,3]
arr1[4,1]    arr1[4,2]    arr1[4,3]
```

Pascal program 9.4 shows an example of filling a 2-dimensional array (arr1) and Test run 9.4 shows a sample run. Note that in this program some of the for loop statements do not need the begin and end keywords as they only contains a single statement.

Program 9.4
```
program prog9_4(input,output);

type arrtype=array[1..4,1..3] of integer;

var arr1:arrtype;
    i,j:integer;

begin
    for i:=1 to 4 do
        for j:=1 to 3 do
            arr1[i,j]:=i*j;

    for i:=1 to 4 do
    begin
        for j:=1 to 3 do
```

```
                    write(arr1[i,j]:8);
          writeln;
      end;
end.
```

```
      1         2         3
      2         4         6
      3         6         9
      4         8        12
```

Pascal program 9.5 shows the equivalent Pascal program with a procedure to fill the array (fill_array) and another procedure to print out its values (show_array). In both cases the dimensions of the array are passed to the procedures with the variables row and col. Both procedures also have the local variables i and j. These variables only exist within these procedures (as do the variables row and col).

Program 9.5

```
program prog9_5(input,output);

type arrtype=array[1..4,1..3] of integer;

var arr1:arrtype;
    i,j:integer;

procedure fill_array(row,col:integer;var arr:arrtype);
var i,j:integer;
begin
     for i:=1 to row do
         for j:=1 to col do
             arr1[i,j]:=i*j;
end;

procedure show_array(row,col:integer; arr:arrtype);
var i,j:integer;
begin

     for i:=1 to row do
     begin
         for j:=1 to col do
             write(arr1[i,j]:8);
         writeln;
     end;

end;

begin

     fill_array(4,3,arr1);
     show_array(4,3,arr1);

end.
```

9.4.1 Write a program, using arrays, with a function that will return the largest value entered by the user. An outline of the program is given next:

```
program test(input,output);

type arrtype=array[1..12] of real;

var   arr1:arrtype;
      largest:real;

function get_largest(num:integer;arr:arrtype):real;
var   large;real;
      i:integer;
begin
   large:=arr[1];
   for i:=2 to num do
   begin
      (* *** to be completed *** *)
   end;
   get_largest:=large;
end;

procedure get_array(num:integer;var arr:arrtype);
var i,j:integer;
begin
      for i:=1 to num do
      begin
         writeln('Enter value >>');
         readln(arr[i]);
      end;
end;

begin
   get_array(12,arr1);
   largest:=get_largest(12,arr1);
   writeln('Largest value is ',largest:8:2);
end.
```

9.4.2 Repeat Exercise 9.4.1 with a smallest value function.

9.4.3 Write a function that will arrange an array in descending values. Refer to Program 9.2.

9.4.4 Modify Program 9.3 so that it determines the nearest preferred resistor value between 10 and 100 Ω for the set of preferred values given in Table 9.1.

Table 9.1 Preferred resistor values

10	16	27	43	68
11	18	30	47	76
12	20	33	51	82
13	22	36	56	91
15	24	39	62	100

9.4.5   Write a function which scales an entered real value so that it scales it between 10 and 100 and displays the number of zeros. A sample run is given in Test run 9.5.

Test run 9.5

```
Enter a value >> 32100
Value is 32.1 with 3 zeros
```

Possible algorithm is:

```
num_zeros:=0;

while (val<=10) do
begin
    val:=val/10;
    num_zeros:=num_zeros+1;
end;
```

where, after these codes are complete, the value of `val` will be between 10 and 100 and the `num_zeros` will have the number of scaling zeros.

9.4.6   Modify Program 9.3 so the user can enter any value of resistance and the program will determine the nearest preferred resistor value. Test run 9.6 gives a sample run. Hint: write a function which scales the entered value between 10 and 100 Ω (as written in Exercise 9.4.5) then pass the scaled value to the preferred value's function.

Test run 9.6

```
Enter resistor value >> 42130
Nearest preferred value is 43000 ohms
```

9.4.7   Write a program which will fill an array with values for the function:

$$y = x^2 + 6x - 2$$

for $x = 1$ to 10 (that is 1, 2, 3, 4, 5, ..., 10).

9.4.8 Modify the program in 9.4.7 for a range of −1 to 1, with a step of 0.1 in between (that is, −1, −0.9, −0.8, ... 0.8, 0.9, 1).

9.4.9 Write a program which fills a two-dimensional array with five rows and four columns. Each row should be filled with row number, the row number squared, the row number cubed and the row number to the forth power. Thus the array will contain:

1	1	1	1
2	4	8	16
3	8	27	81
4	16	64	256
5	25	125	625

Rewrite the program using a procedure to fill the array and another one to display its contents.

9.4.10 Figure 9.5 shows an alternative representation of the program developed in Section 9.3.1 with the array values represented as time sampled values, where the D represents a single time step delay. In this case the input value `value` is delayed by a single time step (Input[i–1]) and two time steps (Input[i–2]). The representation of the output can be written as:

$$Output[i] = \frac{1}{3}\big(Input[i] + Input[i-1] + Input[i-2]\big)$$

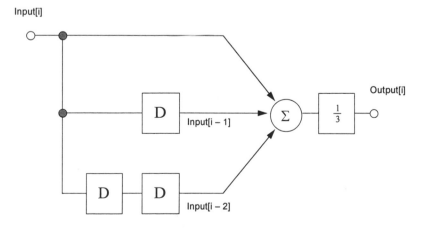

Figure 9.5 Averaging system for time sampling

For the input data of:

Sample	1	2	3	4	5	6	7	8	9	10	11	12
Input	3	4	10	3	-1	-2	-5	-1	4	12	15	20

Determine the output for the following functions:

(i) $Output[i] = \dfrac{1}{2}(Input[i] + Input[i-1])$

(ii) $Output[i] = \dfrac{1}{10}(2\,Input[i] + 6\,Input[i-1] + 2\,Input[i-2])$

(iii) $Output[i] = (Input[i] - Input[i-1])$

Assume that the previous samples to $i=0$ are zero. Test run 9.7 gives a sample run of (i) and Program 9.6 shows a sample program which does not have any functions or procedures.

⊟ **Test run 9.7**

```
I       Input      Output
0       3.00       3.00
1       4.00       3.50
2      10.00       7.00
3       3.00       6.50
4      -1.00       1.00
5      -2.00      -1.50
6      -5.00      -3.50
7      -1.00      -3.00
8       4.00       1.50
9      12.00       8.00
10     15.00      13.50
11     20.00      17.50
```

⌷ **Program 9.6**

```pascal
program prog9_6(input,output);

type arrtype=array[1..12] of real;

var arr1,arr2:arrtype;
    i:integer;

begin
      arr1[1]:=3; arr1[2]:=4; arr1[3]:=10;
      arr1[4]:=3; arr1[5]:=-1;arr1[6]:=-2;
      arr1[7]:=-5; arr1[8]:=-1;arr1[9]:=4;
      arr1[10]:=12; arr1[11]:=15; arr1[12]:=20;

      arr2[1]:=arr1[1];

      for i:=2 to 12 do
```

```
begin
   arr2[i]:=(arr1[i]+arr1[i-1])/2;
end;

writeln('I    Input    Output');

for i:=1 to 12 do
begin
    writeln(i:3,arr1[i]:8:2,arr2[i]:8:2);
end;
end.
```

(10) Strings

10.1 Introduction

Strings are one-dimensional arrays containing characters. In most cases the number of characters a string has will vary, depending on the input. Thus they must be declared with the maximum number of characters that is likely to occur. Typically they are used to store names. They can also be used when numeric values are entered into a program. With this the program reads the value as a string of characters and then converts it into the required numeric format. This allows the program to determine if the user has entered the value in an invalid numeric format, such as with letters.

10.2 Pascal strings

Pascal has a special data type reserved for character arrays, which is string. The string size can be set as the standard form of an array declaration. For example:

```
var   str1:string[100];(* string with up to 100 characters   *)
      str2:string[50];  (* string with up to 50 characters    *)
```

If the string size parameter is excluded, such as:

```
var   str1:string;       (* string with up to 255 characters   *)
```

then the string is assumed to have a size of 255 characters.

Table 10.1 lists the routines (functions and procedures) which are used to manipulate strings and Table 10.2 shows the routines which are used to convert from numeric value into strings, and vice versa.

Program 10.1 shows an example program which uses strings. The assignment operator (:=) is used to assign one string to another (in this case, str1 to str2). The length function is also used to determine the number of characters in the entered string.

A major problem in software development is to guard against incorrect user input. Typically a user may enter a string of characters instead of a numeric value, or a real value instead of an integer. Program 10.2 contains a function (`get_int`) which overcomes this problem. In this function the user enters an input into a string (`inp`). This string is then converted into a numeric value using the `val` function. One of the parameters of the `val` function is *code*. If, after it is called, it is a zero then the string has been successfully converted, else either a string or a real value was entered. The user will be told that the input is invalid and will be reprompted for another value (as the `repeat...until` condition is false). The equivalent function to get a real value is:

```
function get_real(msg:string):real;
var       inp:string;
          code:integer; value:real;
begin

    write(msg);

    repeat

        readln(inp);

        val(inp,value,code);

        if (code<>0) then writeln('Invalid input');
    until (code=0);
    get_real:=value;

end;
```

Table 10.1 Pascal array routines

Routine	Description
```function pos(substr:string; str:string) :byte;```	Searches a string (`str`) for a sub-string (`substr`) and returns its position
```procedure Delete(var str : string; index : Integer; count : Integer);```	Deletes a sub-string (`str`) from a string starting at `index` and ending at `index+count`
```function Copy(str : string; index : Integer; count : Integer) : string;```	Returns a sub-string of a string (`str`) starting at `index` and ending at `index+count`
```function Concat(s1 [, s2, ..., sn]: string): string;```	Concatenates a sequence of strings
```procedure Insert(source : string; var str : string; index : Integer);```	Inserts a sub-string (`str`) into a string (`s`)

Table 10.2 Pascal string conversion routines

Routine	Description

procedure Val(str : string;
  var val;
  var code : Integer);
	Converts a string value (str) to its numeric representation (val), as if it were read from a text file with Read
	code is a variable of type Integer. If it is 0 then there is no error else it displays the position of the error

procedure Str(x [: width [: decimals]]; var str : string);	Converts a numeric value (x) into a string representation (str)

Program 10.1

```
program prog10_1(input,output);

var      str1,str2:string;

begin
     writeln('Enter your name >>');
     readln(str1);

     str2:=str1;
     writeln('String 1 is ',str1);
     writeln('String 2 is ',str2);
     writeln('Number of characters in name is ',length(str1));
end.
```

Program 10.2

```
program prog10_2(input,output);

var      i:integer;

function get_int(msg:string):integer;
var      inp:string;
         code,value:integer;
begin

     write(msg);
     repeat
          readln(inp);
          val(inp,value,code);
          if (code<>0) then writeln('Invalid input');
     until (code=0);
     get_int:=value;

end;

begin
     i:=get_int('Enter an integer >>');
     writeln('Entered value is ',i);
end.
```

```
Enter an integer >> abc
Invalid input
Enter an integer >> 44.4
Invalid input
Enter an integer >> 12
Entered value is 12
```

10.3 Examples

10.3.1 Counting the number of characters

Program 10.3 contains a function (nochars()) which scans a string and determines the number of occurrences of a given character. It uses readln() to read the string as it accepts spaces between words.

The function nochars() uses array indexing to test each of the characters in the array to determine if it has a specific character. Test run 10.2 shows a sample run.

📋 **Program 10.3**
```
program prog10_3(input,output);
(* Find the number of occurrences in a string *)

var str1:string;
    ch:char;

function nochars(str:string; c:char):integer;
var no_occ,i:integer;
begin
   no_occ:=0;
   for i:=1 to length(str) do
   begin
      if (c= str[i]) then no_occ:=no_occ+1;
   end;
   nochars:=no_occ; (* no of characters found *)
end;

begin
   writeln('Enter a string >>');
   readln(str1);

   writeln('Enter a letter to find >>');
   readln(ch);

   writeln('Number of occurrences is ',nochars(str1,ch));
end.
```

```
Enter a string >> resistor 1 is 100 ohms
Enter a letter to find >> s
Number of occurrences is 4
```

10.3.2 Setting up an array of strings

An array of strings can also be set up by declaring a new data type. An example of this is given in Program 10.4. In this case a new data type is declared (`str_arr`) which is an array of strings (in this case 50 strings).

A sample run is given in Test run 10.3. Note that the string "exit" quits the program.

📋 **Program 10.4**
```
program prog10_4(input,output);

const MAX_COMP_NAMES=50;

type str_arr=array[1..MAX_COMP_NAMES] of string;

var components:integer;
    database:str_arr;

procedure get_component_name(var comp:integer; var data:str_arr);
begin
   write('Enter component name >>');
   comp:=comp+1;
   readln(data[comp]);
end;

procedure print_component_names(comp:integer; data:str_arr);
var        i:integer;
begin
   writeln('Component Names');
   for i:=1  to comp do
      writeln(i,' ',data[i]);
end;

begin
    components:=0;

    repeat
       get_component_name(components,database);
       print_component_names(components,database);
    until ((components=MAX_COMP_NAMES) or
                      (database[components]='exit'));

end.
```

⌨ **Test run 10.3**
```
Enter component name >>resistor 1
0           resistor 1
Enter component name >>resistor 2
```

```
Component Names
0               resistor 1
1               resistor 2
Enter component name >>capacitor 1
Component Names
0               resistor 1
1               resistor 2
2               capacitor 1
Enter component name >>capacitor 4
Component Names
0               resistor 1
1               resistor 2
2               capacitor 1
3               capacitor 4
Enter component name >>inductor 5
Component Names
0               resistor 1
1               resistor 2
2               capacitor 1
3               capacitor 4
4               inductor 5
Enter component name >>exit
```

10.3.3 Impedance of a parallel RC circuit

Program 10.5 determines the impedance of a parallel RC circuit. Figure 10.1 gives a schematic of this circuit. The impedance of this circuit can be found using the product of the impedances over the sum. Thus:

$$Z = \frac{R\dfrac{1}{j\omega C}}{R + \dfrac{1}{j\omega C}} = \frac{R}{j\omega C(R + \dfrac{1}{j\omega C})} = \frac{R}{j\omega CR + 1}$$

The magnitude of the impedance is thus:

$$|Z| = \frac{R}{\sqrt{1 + (\omega RC)^2}}$$

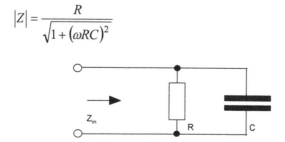

Figure 10.1 Parallel RC circuit

A structure chart for this program which determines this magnitude is given in Figure 10.2 (note that for clarity the parameters passed to the two of the calls to the get_real() function have not been included). The get_parameters() function gets three variables (Res, Cap and freq); parallel_impedance() determines the input impedance and returns it back into the variable Zin. Finally, print_impedance() displays the input parameters and calculated impedance.

The get_real() function gets a value by first putting the entered information into a string and then converting it into a floating point value. If the conversion fails then the user is asked to re-enter the value. It also contains a check for the minimum and maximum value of the entered value.

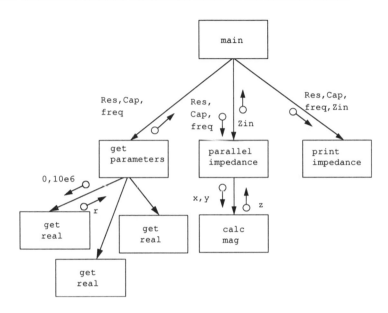

Figure 10.2 Structure chart for Program 10.5

Test run 10.4 shows that the user can enter a value in the incorrect format and the program will re-prompt for another. Notice that the user has entered the strings 'none' and 'fred'; the program copes with these and re-prompts for an input.

🖵 **Test run 10.4**

```
Enter resistance    >>none
Invalid input <none>
Enter resistance    >>fred
Invalid input <fred>
Enter resistance    >>-100
Invalid input <-100>

Enter resistance >>1000
Enter capacitance >>1e-6
Enter frequency       >>1e3
R=1000.000 ohms C=    1.00 uF f=1000.000 Hz
Zin = 24.704565 ohms
```

📋 **Program 10.5**

```pascal
program prog10_5(input,output);

const PI=3.14159; MICRO=1e-6;

var    Res,Cap,freq,Zin:real;

procedure get_real(msg:string; min, max:real; var value:real);
var instr:string;
    code:integer;
    okay:boolean;
begin
  repeat
    write(msg);
    readln(instr);
    val(instr,value,code);
    if (code<>0) then         (* invalid input   *)
    begin
       okay:=FALSE;
       writeln('Invalid input <',instr,'>');
    end
    else okay:=TRUE;

  until (okay=TRUE);
end;

procedure get_parameters(var r,c,f:real);
begin
  get_real('Enter resistance  >> ',0,10e6,r);
  get_real('Enter capacitance >> ',0,1,c);
  get_real('Enter frequency   >> ',0,1e7,f);
end;

procedure print_impedance(r,c,f,Z:real);
begin
  writeln('R=',r,' ohms C=',c/MICRO,' uF f=',f,'Hz');
  writeln('Zin = ',Z,' ohms');
end;

function calc_mag(x,y:real):real;
begin
  calc_mag:=x*x+y*y;
end;

procedure parallel_impedance(r,c,f:real;var Z:real);
begin
  Z:=r/(calc_mag(1,2*PI*f*r*c));
end;

begin
  get_parameters(Res,Cap,freq);
  parallel_impedance(Res,Cap,freq,Zin);
  print_impedance(Res,Cap,freq,Zin);
end.
```

10.4.1   Explain why it is better to input numeric values as a string and then converting it to a numeric value rather than entering it with `readln()`.

10.4.2   Write a program that declares the following seven strings.

```
'Option 1','Option 2','Option 3',
'Option 4','Option 5','Option 6', 'EXIT'
```

Store these strings as a single array of strings named `menu` by declaring an array of strings. The program should display these strings as menu options using a `for` loop. Test run 10.5 shows a sample run.

⌨   **Test run 10.5**
```
Menu Options
    Option 1
    Option 2
    Option 3
    Option 4
    Option 5
    Option 6
    EXIT
```

10.4.3   Modify the program in Exercise 10.4.2 so that the user can enter the menu option. The program will display a message on the option selected. Test run 10.6 shows a sample run.

⌨   **Test run 10.6**
```
Menu Options
    Option 1
    Option 2
    Option 3
    Option 4
    Option 5
    Option 6

    EXIT
Enter option >> Option 2
    >>> Option 2 selected
Menu Options
    Option 1
    Option 2
    Option 3
    Option 4
    Option 5
    Option 6
    EXIT
Enter option >> EXIT
```

10.4.4 Modify some programs in previous chapters so that program parameters are entered using the `get_real()` function.

10.4.5 Write a function that will capitalize all the characters in a string.

10.4.6 Repeat Exercise 10.4.5 but make the characters lower case.

10.4.7 Write a function that determines the number of words in a string.

10.4.8 Write a program in which the user enters a string of text and then presses the RETURN key. The program will then display the number of characters in the entered text. A sample run is shown in Test run 10.7.

🖳 **Test run 10.7**
```
Enter some text >> This is some sample text

This string has 24 characters
```

10.4.9 Write a program in which the user enters a string of either "sin", "cos" or "tan" and then a value. The program will then determine the corresponding sine, cosine or tan of the value. A sample run is shown in Test run 10.8.

🖳 **Test run 10.8**
```
Enter a math function
    Sin
    Cos
    Tan
    Exit

>> Sin
Enter a value (in degrees) >> 30
Sin of 30 degrees is 0.5
Enter a math function
    Sin

    Cos

    Tan
    Exit

>> Exit
```

10.4.10 Modify the program in 10.4.9 so that the program reads in the entered value as a string and converts it to a real value. The program should re-prompt if the value is invalid.

10.4.11 Write a program in which the user enters a number of names, each followed by the RETURN key. The end of the names is signified by entering no characters. The program should store these in an array of strings and then display them to the user. A sample run is shown in Test run 10.9.

11 File I/O

11.1 Introduction

Information on computers is organized into directories and files. Typically files have a filename followed by a filename extension which identifies the type of file. This file extension is important in some operating systems, such as Windows 95 and Windows NT, as it identifies the application program which is associated with the file. Table 11.1 shows some typical file types.

Table 11.1 Typical file types

File extension	File type	File extension	File type
`.c`	C program	`.jpg`	JPEG file (compressed image)
`.doc`	Word processor	`.txt`	Text file (ASCII coding)
`.bmp`	Bitmapped graphics file	`.exe`	PC executable file
`.gif`	GIF file (compressed image file)	`.obj`, `.o`	Object code
`.avi`	Motion video	`.xls`	Microsoft Excel spreadsheet
`.ps`	Postscript file (printer output)	`.hlp`	Help files
`.au`	Compressed sound file	`.for`	FORTRAN program
`.wav`	Sound file	`.pas`	Pascal program
`.mpg`	Compressed motion video	`.java`	Java program

Files either contain text in the form of ASCII (a text file) or binary data. A text file uses ASCII characters and a binary file uses the binary digits which the computer uses to store values. It is not normally possible to view a binary file without a special program, but a text file can be viewed with a text editor.

Figure 11.1 shows an example of two files which contain four integer values. The binary file stores integers using two bytes in 2s complement signed notation (refer to Appendix C.3), whereas the text file uses ASCII characters to represent the values. For example, the value of −1 is represented as 11111111 11111111 in 2s complement. This binary pattern is stored to the binary file. The text file uses ASCII characters to represent −1 (these will be '−' and '1'), and the bit pattern stored for the text file will thus be 0010

103

1101 (ASCII '–') and 0011 0001 (ASCII '1'). If a new line is required after each number then a new-line character is inserted after it. Note, there is no new-line character in ASCII and it is typical to represent a new-line with two characters, a carriage return (CR) and a line feed (LF).

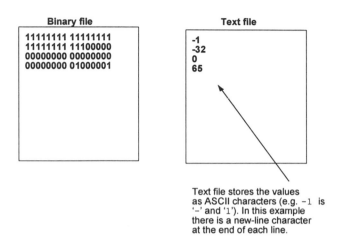

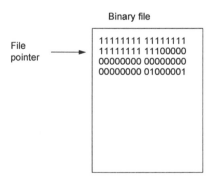

Text file stores the values as ASCII characters (e.g. –1 is '–' and '1'). In this example there is a new-line character at the end of each line.

Figure 11.1 Binary and text files

The file pointer moves as each element is read/written. Figure 11.2 shows a file pointer pointing to the current position within the file.

The number of bytes used to store each of the elements will depend on the data type of the variable. For example, a long integer will be stored as four bytes, and a floating point value can also be stored as four bytes (on some systems). The floating point format differs from an integer format; the standard floating point format uses a sign-bit, a significand and an exponent. The end of the file is signified by an EOF character.

Binary file

File pointer →

```
11111111 11111111
11111111 11100000
00000000 00000000
00000000 01000001
```

Figure 11.2 File pointer

11.2 Pascal file I/O

Pascal has a very basic set of file input/output. The functions used are defined in Table 11.2. A file pointer is defined either with the text keyword (for a text file) or with:

```
var fptr: file of type;
```

Thus a file pointer for an integer file would use the following:

```
var fptr: file of integer;
```

Pascal Program 11.1 reads in a number of integer values and writes each one in turn to a file ('out.dat'). The program initially assigns the filename to the file pointer (fout) using the assign function. Next the file is created with the rewrite function. Each value that is entered is then written to the file using the write function. The program keeps prompting for values until the user enters a −1 value. When this happens the program will exit the re-peat...until loop. The file pointer is then reset to the start of the file with the reset function. Next the values are read back using the read function. Finally, after the −1 value is read in, the file is closed with the close routine.

Table 11.2 Pascal file I/O functions

Function	Description
assign (*fptr, fname*)	Assigns a file pointer (*fptr*) to a file (*fname*)
rewrite (*fptr*)	Creates and opens a file which has been assigned with *fptr* for output
reset (*fptr*)	Opens an existing file which has been assigned with *fptr* for input
write (*fptr, val*)	Writes a value (*val*) to a file which has been assigned with *fptr*
read (*fptr, val*)	Reads a file which has been assigned with *fptr* and puts the value into *val*

Program 11.1
```
program prog11_1(input,output);
var   fout : text;
      val:integer;
```

```
begin
   assign(fout,'out.dat');

   rewrite(fout); (* create new file *)

   repeat
      write('Enter a value');
      readln(val);
      writeln(fout,val);
   until (val=-1);

   reset(fout); (* set file pointer back to the start of the file *)

   writeln('Values in file are:');

   repeat
      readln(fout, val);
      if (val<>-1) then writeln(val);
   until (val=-1);

   close(fout);
end.
```

11.3 Examples

11.3.1 Averages program

Pascal Program 11.2 uses text files to determine the average value of a number of floating point values contained in a file. The `get_values()` function is used to read the values from a file, in this case, *IN.DAT*. This file can be created using a text editor. An example of the contents of the *IN.DAT* file are given next.

```
3.240
1.232
6.543
-1.432
```

A sample run using this file is given in Test run 11.1.

Test run 11.1
```
INPUT VALUES ARE:
   3.240
   1.232
   6.543
  -1.432
Average is     2.396
```

Program 11.2

```pascal
program prog11_2(input,output);
(* Program to determine the average of a file      *)
(* containing a number of floating point values    *)

const NOVALUES=100; (* max. number of entered values *)

type arrtype=array[1..NOVALUES] of real;

var values:arrtype;
    average:real;
    nvalues:integer;

procedure get_values(maxvals:integer; fname:string; var n:integer;
                     var arr:arrtype);
var infile:text;
begin
     n:=0;
     assign(infile,fname);
     reset(infile);
     while ( (not eof(infile)) and (n<maxvals)) do
     begin
          if (not eof(infile)) then n:=n+1;
          read(infile,arr[n]);
     end;
     close(infile);
end;

function calc_average(nval:integer; arr:arrtype):real;
var i:integer;
    running_total:real;
begin
     running_total:=0;
     for i:=1 to nval do
         running_total:=running_total+arr[i];

     (* note there is no test for a divide by zero *)
     calc_average:=running_total/nval;
end;

procedure display_average(nval:integer; arr:arrtype; aver:real);
var      i:integer;
begin

   writeln('INPUT VALUES ARE:');

   for i:=1 to nval do
     writeln(arr[i]:8:3);

   writeln('Average is ',aver:8:3);
end;

begin
   get_values(NOVALUES,'IN.DAT',nvalues,values);
   average:=calc_average(nvalues,values);
   display_average(nvalues,values,average);
end.
```

11.3.2 Binary read/write

Pascal Program 11.3 is an example of how an array of floating point values is written to a binary file. In the Pascal program the values are written to the file using `write` and read using the `read` routine. A sample test run is given in Test run 11.2.

```
Enter file name >>number.dat
Number of values to be entered >>5
Enter value 0 >>1.435
Enter value 1 >>0.432
Enter value 2 >>-54.32
Enter value 3 >>-1.543
Enter value 4 >>100.01
Values are:
0     1.435
1     0.432
2    -54.320
3    -1.543
4   100.010
```

📋 **Program 11.3**

```pascal
program prog11_3(input,output);
(*       Writes and reads and array of floats           *)
(*       to and from a binary file                      *)
const MAXVALUES=100; (* max. number of floats in array  *)

type float_file=file of real;
     float_arr=array[1..MAXVALUES] of real;

var  fname:string;
     values:float_arr;
     no_values:integer;

procedure get_filename(var fname:string);
begin
   write('Enter file name >>');
   readln(fname);
end;

procedure get_values(maxvals:integer; var vals:
                              float_arr;var nov:integer);
var i:integer;
begin

   repeat
     write('Number of values to be entered >>');
     readln(nov);
     if (nov>maxvals) then
                 writeln('Too many values: MAX:',MAXVALUES);
   until ((nov>0) and (nov<maxvals));

   for i:=1 to nov do
```

```
        begin
                write('Enter value ',i,' >>');
                readln(vals[i]);
        end;
end;

procedure dump_data(fname:string;arr:float_arr;nov:integer);
var outfile:float_file;
    i:integer;
begin

    assign(outfile,fname);  (* assign binary file *)
    rewrite(outfile);

    for i:=1 to nov do
        write(outfile, arr[i]);
    close(outfile);
end;

procedure read_data(fname:string; var arr:float_arr;var nov:integer);
var infile:float_file;
begin
   nov:=0;    (* number of values in the array *)

   assign(infile,fname);
   reset(infile);

   while ( not eof(infile)) do
   begin
      nov:=nov+1;
      read(infile,arr[nov]);
   end;

   close(infile);
end;

procedure print_values(arr:float_arr;nov:integer);
var i:integer;
begin
   writeln('Values are:');

   for i:=1 to nov do
      writeln(i:3,arr[i]:8:3);
end;

begin
   get_filename(fname);
   get_values(MAXVALUES,values,no_values);
   dump_data(fname,values,no_values);
   read_data(fname,values,no_values);
   print_values(values,no_values);
end.
```

11.3.3 Reading and writing one character at a time

In Pascal Program 11.4 a single character is read from a file. It reads a character, one at a time, from a file and writes it to another file. It uses the read and write routines.

```
program copytext(input,output);
var  inf,outf:text;
     ch:char;
begin
     assign(inf,'in.dat');
     reset(inf);

     assign(outf,'out.dat');
     rewrite(outf);          (* create file              *)

     while (not eof(inf)) do
     begin
           read(inf,ch);     (* read character           *)
           write(ch);        (* show character to screen *)
           write(outf,ch);   (* write character          *)
     end;
     close(inf); close(outf);
end.
```

11.4 Exercises

11.4.1   Write a program in which the user enters any character and the program will determine the number of occurrences of that character in the specified file. For example:

```
Enter filename: fred.dat
Enter character to search for: i
There are 14 occurrences of the character i in the file
fred.dat.
```

11.4.2   Write a program which determines the number of words in a file. One possible method is to assume that each word is seperated by a single space character, thus the number of words is equal to the number of spaces plus one. An outline of the code, using this method, is given next:

```
words:=0;

while (not eof(inf)) do
begin
      read(inf,ch);
      if (ch=' ') then
            words:=words+1;
end;
writeln('Words found =',words+1);
```

11.4.3   Write a program which will determine the number of lines in a file. A possible method is to count the number of new-line characters. A

A new-line in a text file is identified with the LF (which has an ASCII decimal value of 10) and CR (which has a ASCII decimal value of 13) characters. An outline of the code is given next:

```
newline:=0;

while (not eof(inf)) do
begin
     read(inf,ch);
     if (ch=#13) then
     begin
          writeln('New-line found');
          newline:=newline+1;
     end;
end;
writeln('New lines found =',newline);
```

11.4.4 Write a program which reads a text file and modify it so that it displays new-line characters with a special character. A text file has the stored ASCII characters LF (#10) and CR (#13), as defined in Appendix B). One possible method is to display the LF and CR characters to the screen with a special character, such as '#'. An outline of the code is given next:

```
while (not eof(inf)) do
begin
     read(inf,ch);
     if ((ch=#13) or (ch=#10)) then write('#')
     else write(ch);
end;
```

11.4.5 Write a program which will determine the average, the largest and the smallest values of a text file containing floating point values in a text form.

11.4.6 Write a program which will count the number of characters in a file. Hint: read the file one character at a time.

11.4.7 Write a program which will count the occurrences of the letter 'a' in a file. Hint: read the file one character at a time.

11.4.8 Write a program which will get rid of blank lines in an input file and write the processed file to an output file. Example input and output files are given next (Hint: read one character at a time and write them to the file, but do not write the new-line characters, unless they are at the end of a line of characters).

Input file:

Value 1	Value 2
100	101.1
150	165.1
200	300.5

Output file:

Value 1	Value 2
100	101.1
150	165.1
200	300.5

12 Records

12.1 Introduction

A record is an identifiable object that contains items which define it. These items are linked under a common grouping. For example, an electrical circuit has certain properties that define it. These could be:

- A circuit title.
- Circuit components with identifiable names.
- Circuit components with known values.

For example, a circuit may have a title of 'RC Filter Circuit', the circuit components are named 'R1', 'R2' and 'C1' and the values of these are $4320\ \Omega$, $1200\ \Omega$ and $1\ \mu F$, respectively. The title and the component names are character strings, whereas the component values are floating points. A structure (or record) groups these properties into a single entity. These groupings are referred to as fields and each field is made up of members.

12.2 Records in Pascal

A structure is a type that is a composite of elements that are distinctive and perhaps of different data types. The following is an example of a structure which will store a single electrical component. The record variable declared, in this case, is Component. It has three fields of differing data types; cost (a real value), code (an integer) and name (a character string).

```
type
   comp = record
     cost:real;
     code:integer;
     name:string;
   end;

var Component:comp;
```

The dot notation (.) accesses each of the members within the record. For example:

```
Component.cost:=30.1;
Component.code:=32201;
Component.name:='Resistor 1';
```

Pascal Program 12.1 is a simple database program. The database stores a record of a single electrical component which includes its name (Component.name), its cost (Component.cost) and its code number (Component.code). The name is a string, the code a signed integer and the cost a floating point value.

Program 12.1

```
program prog12_1(input,output);
type
   comptype = record
      cost:real;
      code:integer;
      name:string;
   end;

var   Component:comptype;

begin
     Component.cost:=30.1;
     Component.code:=32201;
     Component.name:='Resistor 1';
     writeln('Name ',Component.name,' Code ',Component.code,
                ' Cost ',Component.cost);
end.
```

Test run 12.1 shows a sample run.

Test run 12.1
```
Name Resistor 1 Code 32201 Cost 30.100000
```

Pascal Program 12.2 contains a procedure to print the record (print_component()). To pass a structure into a function the data type of the parameter passed must be defined. For the purpose the type keyword is used to define a new data type, in this case, it is named comp.

Program 12.2

```
program prog12_2(input,output);

type
   comptype = record
      cost:real;
```

```
      code:integer;
      name:string;
   end;
var      Component:comptype;

procedure print_component(comp:comptype);
begin
   writeln('Name ',Comp.code, ' Code ',Comp.code,' Cost
',Comp.cost);
end;

begin
     Component.cost:=30.1;
     Component.code:=32201;
     Component.name:='Resistor 1';
     writeln('Name ',Component.name,' Code ',Component.code,
                 ' Cost ',Component.cost);
end.
```

Test run 12.2 shows a sample run.

🖳 Test run 12.2

```
Name Resistor 1 Code 32201 Cost 30.100000
```

Pascal Program 12.3 uses a function to get data into the record (get_component()). The parameter passed into this function has a var in front of the parameter so that it can be passed back to the calling routine.

📋 Program 12.3

```
program prog12_3(input,output);

type
   comptype = record
      cost:real;
      code:integer;
      name:string;
   end;

var   Component:comptype;

procedure get_component(var comp:compType);
begin
   Comp.cost:=30.1;
   Comp.code:=32201;
   Comp.name:='Resistor 1';
end;

procedure print_component(comp:comptype);
begin
   writeln('Name ',Comp.name,' Code ',Comp.code,
                         ' Cost ',Comp.cost);
end;
```

```
begin
   get_component(Component);
   print_component(Component);
end.
```

Test run 12.3 shows that the results are identical to the previous run.

12.3 Array of structures

An array of structures can be set up in a way similar to normal array indexing. When an array is declared the compiler assigns enough memory to hold all its elements. Program 12.4 is similar to Program 12.3, but uses an array of structures to store up to five electrical components. Figure 12.1 shows a structure chart of this program. It uses get_real() and get_int() to filter any invalid inputs for the cost and code of a component. These functions were developed in Chapter 10 and have been reused as they have been well tested and are easily ported into any program. The cost of the electrical components is now limited between 0 and 1000 and the component code from 0 to 32 767. A get_string() function has also been added to get the name of the component. Test run 12.4 shows a sample run.

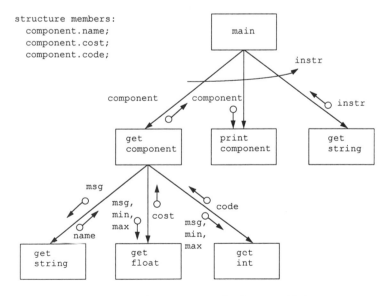

Figure 12.1 Structure chart for Program 12.4

```
Enter name of component >> resistor 1
Enter cost of component >> 1.23
Enter component code >> 32455
Name    resistor 1 Code    32455 Cost    1.23
Do you wish to continue (type 'exit' to leave)y
Enter name of component >> capacitor 1
Enter cost of component >> 2.68
Enter component code >> 32456
Name    resistor 1 Code    32455 Cost    1.23
Name    capacitor 1 Code    32456 Cost    2.68
Do you wish to continue (type 'exit' to leave)y
Enter name of component >> inductor 2
Enter cost of component >> 6.32
Enter component code >> 32457
Name    resistor 1 Code    32455 Cost    1.23
Name    capacitor 1 Code    32456 Cost    2.68
Name    inductor 2 Code    32457 Cost    6.32
Do you wish to continue (type 'exit' to leave)exit
```

📋 **Program 12.4**

```pascal
program prog12_4(input,output);
const MAXCOMPONENTS=50;

type
   comptype = record
      cost:real;
      code:integer;
      name:string;
   end;

   comp_arr=array[1..MAXCOMPONENTS] of comptype;

var   Component:comp_arr;
      NumComponents:integer;
      instr:string;

procedure print_component(n:integer;comp:comp_arr);
var       i:integer;
begin
   for i:=1 to n do
      writeln('Name ',Comp[i].name,' Code ',Comp[i].code,
         ' Cost ',Comp[i].cost);
end;

procedure get_string(msg:string;var ins:string);
begin
   write(msg);
   readln(ins);
end;

procedure get_real(msg:string; min, max:real; var value:real);
var instr:string;
    code:integer;
    okay:boolean;
begin
   repeat
      write(msg);
```

```
      readln(instr);
      val(instr,value,code);
      if (code<>0) then
      begin
         okay:=FALSE;
         writeln('Invalid input <',instr,'>');
      end
      else okay:=TRUE;

   until (okay=TRUE);
end;

procedure get_int(msg:string; min, max:integer; var value:integer);
var instr:string;
    code:integer;
    okay:boolean;
begin
   repeat
      write(msg);
      readln(instr);
      val(instr,value,code);
      if (code<>0) then
      begin
         okay:=FALSE;
         writeln('Invalid input <',instr,'>');
      end
      else okay:=TRUE;

   until (okay=TRUE);
end;

procedure get_component(var n:integer; var Comp:Comp_arr);
begin
   n:=n+1;
   get_string('Enter name of component >> ',Comp[n].name);
   get_real('Enter cost of component >> ',0.0,1000.0,Comp[n].cost);
   get_int('Enter component code >> ',0,1000,Comp[n].code);
end;

begin

   NumComponents:=0;

   repeat
      get_component(NumComponents,Component);
      print_component(NumComponents,Component);
      get_string('Do you wish to continue (type "exit" to leave)',
                               instr);
   until (instr='exit');

end.
```

12.3.1 Complex arithmetic

Program 12.5 uses a structure (or record) to multiply to complex numbers. If these complex numbers are $a+jb$ and $c+jd$ and the result is z then:

$$z = (a + jb)(c + jd)$$
$$= ac + jad + jbc - bd$$
$$= (ac - bd) + j(ad + bc)$$
$$\mathrm{Re}(z) = ac - bd$$
$$\mathrm{Im}(z) = ad + bc$$

This operation is implemented in the procedure multi_rect(). Test run 12.5 gives a test run for the result of *3+j4* and *6+j2*.

Program 12.5

```
program prog12_5(input,output);
type
   rect=record
          x,y:real;
   end;

var z1,z2,z3:rect;

procedure multi_rect(a,b:rect;var c:rect);
begin
     c.x:=a.x*b.x-a.y*b.y;
     c.y:=a.x*b.y+a.y*b.x;
end;

procedure show_rect(a:rect);
begin
     writeln(a.x:8:2,'+j ',a.y:8:2);
end;

begin
     z1.x:=3; z1.y:=4;
     z2.x:=6; z2.y:=2;
     multi_rect(z1,z2,z3);
     show_rect(z3);
end.
```

Test run 12.5
```
10 + j 30
```

12.4 Exercises

12.4.1 Write a database program with a single structure in which the user enters their name, the age and their height. The program should display the entered data.

12.4.2   Modify the program in Exercise 12.4.1 so that it uses a procedure to enter the data into the structure and another which displays the entered data (if the program in Exercise 12.4.1 does not already contain procedures). The following is an outline of the code:

```
program test(input,output);

type
   usertype = record
      height:real;
      age:integer;
      name:string;
   end;

var   user:usertype;

procedure get_user(var use:usertype);
begin
(* *** to be completed *** *)
end;

procedure print_user(use:usertype);
begin
(* *** to be completed *** *)
end;

begin
   get_user(user);
   print_user(user);
end.
```

12.4.3   Modify the program in Exercise 12.4.2 so that the user enters 4 different entries. The program should display the entered data. The following is an outline of the code:

```
program test(input,output);

const MAXUSERS=4;

type
   usertype = record
      height:real;
      age:integer;
      name:string;
   end;

   user_arr=array[1..MAXUSERS] of usertype;

var   user:usertype;

procedure get_user(var use:usertype);
begin
(* *** to be completed *** *)
end;
```

```
procedure print_user(use:usertype);
begin
(* *** to be completed *** *)
end;

begin
   for i:=1 to MAXUSERS do
      get_user(user[i]);
   for i:=1 to MAXUSERS do
      print_user(user[i]);
end.
```

12.4.4 Modify the program in Exercise 12.4.3 so that the program determines the average age and also the average height.

12.4.5 Modify the program in Exercise 12.4.3 so the names in the structure are ordered alphabetically.

12.4.6 Write a database program, based on Program 12.4, which gives a menu choice as to whether the user wishes to enter a new electric component, to list all the components already in the database, or to exit the program. A sample run is given in Test run 12.6.

🖥 **Test run 12.6**
```
Do you wish to
(1)    Input a component
(2)    List all components
(3)    Exit from program
Enter option >>>
```

12.4.7 Write a program which converts from rectangular notation to polar form. In rectangular notation:

$$z = x + \mathbf{i}y$$

in polar form this is:

$$Z = |z|\langle z \rangle$$

were $|z| = \sqrt{x^2 + y^2}$ and $\langle z \rangle = \tan^{-1}\left(\dfrac{y}{x}\right)$

12.4.8 Modify the database program in the text so that the user can select an option which will order the component names in alphabetic order.

12.4.9 Modify Program 12.5 so that it adds two complex numbers. The procedure added should be called `add_complex()`.

12.4.10 Modify Program 12.5 so that it subtracts two complex numbers. The procedure added should be called `sub_complex()`.

12.4.11 Modify Program 12.5 so that it divides two complex numbers. The procedure added should be called `div_complex()`. Hint:

$$z = \frac{a + jb}{c + jd}$$

$$= \sqrt{\frac{a^2 + b^2}{c^2 + d^2}} \left\langle \tan^{-1}\left(\frac{b}{a}\right) - \tan^{-1}\left(\frac{d}{c}\right) \right\rangle$$

which is in the form of A<θ>. In a complex form this is given by:

$$z = A\cos\theta + jA\sin\theta$$

13 Graphics

13.1 Introduction

Displays can normally be used either in a text or a graphics mode. Programs which output to text displays are generally much faster than graphic displays because the characters displayed on a text display are preprogrammed into the hardware of the computer. Whereas, on graphics displays the program must map each dot (pixel) onto the screen. A PC text display typically displays characters in an array of 80 columns by 25 rows, whereas in graphics mode the screen is made up of individual pixels, such as 640 pixels in the x-direction and 480 in the y-direction. Many currently available software packages display information in graphical form. If the basic interface is displayed in graphical form it is known as a graphical user interface (or GUI). Popular GUIs include Microsoft Windows and X-Windows. Typically, graphics are used in applications which require high-resolution images. These include schematic diagrams, circuit simulation graphs, animation, and so on.

Graphics are not an intrinsic part of most programming languages. They are normally found in a graphics library. These contain functions that can range from the generation of simple line drawings to 3D bitmapped graphics manipulation. Many different libraries can be purchased but this chapter discusses Turbo/Borland C graphics.

To make use of the Turbo Pascal graphics library the statement `uses graph;` must be inserted near the top of the program.

```
Program temp(input,output);

uses graph;

VAR
```

The Turbo Pascal libraries implement a complete library of more than 50 graphics routines. The main operations are as follows:

- Simple graphics operations, such as `putpixel`, `line` and `rectangle`;
- High-level calls, such as `setviewport`, `circle`, `bar3d`, and `drawpoly`;
- Several fill and line styles;

123

- Bit-oriented routines, such as `getimage` and `putimage`;
- Several fonts that may be magnified, justified and oriented.

The basic graphics screen is made up of pixels, which are accessed using an *x-y* co-ordinate system. The *x*-direction is horizontally across the screen and the *y*-direction is vertically down the screen. The top left-hand corner is the (0,0) *x-y* point and the bottom of the screen is the (MaxX, MaxY) point. A diagram of this is shown in Figure 13.1.

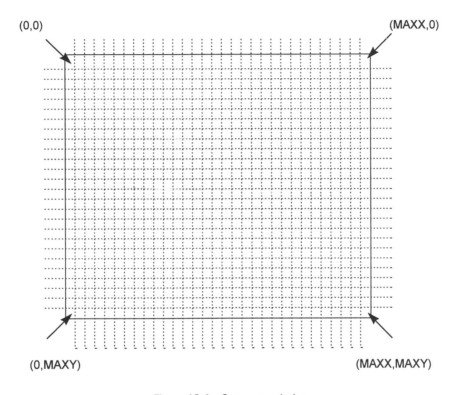

Figure 13.1   Screen resolution

A graphics display is interfaced to the PC system using a video driver card. The resolution and the number of displayable colours depends on the type of graphics driver and display used. A program can automatically detect the graphics driver and load the required file that contains information on how the program interfaces to the driver. This file is called a driver file. Table 13.1 shows typical graphics drivers and their associated driver files. A program uses the graphics driver file when the program is run. This allows a single program to be used with several different types of graphics displays. Driver files are identified with a *BGI* filename extension (see Figure 13.2). It is advisable to copy the standard graphics drivers onto a disk or into the current working directory. A listing of these BGI files is shown next.

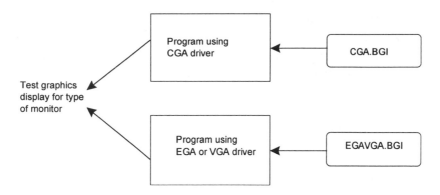

Figure 13.2 BGI files required for CGA and EGA/VGA graphics drivers

Table 13.1 Typical graphics drivers

Graphics driver	Resolution	Colours	Driver file
CGA	320×200 (CGAC0)	4	CGA.BGI
	320×200 (CGAC1)	4	
	320×200 (CGAC2)	4	
	320×200 (CGAC3)	4	
	640×200 (CGAHI)	2	
EGA	640×200 (EGALO)	16	EGAVGA.BGI
	640×350 (EGAHI)	(BLACK...WHITE)	
		16	
VGA	640×200 (VGALO)	16	EGAVGA.BGI
	640×350	16	
	(VGAMED)	16	
	640×480 (VGAHI)		
SVGA	800×600	256	SVGA256.BGI
	1024×768	16	SVGA16.BGI

Typically, these files will be found in the \TC or \BORLANDC\BGI directory.

```
E:\TURBO>dir *.bgi
ATT      BGI      6,269   20/04/90    9:23 ATT.BGI
CGA      BGI      6,253   20/04/90    9:23 CGA.BGI
EGAVGA   BGI      5,363   02/05/89    5:50 EGAVGA.BGI
HERC     BGI      6,125   02/05/89    5:50 HERC.BGI
IBM8514  BGI      6,665   02/05/89    5:50 IBM8514.BGI
PC3270   BGI      6,029   02/05/89    5:50 PC3270.BGI
         6 file(s)            36,704 bytes
         0 dir(s)         2,375,680 bytes free
```

Other drivers are available such as *SVGA.BGI* (16-colour SVGA) and *SVGA256.BGI* (256-colour SVGA). EGA and VGA monitors can display at least 16 colours. Within a program these are accessed either as a numerical value or by a symbolic name, as given in Table 13.2.

The `setcolor()` function sets the current drawing colour. For example, to set the drawing colour to white the `setcolor(WHITE);` or `setcolor(15);` statement is used. The former is preferable as it is self-documenting.

Table 13.3 outlines the basic graphics functions. An on-line help facility is available by placing the cursor on the function name then pressing the CNTRL and function key F1 (CNTRL-F1) at the same time, or by pressing F1 for more general help.

Table 13.2 Displayable colours

Numeric value	Symbolic name	Numeric value	Symbolic name
0	BLACK	8	DARKGRAY
1	BLUE	9	LIGHTBLUE
2	GREEN	10	LIGHTGREEN
3	CYAN	11	LIGHTCYAN
4	RED	12	LIGHTRED
5	MAGENTA	13	LIGHTMAGENTA
6	BROWN	14	YELLOW
7	LIGHTGRAY	15	WHITE

Table 13.3 Sample Borland graphics routines

Graphic routine	Function	Description
arc	Draws a circular arc	`arc(x,y,stangle,endangle,radius)` draws an arc with centre point x,y at a start angle `stangle`, and end angle `endangle` and the radius is `radius`
bar	Draws a 2D bar	`bar(left,top,right,bottom)` draws a solid rectangular bar from (`left`,`right`) to (`right`,`bottom`) using current drawing colour
circle	Draws a circle of a given radius and centre	`circle(x,y,radius)`

`cleardevice`	Clears the graphic screen	`cleardevice()` erases the entire graphics screen
`closegraph`	Shuts down the graphics screen	`closegraph()` returns the screen to text mode
`drawpoly`	Draws the outline of a polygon	`drawpoly(numpoints,polypoints)` draws a polygon with `numpoints` using array `polypoints`. This array has consecutive x,y points. The number of values in the array will be twice the number of points to be displayed. For example, to display the polygon at the points (5,10), (50,100), (40,30) then an array needs to be filled with the values 5, 10, 50, 100, 40, 30
`floodfill`	Flood fills a bounded region	`floodfill(x,y,border)` fills an enclosed area where x,y is the seed point with the enclosed area to be filled. The floodfill continues outwards until the `border` colour is reached
`getimage`	Gets an image from the screen	`getimage(x1,y1,x2,y2,ptr)`
`getmaxx`	Gets maximum x-co-ordinate of the screen	`x=getmaxx()`
`getmaxy`	Gets maximum y-co-ordinate of the screen	`y=getmaxy()`
`grapherrormsg`	Displays error message generated by `graphresult()`	`grapherrormsg(err)`
`graphresult`	Determines if the graphics screen has been initialized correctly	`err=graphresult()` Return codes include: `grOk`, `grNoInit-Graph`, `grNotDetected`, `grFileNot-Found`, `grInvalidDriver`, `grFontNot-Found`, `grInvalidMode`, `grError`, `grIOerror`, `grInvalidFont`
`imagesize`	Determines the size of a graphics object	`imagesize(ptr)`

`initgraph`	Initializes graphics. It can determine the graphics driver and graphics mode to use by checking the hardware	`initgraph(*gdriver,*gmode, pathtodriver)` `gmode` returns the graphics driver, if `gmode` is set as `DETECT` then the graphics mode will be set to the highest possible resolution. Settings for `gmode` are `DETECT`, `CGA`, `EGA`, `EGA64` and `VGA`.Typical settings for `gdriver` are given in Table 13.1. For example, `VGALO`(640×200, 16 colour), `VGAMED` (640×350, 16 colour), `VGAHI` (640×480, 16 colour)
`line`	Draws a line with the current drawing colour	`line(x1,y1,x2,y2)`
`outtextxy`	Displays a string of text to the graphics screen	`outtextxy(x,y,str)` displays the text `str` and co-ordinate `x,y`
`putimage`	Puts an image from memory onto the screen	`putimage(x,y,ptr,mask)`
`putpixel`	Puts a single pixel to the screen	`putpixel(x,y,col)` puts a pixel at (x,y) of colour `col`
`rectangle`	Draws a rectangle of the current drawing colour	similar to `bar()` but no fill
`setbkcolor`	Sets the current background colour	`setbkcolour(colour)`
`setcolor`	Sets the current drawing colour	`setcolor(colour)` available colours on EGA/VGA are from BLACK to WHITE

13.2 Basic graphics routines

13.2.1 Closing graphics

The `closegraph()` function shuts down the graphics system. The standard format is given next:

```
procedure    closegraph;
```

13.2.2 Initializing graphics

This procedure initializes the graphics system and puts the hardware into graphics mode. The standard format for the `initgraph()` routine is given next:

```
InitGraph(VAR GraphDriver:Integer;VAR GraphMode: Integer;
                  PathToDriver: string);
```

PCs can have different graphics drivers, for example:

- CGA (Colour Graphics Adapter);
- EGA (Enhanced Graphics Adapter);
- VGA (Video Graphics Adapter);
- SVGA (Super Video Graphics Adapter);

It is possible for this function to automatically detect the graphics driver by setting the `graphdriver` parameter to DETECT. This has the advantage of setting the display to the maximum possible graphics range. The `pathtodriver` string informs the program as to where it will find the graphics driver file. This file is loaded when the program is run. If the string is a null (or empty) string " then the program will assumes that it will be found in the current working directory. Otherwise, if the driver file is to be found in the directory `\TURBO` on the `C:` drive then the string will contain 'C:\TURBO'.

Program 13.1 displays a diagonal line from the top corner to the bottom corner of the screen. The graphics driver is initialized using `initgraph()`. After initialization the `graphresult()` routine is used to determine if there were any errors in initializing the driver. A return of grOk indicates that there have been no problems and the graphics screen can now be used. If it does not return grOk then `grapherrormsg()` is used to display the error. Typical errors are 'BGI File not found', 'Graphics not initialised', 'Invalid Font', etc.

The `getmaxx()` and `getmaxy()` functions return the maximum screen size in the x- and y-directions, respectively. For a typical VGA display the maximum number of pixels in the x-direction will be 640 and in the y-direction 480.

▢ **Program 13.1**

```
program prog13_1(input,output);

uses graph;

var   grDriver,grMode,errorcode : Integer;
```

```
begin
   grDriver := Detect;
   InitGraph(grDriver,grMode,'');
   ErrorCode := GraphResult;
   if (errorcode = grOk) then
    begin
       setcolor(WHITE);
       line(0,0,getmaxx,getmaxy);
       readln;
       closegraph;
    end
    else writeln('Graphics error: ',grapherrormsg(errorcode));
end.
```

13.2.3 Drawing a pixel

The putpixel() procedure plots a pixel at a given position and colour. The standard format is given next:

```
procedure PutPixel(X, Y, Color:integer);
```

Program 13.2 displays pixels of a random colour at a random location. The function random(X) returns a random value from 0 to X-1. This random value is based upon the system timer. The initial value of the timer is set by calling randomize at the start of the program.

The graphics display is initialized in open_graphics(). The function keypressed is used for this purpose. It returns a TRUE value when a key is pressed, thus the loop repeat...until keypressed will continue until the user presses a key.

Program 13.2

```
program prog13_2(input,output);

uses graph,crt;

var x,y:integer;

procedure open_graphics;
var    grDriver,grMode,errorcode : Integer;
begin
    grDriver := Detect;
    InitGraph(grDriver,grMode,'');
    ErrorCode := GraphResult;
    if (errorcode <> grOk) then
    begin
      writeln('Graphics error: ',grapherrormsg(errorcode));
      closegraph;
      exit;
    end;
end;

begin
```

```
   open_graphics;
   randomize;

   repeat
      x:=random(getmaxx);
      y:=random(getmaxy);
      putpixel(x,y,random(15));
   until keypressed;

   closegraph;
end.
```

13.2.4 Drawing a line

The line() procedure draws a line of the current drawing colour from (*x1*, *y1*) to (*x2*, *y2*). The standard format for line() is:

```
procedure Line(x1, y1, x2, y2 : Integer);
```

Program 13.3 draws many random lines of random colours.

Program 13.3

```
program prog13_3(input,output);

uses graph,crt;

var maxX,maxY:integer;

procedure open_graphics;
var    grDriver,grMode,errorcode : Integer;
begin
    grDriver := Detect;
    InitGraph(grDriver,grMode,'');
    ErrorCode := GraphResult;
    if (errorcode <> grOk) then
    begin
      writeln('Graphics error: ',grapherrormsg(errorcode));
                closegraph;
                exit;
    end;
end;

begin
   open_graphics;
   randomize;

   maxX:=getmaxx;
   maxY:=getmaxy;

   repeat
      setcolor(random(15));
      line(random(maxX),random(maxY),random(maxX),random(maxY));
   until keypressed;
   closegraph;
end.
```

13.2.5 Drawing a rectangle

The `rectangle` procedure draws a rectangle using the current drawing colour. The standard format for the `rectangle()` routine is given next:

```
procedure Rectangle(x1, y1, x2, y2: Integer);
```

Program 13.4 displays a single resistor on the screen. The `draw_resistor(x,y)` function draws this resistor at a point starting at (*x,y*). One problem in displaying graphics is that graphics displays can vary in the number of displayable pixels. If absolute co-ordinates are used then the object will appear relatively small on a high-resolution display or relatively large on a low-resolution display. For this reason the resistor is scaled with respect to the maximum *x*- and *y*-co-ordinates, this makes its co-ordinates relative to the screen size. The scaling of the resistor is given in Figure 13.3.

13.2.6 Displaying text

The `outtextxy()` function sends a string to the output device. Numerical values cannot be displayed to the screen directly and must be converted into a string before they are displayed. The standard format for the `outtextxy()` routine is given next:

```
procedure  outtextxy(x,y:integer,textstr:string);
```

Program 13.5 uses `outtextxy()` to display a resistor value string within the `draw_resistor()` procedure.

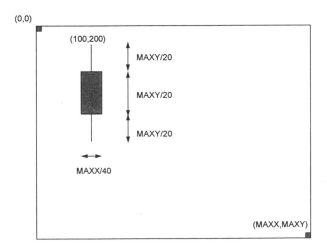

Figure 13.3 Layout of resistor graphic

Program 13.4

```pascal
program prog13_4(input,output);

uses graph,crt;

var maxX,maxY:integer;

procedure open_graphics;
var    grDriver,grMode,errorcode : Integer;
begin
    grDriver := Detect;
    InitGraph(grDriver,grMode,'');
    ErrorCode := GraphResult;
    if (errorcode <> grOk) then
    begin
      writeln('Graphics error: ',grapherrormsg(errorcode));
                closegraph;
                exit;
    end;
end;
procedure draw_resistor(x,y:integer);
type resistor = record
       length,width,connectline:integer;
       end;
var   res:resistor;
begin
    maxx:=getmaxx;
    maxy:=getmaxy;
    res.length:=maxy div 20;
    res.width:=maxx div 40;
    res.connectline:=maxy div 20;

    line(x,y,x,y+res.length);
    rectangle(x-res.length div 2,y+res.connectline,
    x+res.width div 2, y+res.connectline+res.length);
    line(x,y+res.connectline+res.length,
    x,y+res.length+2*res.connectline);
end;

begin
        open_graphics;
        draw_resistor(100,200);
        readln;
        closegraph;
end.
```

Program 13.5

```pascal
program prog13_5(input,output);
uses graph,crt;

var maxX,maxY:integer;

procedure open_graphics;
var    grDriver,grMode,errorcode : Integer;
begin
    grDriver := Detect;
```

```
        InitGraph(grDriver,grMode,'');
        ErrorCode := GraphResult;
        if (errorcode <> grOk) then
        begin
          writeln('Graphics error: ',grapherrormsg(errorcode));
                  closegraph;
                  exit;
        end;
end;

procedure draw_resistor(x,y:integer;  str:string);
type resistor = record
        length,width,connectline:integer;
        end;
var   res:resistor;
begin
      maxx:=getmaxx;
      maxy:=getmaxy;
      res.length:=maxy div 20;
      res.width:=maxx div 40;
      res.connectline:=maxy div 20;

      line(x,y,x,y+res.length);
      rectangle(x-res.length div 2,y+res.connectline,
      x+res.width div 2,  y+res.connectline+res.length);
      line(x,y+res.connectline+res.length,
      x,y+res.length+2*res.connectline);
      outtextxy(x+res.width,y+res.length div 2+res.connectline,
                                        str);
end;

begin
        open_graphics;
        draw_resistor(100,200,'100K');
        draw_resistor(200,200,'200K');
        readln;
        closegraph;
end.
```

13.2.7 Drawing a circle

The circle() procedure draws a circle at a centre (*x,y*) of a given radius.
The standard format for the circle() routine is given next:

```
procedure Circle(X,Y,Radius : Integer);
```

Program 13.6 uses circle() to display a voltage source.

📋 **Program 13.6**
```
program prog13_6(input,output);

uses graph,crt;

var maxX,maxY:integer;
```

```pascal
procedure open_graphics;
var    grDriver,grMode,errorcode : Integer;
begin
    grDriver := Detect;
    InitGraph(grDriver,grMode,'');
    ErrorCode := GraphResult;
    if (errorcode <> grOk) then
    begin
     writeln('Graphics error: ',grapherrormsg(errorcode));
                closegraph;
                exit;
    end;
end;
procedure draw_resistor(x,y:integer; str:string);
type resistor = record
      length,width,connectline:integer;
      end;
var  res:resistor;
begin
    maxx:=getmaxx;
    maxy:=getmaxy;
    res.length:=maxy div 20;
    res.width:=maxx div 40;
    res.connectline:=maxy div 20;

    line(x,y,x,y+res.length);
    rectangle(x-res.length div 2,y+res.connectline,
    x+res.width div 2, y+res.connectline+res.length);
    line(x,y+res.connectline+res.length,
    x,y+res.length+2*res.connectline);
    outtextxy(x+res.width,y+res.length div 2+res.connectline,str);
end;

procedure draw_voltage_source(x,y:integer; str:string);
type voltage = record
      radius,connectline:integer;
      end;
var    volt:voltage;
   maxy:integer;
begin
   maxy:=getmaxy;
   volt.radius:=maxy div 40;
   volt.connectline:=maxy div 20;

   line(x,y,x,y+volt.connectline);
   circle(x,y+volt.connectline+volt.radius,volt.radius);
   line(x,y+volt.connectline+2*volt.radius,
   x,y+2*volt.radius+2*volt.connectline);

   outtextxy(x+volt.connectline+volt.radius,
   y+volt.radius+volt.connectline,str);
end;

begin
        open_graphics;
        draw_resistor(200,200,'100K');
        draw_resistor(300,200,'200K');
        draw_voltage_source(100,200,'5V');
```

```
        readln;
        closegraph;
end.
```

13.2.8 Bitmapped graphics

Program 13.7 displays a face which can be moved around the screen using the
arrowkeys. Figure 13.4 shows a sample screen.

   The `readkey` function gets a single keystroke from the keyboard. If the
return value is a 0 then the keystroke is an extended character, such as a function key (F1...F12), page up, page down, arrowkeys, and so on. The extended
character can be determined by calling `getch()` again. Sample return values
are given in Table 13.4.

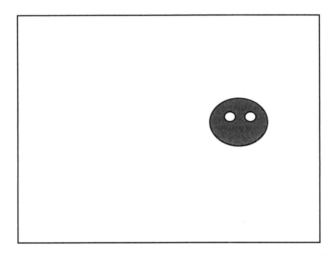

Figure 13.4   Face to be displayed

Table 13.4   Sample returns for extended characters

Return value	Key
Up arrow	72
Down arrow	80
Left arrow	75
Right arrow	77
Escape key	27

The following code determines whether a function key has been pressed.

```
ch:=readkey; if (ch=#0) then ch:=readkey;
```

For example, if the Escape key is pressed then `ch` stores the value 27.

   The `getimage(x1,y1,x2,y2)` function captures the image from the
co-ordinates `(x1,y1) to (x2,y2)` into memory and `putimage(x,y,`

BITMASK) is used to display the image and to clear it from the screen. The quickest way of erasing a graphics object is to exclusive-OR all the bits in the object bitmapped with itself. The putimage(x,y,BITMASK) function allows a bitmask to be applied to the image. An exclusive-OR function is defined with XORPUT. For example, if the bits on a section of the screen are 11001010, then when this is exclusive-ORed with itself the result will be 00000000.

Program 13.7

```pascal
program prog13_7(input,output);
(*********************************************)
(* FACE.PAS                                  *)
(* Title: Shape moving program              *)
(* Function: Program to display a shape which *)
(* can be moved using the arrow-keys        *)
(*********************************************)

uses graph,crt;

const UPARROW=#72;DOWNARROW=#80;LEFTARROW=#75;RIGHTARROW=#77;
      ESC=#27;INCREMENT=4;
      NO_ERROR=0;GRAPHICS_ERROR=1;GRAPHICS_MEM_ERROR=2;

var shape:pointer;
    x,y:integer;
    ch:char;

procedure open_graphics;
var    grDriver,grMode,errorcode : Integer;
begin
    grDriver := Detect;
    InitGraph(grDriver,grMode,'');
    ErrorCode := GraphResult;
    if (errorcode <> grOk) then
    begin
      writeln('Graphics error: ',grapherrormsg(errorcode));
                closegraph;
                exit;
    end;
end;

function   get_shape:pointer;
var startx,starty,ulx, uly, lrx, lry, size, buffsize:integer;
  al:pointer;
begin
    (* Draw shape *)

          setfillstyle( SOLIDFILL,WHITE );

  startx:=getmaxx div 2; starty:=getmaxy div 2;
  size:=getmaxx div 20;

      (* draw face outline *)
  circle(startx,starty,size);
```

```
        floodfill(startx,starty,WHITE);

        (* draw eyes        *)
        setcolor(RED);
        circle(startx+size div 3,starty,size div 3);
        floodfill(startx+size div 3,starty,WHITE);

        circle(startx-size div 3,starty,size div 3);
        floodfill(startx+size div 3,starty,WHITE);

        (* get size of face   *)
        ulx := startx-size;
        uly := starty-size;
        lrx := startx+size;
        lry := starty+size;

        buffsize := imagesize(ulx, uly, lrx, lry);

            getmem(al,buffsize);

        getimage(ulx, uly, lrx, lry, al^);
        putimage(ulx, uly, al^, xorput);
            get_shape:=al;

end;

begin
    open_graphics;
    shape:=get_shape;
        x:=getmaxx div 2; y:=getmaxy div 2;  (* start co-ordinates *)

    repeat
        putimage(x, y, shape^, XORPUT);        (* draw image    *)
        ch:=readkey; if (ch=#0) then ch:=readkey; (* get extended key *)
        putimage(x, y, shape^, XORPUT);        (* erase image     *)

        if    (ch=UPARROW) then  y:=y-INCREMENT
        else if (ch=DOWNARROW) then  y:=y+INCREMENT
        else if (ch=LEFTARROW)  then x:=x-INCREMENT
        else if (ch=RIGHTARROW) then x:=x+INCREMENT;

            (* test if shape is off the screen *)
        if (x>0.9*getmaxx) then x:=9*getmaxx div 10;
        if (x<0) then x:=0;
        if (y>0.9*getmaxy) then y:=9*getmaxy div 10;
        if (y<0) then y:=0;
    until (ch=ESC);
    closegraph;
end.
```

13.3 Exercises

13.3.1   Draw a cross which touches each corner of the screen.

13.3.2 Draw a triangle with its base on the bottom of the screen and an apex which reaches the centre of the top of the screen.

13.3.3 Write a program that draws circles of radius 1, 2, 4, 8, 16, 32, 64... units. Each of the circles should be drawn one at a time with a delay of one second between updates. The function `de-lay(milliseconds)` delays the program for a number of milliseconds; for example, `delay(1000)` delays for one second.

13.3.4 Write a program that covers the screen with random blue pixels.

13.3.5 Write a program that moves a red rectangle across the screen from left to right. Use the `delay()` function to animate it. The rectangle should physically move. A possible method could be:

(a) display the rectangle in red at *x,y* coordinates;
(b) delay for a small time period;
(c) display the rectangle in black (which erases the red rectangle);
(d) increment the *x*- co-ordinate and go back to (a).

13.3.6 Write a program in which the user enters the values of the resistor colour bands and the program displays the resistor with the correct colour bands.

13.3.7 Write a program that displays the schematic given in Figure 13.5.

Figure 13.5 Schematic

13.3.8 Write a program that draws a graph axis for *x* and *y* with a given maximum *x* and *y*. For example,

```
procedure drawaxis(maxx,maxy:integer);
```

13.3.9 Change the program in Exercise 13.3.8 so that it draws text to the graph (for example, with maximum *x* and *y* values).

14 Software Interrupts

14.1 Introduction

An interrupt allows a program or an external device to interrupt the execution of a program. The generation of an interrupt can occur by hardware (hardware interrupt) or software (software interrupt). When an interrupt occurs an interrupt service routine (ISR) is called. For a hardware interrupt the ISR then communicates with the device and processes any data. When it has finished the program execution returns to the original program. A software interrupt causes the program to interrupt its execution and goes to an interrupt service routine. Typical software interrupts include reading a key from the keyboard, outputting text to the screen and reading the current date and time.

14.2 BIOS and the operating system

The Basic Input/Output System (BIOS) communicates directly with the hardware of the computer. It consists of a set of programs which interface with devices such as keyboards, displays, printers, serial ports and disk drives. These programs allow the user to write application programs that contain calls to these functions, without having to worry about controlling them or which type of equipment is being used. Without BIOS the computer system would simply consist of a bundle of wires and electronic devices.

There are two main parts to BIOS. The first is the part permanently stored in a ROM (the ROM BIOS). It is this part that starts the computer (or boots it) and contains programs which communicate with resident devices. The second stage is loaded when the operating system is started. This part is non-permanent.

An operating system allows the user to access the hardware in an easy-to-use manner. It accepts commands from the keyboard and displays them to the monitor. The Disk Operating System, or DOS, gained its name from its original purpose of providing a controller for the computer to access its disk drives. The language of DOS consists of a set of commands which are entered directly by the user and are interpreted to perform file management tasks, program execution and system configuration. It makes calls to BIOS to execute these. The main functions of DOS are to run programs, copy and remove files, create directories, move within a directory structure and to list files. Microsoft Windows 95 calls BIOS programs directly.

14.3 Interrupt vectors

Interrupt vectors are addresses which inform the interrupt handler as to where to find the ISR. All interrupts are assigned a number from 0 to 255. The interrupt vectors associated with each interrupt number are stored in the lower 1024 bytes of PC memory. For example, interrupt 0 is stored from `0000:0000` to `0000:0003`, interrupt 1 from `0000:0004` to `0000:0007`, and so on. The first two bytes store the offset and the next two store the segment address. Each interrupt number is assigned a predetermined task, as outlined in Table 14.1. An interrupt can be generated either by external hardware, software, or by the processor. Interrupts 0, 1, 3, 4, 6 and 7 are generated by the processor. Interrupts from 8 to 15 and interrupt 2 are generated by external hardware. These get the attention of the processor by activating a interrupt request (IRQ) line. The `IRQ0` line connects to the system timer, the keyboard to `IRQ1`, and so on. Most other interrupts are generated by software.

Table 14.1   Interrupt handling

Interrupt	Name	Generated by
00 (00h)	Divide error	processor
01 (00h)	Single step	processor
02 (02h)	Non-maskable interrupt	external equipment
03 (03h)	Breakpoint	processor
04 (04h)	Overflow	processor
05 (05h)	Print screen	Shift-Print screen key stroke
06 (06h)	Reserved	processor
07 (07h)	Reserved	processor
08 (08h)	System timer	hardware via IRQ0
09 (09h)	Keyboard	hardware via IRQ1
10 (0Ah)	Reserved	hardware via IRQ2
11 (0Bh)	Serial communications (COM2)	hardware via IRQ3
12 (0Ch)	Serial communications (COM1)	hardware via IRQ4
13 (0Dh)	Reserved	hardware via IRQ5
14 (0Eh)	Floppy disk controller	hardware via IRQ6
15 (0Fh)	Parallel printer	hardware via IRQ7
16 (10h)	BIOS – Video access	software
17 (11h)	BIOS – Equipment check	software

18 (12h)	BIOS – Memory size	software
19 (13h)	BIOS – Disk operations	software
20 (14h)	BIOS – Serial communications	software
22 (16h)	BIOS – Keyboard	software
23 (17h)	BIOS – Printer	software
25 (19h)	BIOS – Reboot	software
26 (1Ah)	BIOS – Time of day	software
28 (1Ch)	BIOS – Ticker timer	software
33 (21h)	DOS – DOS services	software
39 (27h)	DOS – Terminate and stay resident	software

14.4 Processor interrupts

The processor-generated interrupts normally occur either when a program causes a certain type of error or if it is being used in a debug mode. In the debug mode the program can be made to break from its execution when a breakpoint occurs. This allows the user to test the current status of the computer. It can also be forced to step through a program one operation at a time (single step mode).

14.5 Generating software interrupts

Turbo Pascal provides access to the processor throught the routine named Intr(). To use this procedure the *uses dos;* statement is placed near the top of the program. A data type named Registers has also been predefined, as shown below.

```
type
   Registers = record
                    case Integer of
                      0: (AX,BX,CX,DX,BP,SI,DI,DS,ES,Flags: Word);
                      1: (AL,AH,BL,BH,CL,CH,DL,DH: Byte);
   end;
```

Registers are accessed either as 8-bit registers (such as AL, AH) or 16-bit registers (such as AX, BX). If a structure name regs is declared, then:

regs.al   accesses the 8-bit AL register
regs.ax   accesses the 16-bit AX register.

The syntax of the intr() function is:

```
intr(intno:integer; regs:register);
```

where the first argument is the interrupt number and the second argument is the settings for the registers.

14.5.1 Interrupt 10h: BIOS video mode

Interrupt 10h allows access to the video display. Table 14.2 outlines typical interrupt calls. Program 14.1 uses the BIOS video interrupt to display a border around the screen which changes colour each second from black to light blue. These colours are set up with an enum data type definition. In this case, BLACK is defined as 0, BLUE as 1, and so on.

To display a border the AH register is loaded with 0Bh, BH with 00h and BL with the border colour. Next, the interrupt 10h is called with these parameters. Typical Turbo Pascal procedures which use this interrupt are textcolor(), textbackground(), textattr(), gotoxy(), wherex(), wherey(), textmode() and gettextinfo(). Figure 14.1 shows the bit definition for the colours.

Table 14.2 BIOS video interrupt

Description	Input registers	Output registers
Set video mode	AH=00h	AL = video mode flag 0 (Text:40×25 B/W) 1 (Text:40×25 B/W) 2 (Text:80×25 Colour) 3 (Text:60×25 Colour) 4 (Graphics:320×200 Colour) 5 (Graphics:320×200 B/W) 6 (Graphics: 640×200 Colour)
Set cursor position	AH = 02h, BH = 00h DH = row (00h is top) DL = column (00h is left)	
Read cursor position	AH = 02h, BH = 00h	DH = row (00h is top) DL = column (00h is left)
Write character and attribute at cursor position	AH = 09h, AL = character to display, BH = 00h, BL = attribute (text mode) or colour (graphics mode) if bit 7 set in graphics mode, character is Exclusive-ORed on the screen, CX = number of times to write characters	

| Read character and attribute at cursor position | AH = 08h BH = 00h | AH = attribute (see Figure 14.1 AL = character |
| Set background/ border colour | AH = 0Bh BH = 00h BL = background/border colour (border only in text modes) | |

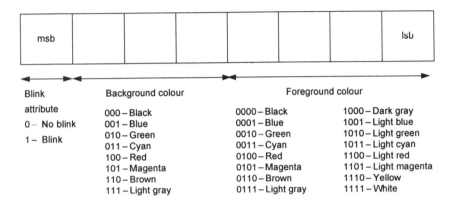

Blink attribute	Background colour	Foreground colour	
0 – No blink	000 – Black	0000 – Black	1000 – Dark gray
1 – Blink	001 – Blue	0001 – Blue	1001 – Light blue
	010 – Green	0010 – Green	1010 – Light green
	011 – Cyan	0011 – Cyan	1011 – Light cyan
	100 – Red	0100 – Red	1100 – Light red
	101 – Magenta	0101 – Magenta	1101 – Light magenta
	110 – Brown	0110 – Brown	1110 – Yellow
	111 – Light gray	0111 – Light gray	1111 – White

Figure 14.1 Character attribute

Program 14.1

```
program prog14_1(input,output);

uses DOS,CRT;

var  colour:integer;

procedure setborder( col:integer);
var inregs:registers;
begin
   inregs.ah:=$0b;
   inregs.bh:=$00;
   inregs.bl:=col;
   intr($10,inregs);
end;

begin

   writeln('Program to display borders from black to light blue');

   for colour:=BLACK to LIGHTBLUE do
   begin
      setborder(colour);
      delay(1000);
   end;

end.
```

14.5.2 Interrupt 11h: BIOS equipment check

Interrupt 11h returns a word which gives a basic indication of the types of equipment connected. It is useful in determining if there is a math co-processor present and the number of parallel and serial ports connected. A program and test run using this interrupt are given in Program 14.2 and Test run 14.1. Table 14.3 shows the format of the call.

Table 14.3 BIOS equipment check interrupt

Description	Input registers	Output registers
Get equipment list		AX = BIOS equipment list word
		see Table 14.5 for bit definitions

Program 14.2

```
program prog14_2(input,output);

uses dos;

var inregs: registers;
    ax,printers,vmode,nfloppies:integer;
begin
   intr($11,inregs);

   ax:=inregs.ax;

   printers:=(ax and $B000) shr 13;

   vmode:=((ax and $0030) shr 4)+1;

   nfloppies:=((ax and $00C0) shr 6)+1;

   if (ax and $01=$01) then writeln('Floppy disk present');

   if (ax and $02=$01) then writeln('Math coprocesser present');

   writeln('No. of printers is ',printers);

   writeln('Video mode ',vmode);

   writeln('No. of floppies is(are) ',nfloppies);
end.
```

Test run 14.1
```
Floppy disk present
Math coprocesser present
No. of printers is 4
Video mode 3
No. of floppies is(are) 1
```

14.5.3 Interrupt 13h: BIOS disk access

Interrupt 13h allows access to many disk operations. Table 14.4 lists two typical interrupt calls.

Table 14.4 BIOS disk access interrupt

Description	Input registers	Output registers
Reset disk system	AH = 00h DL = drive (if bit 7 is set both hard disks and floppy disks are reset)	Return: AH = status
Get status of last operation	AH = 01h DL = drive (bit 7 set for hard disk)	Return: AH = status

14.5.4 Interrupt 14h: BIOS serial communications

In Chapter 16 serial communications will be discussed in some detail. BIOS interrupt 14h can be used to transmit and receive characters and also to determine the status of the serial port. Table 14.5 lists the main interrupt calls. Program 14.3 initializes COM2: with 4800 baud, even parity, 1 stop bit and 7 data bits.

Table 14.5 BIOS serial communications interrupt

Description	Input registers	Output registers
Initialize serial port	AH = 00h AL = port parameters (see Figure 14.2) DX = port number (00h–03h)	AH = line status (see get status) AL = modem status (see get status)
Write character to port	AH = 01h AL = character to write DX = port number (00h–03h)	AH bit 7 clear if successful AH bit 7 set on error AH bits 6–0 = port status (see get status)
Read character from port	AH = 02h DX = port number (00h–03h)	Return: AH = line status (see get status) AL = received character if AH bit 7 clear

Get port status	AH = 03h DX = port number (00h–03h)	AH = line status bit 7: timeout 6: transmit shift register empty 5: transmit holding register empty 4: break detected 3: framing error 2: parity error 1: overrun error 0: receive data ready

Program 14.3

```
program prog14_3(input,output);
uses DOS;

var inregs:registers;

begin
   inregs.ah:=$00;
   inregs.al:=$D2;        (*    1101 0010                            *)
                          (*    110 - 4800 bps, 10 - even parity,    *)
                          (*    0 - 1 stop bit, 10 - 7 data bits     *)
   inregs.dx:=$01;        (*    COM2:                                *)
   intr($14,inregs);
end.
```

14.5.5 Interrupt 16h: BIOS keyboard

Interrupt 16h allows access to the keyboard, Table 14.6 shows typical interrupt calls. Program 14.4 uses the BIOS keyboard interrupt to display characters, entered from the keyboard, to the screen. A function khit() determines if there is a character in the keyboard buffer. If there is then it returns a TRUE otherwise it returns a FALSE. The check for keystroke interrupt call sets the zero flag (ZF) if there are no characters in the buffer, otherwise it will be a 0.

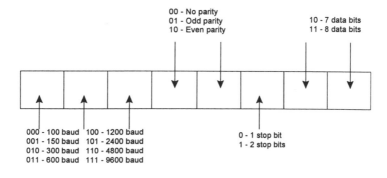

Figure 14.2 Bit definitions for serial port initialization

Table 14.6 BIOS keyboard interrupt

Description	Input registers	Output registers
Get keystroke	AH = 00h	AH = scan code AL = ASCII character
Check for keystroke	AH = 01h	Return: ZF set if no keystroke available ZF clear if keystroke available AH = scan code AL = ASCII character
Get shift flags	AH = 02h	AL = shift flags bit 7: Insert active 6: CapsLock active 5: NumLock active 4: ScrollLock active 3: Alt key pressed 2: Ctrl key pressed 1: left shift key pressed 0: right shift key pressed

Program 14.4

```
program prog14_4(input,output);

uses DOS;

var ch:char;

function khit:boolean;
var inregs:registers;
    zf:integer;
begin
   inregs.ah:=1;
   intr($16,inregs);
   zf:=inregs.flags and $40;
   if (zf>0) then khit:=FALSE
   else khit:=TRUE;
end;

function get_character:char;
var inregs:registers;
    ch:char;
begin
   inregs.ah:=0;
   intr($16,inregs);
   ch:=chr(inregs.al);
   get_character:=ch;
end;

begin
   writeln('Enter x to exit');
```

```
repeat
      if (khit) then
      begin
         ch:=get_character;
         write(ch);
      end;
   until (ch='x');
end.
```

14.5.6 Interrupt 17h: BIOS printer

The BIOS printer interrupts allow a program either to get the status the printer or to write a character to it. Table 14.7 outlines the interrupt calls.

Table 14.7 BIOS printer interrupt

Description	Input registers	Output registers
Initialize printer port	AH = 01h DX = printer number (00h-02h)	AH = printer status bit 7: not busy 6: acknowledge 5: out of paper 4: selected 3: I/O error 2: unused 1: unused 0: timeout
Write character to printer	AH = 00h AL = character to write DX = printer number (00h-02h)	AH = printer status
Get printer status	AH = 02h DX = printer number (00h-02h)	AH = printer status

14.5.7 Interrupt 21h: DOS services

Programs access DOS functions using interrupt 21h. The functionality of the call is set by the contents of the AH register. Other registers are used either to pass extra information to the function or to return values back. For example, to determine the system time the AH is loaded with the value 2Ah. Next, the processor is interrupted with interrupt 21h. Finally, when the program returns from this interrupt the CX register will contain the year, DH the month, DL the day and AL the day of the week.

Table 14.8 is only a small section of all the DOS related interrupts. For example, function 2Fh contains many functions that control the printer. Note that for the *Get free disk space* function the total free space on a drive is AX×BX×CX and total space on disk, in bytes, is AX×CX×DX.

Table 14.8 DOS interrupts

Description	Input registers	Output registers
Read character from keyboard with echo	AH=01h	AL=character returned
Write character to output	AH=02h DL=character to write	
Write character to printer	AH=05h DL=character to print	
Read character with no echo	AH=07h	AL=character read from keyboard
Get k/b status	AH=0Bh	AL=0 no characters AL=FFh characters
Get system date	AH=2Ah	CX=year, DH=month DL=day, AL=day of week (0–Sunday, and so on)
Set system date	AH=2Bh, CX=year, DH=month, DL=day	
Get system time	AH=2Ch	CL=hour CL=minute DH=second DL=1/100 seconds
Set system time	AH=2Dh, CH=hour CL=minute, DH=second DL=1/100 second	
Get DOS version	AH=30h	AL=major version number AH=minor version number
Terminate and stay resident	AH=32h DL=driver (0–default, 1– A,and so on)	
Get boot drive	AX=3305h	DL=boot drive (1–A, and so on)
Get free disk space	AL=36h DL=drive number (0–A, etc.)	AX=sectors per cluster BX=number of free clusters CX=bytes per sector DX=total clusters on driver
DOS exit	AH=4ch	

In Program 14.5, function 02h (write character to the output) is used to display the character 'A'. It uses the ord() function which converts a chararacter into an equivalent decimal value. In this case, the function number 02h is loaded into AH and the character to be displayed is loaded into DL. Program 14.6 shows an equivalent program without the ord() function.

📋 **Program 14.5**
```
program prog14_5(input,output);

uses DOS;

var inregs:registers;

begin
   inregs.ah:=$02;
   inregs.dl:=ord('A');
   intr($21,inregs);
end.
```

📋 **Program 14.6**
```
program prog14_6(input,output);
(*         Program to display 'A' using DOS interrupt          *)

uses dos;

var REGS:registers;

begin
     regs.ah:=$02;
     regs.dl:=65;

     intr($21,regs);
end.
```

Program 14.7 uses the function 01h to get a character from the keyboard.

📋 **Program 14.7**
```
program prog14_7(input,output);
(* Program using DOS interrupt to get a character from the   *)
(* keyboard.  Interrupt 21h is used and AH=02h               *)
uses DOS;

var ch:char;
    inregs:registers;

begin
   inregs.ah:=$01;
   write('Enter character >> ');
   intr($21,inregs);
   ch:=chr(inregs.al);
   writeln('Character entered was ',ch);
end.
```

Program 14.8 uses 01h and 02h functions to read and write a character from/to the input/output.

📋 **Program 14.8**

```
program prog14_8(input,output);

(* Program using DOS interrupt to get a character from    *)
(* the keyboard and display it. Interrupt 21h is          *)
(* used and AH=01  (read)and AH=02h (display)             *)

uses DOS;

var inregs:registers;
begin
   inregs.ah:=$01;
   write('Enter character >> ');
   intr($21,inregs);

      (* Display character *)
   inregs.ah:=$02;
   inregs.dl:=inregs.al;
   intr($21,inregs);
end.
```

Program 14.9 shows how a program can gain access to the system date. The function used in this example is 2Ah.

📋 **Program 14.9**

```
program prog14_9(input,output);
uses dos;

var REGS:registers;
    day,month,year,day_of_week:integer;

begin
    regs.ah:=$2a;
    intr($21,regs);
    day:=regs.dl;
    month:=regs.dh;
    year:=regs.cx;
    day_of_week:=regs.al;

    writeln('Date is ',day,'/',month,'/',year);
    writeln('Day of week is ',day_of_week);
end.
```

Test run 14.2 gives a sample run.

💻 **Test run 14.2**

```
Date is 8/9/1993
Day of week is 3
```

14.5.8 Interrupt 19h: BIOS reboot

Interrupt 19h reboots the system without clearing memory or restoring interrupt vectors. For a warm boot, equivalent to Ctrl-Alt-Del, then 1234h should be stored at 0040h:0072h. For a cold boot, equivalent to a reset, then 0000h is stored at 0040h:0072h. Care should be taken with this interrupt as it may cause the PC to 'hang'.

14.5.9 Interrupt 1Bh: BIOS control-break handler

This interrupt invokes the interrupt handling routine for the Cntrl-C keystroke. Turbo Pascal makes use of this for the function ctrlbrk().

14.5.10 Interrupt 1Ch: BIOS system timer tick

The PC system clock is updated 18.2 times every second. This clock update is automatically generated by the system timer tick interrupt. It is possible to use it to create a multi-tasking system. To achieve this the timer ISR is redirected from the system time update to a user-defined routine. This is achieved using the function setintvec(int,handler), where int is the interrupt number and handler is the name of the new ISR for this interrupt.

In Program 14.10, the function my_interrupt() is called 18.2 times every second. Each time it is called a variable named count is incremented by one (notice in the main program there are no calls to this function). The main program tests the variable count and if it is divisible by 18 then the program displays a new count value.

In order to leave the system in the way in which it was started then the old ISR address must be restored. To achieve this the getintvec() function is used to get the address of the interrupt routine at the start of the program. This is then restored with setintvec() at the end. A test run is shown in Test run 14.3.

Program 14.10
```
program prog14_10(input,output);
uses DOS,CRT;

var count, oldcount,newcount:longint;
        old_int:pointer;

procedure my_interrupt;interrupt;
begin
   count:=count+1;
end;

begin
     oldcount:=0; count:=0;

   writeln('Press any key to exit');
   getintvec($1C,old_int); (* save the old interrupt vector  *)
```

```
    setintvec($1C,addr(my_interrupt));
                        (* install the new interrupt handler *)
    repeat
       if ((count mod 18)=0) then
       begin
          newcount:=count;
          if (oldcount<>newcount) then writeln(count);
          oldcount:=count;
       end;
    until keypressed;
    (* set the old interrupt handler back *)
    setintvec($1c, old_int);
end.
```

💻 **Test run 14.3**
```
Press any key to exit
18
36
54
72
90
108
126
144
162
180
198
216
```

14.5.11 Interrupt 1Ah: BIOS system time

The BIOS system time interrupt allows a program to get access to the system timer. Table 14.9 outlines the interrupt calls.

Table 14.9 BIOS system time interrupt

Description	Input registers	Output registers
Get system time	AH = 00h	CX:DX = number of clock ticks since midnight AL = midnight flag, non-zero if midnight passed since time last read
Set system time	AH = 01h	CX:DX = number of clock ticks since midnight
Set real-time clock time	AH = 03h CH = hour (BCD) CL = minutes (BCD) DH = seconds (BCD) DL = daylight savings flag (00h standard time, 01h daylight time)	

Get real-time AH = 02h		Return: CF clear if successful
clock time		CH = hour (BCD)
		CL = minutes (BCD)
		DH = seconds (BCD)
		DL = daylight savings flag
		(00h standard time, 01h day-
		light time)
		CF set on error

14.6 Exercises

14.6.1 Using BIOS interrupt 10h, write a program that contains the following functions.

Function	Description
ch=read_character(x,y)	read character from screen position (x,y) and put the result into ch.
moveto(x,y)	move the screen cursor to position (x,y)
get_cursor(&x,&y)	get the current cursor postion and return it in x and y.

14.6.2 Using DOS interrupt (21h) write a program that determines the
DOS version. Note that DOS uses a major and minor number for
version control. The general format is VER MAJOR.MINOR. For
example,

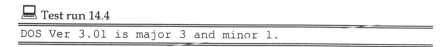
Test run 14.4

```
DOS Ver 3.01 is major 3 and minor 1.
```

Check the version number using the DOS command *VER*.

14.6.3 Using DOS interrupt (21h) write a program that determines the
amount of free and total disk space on the default disk drive.

14.6.4 Using DOS interrupts, write a program that determines the system
time.

14.6.5 Modify the DOS interrupt program that displays the date so that it will display the actual day (e.g. SUNDAY, etc.) and not the day of the week. For example

---

🖥 **Test run 14.5**
```
Current Date is WEDNESDAY 9/9/1993
```

14.6.6 Using DOS interrupts write a program that displays if a key has been pressed.

14.6.7 Program 14.11 uses a DOS interrupt. When it is run it prints the text PROGRAM START but does not print the text PROGRAM END. Explain why?

📋 **Program 14.11**
```
program prog14_11(input,output);

var inregs:registers;

begin

  puts("PROGRAM STARTED");

  inregs.ah=$4c;
  intr($21,inregs);
  writeln('PROGRAM END');
end.
```

14.6.8 Using BIOS video interrupt 10h write programs which perform the following:

    (a)   fill a complete screen with the character 'A' of a text colour of red with a background of blue;

    (b)   repeat (a), but the character displayed should cycle from 'A' to 'Z' with a one-second delay between outputs;

    (c)   repeat (a), but the foreground colour should cycle through all available colours with a one-second delay between outputs;

    (d)   repeat (a) so that the background colour cycles through all available colours with a one-second delay between outputs.

14.6.9 Using BIOS keyboard interrupt 16h write a program that displays the status of the Shift, Caps lock, Cntrl, Scroll and Num keys.

14.6.10 If there is a line printer connected to the parallel port then write a program which sends text entered from a keyboard to the printer. The message should be entered followed by a CNTRL-D (4 ASCII). Use BIOS printer interrupt 17h.

The program should also contain error checking of each character sent. Errors should include printer out-of-paper, printer time-out and printer I/O error. If possible, test the program by switching the printer off while it is printing.

15 Interfacing

15.1 Introduction

There are two main methods of communicating external equipment, either they are mapped into the physical memory and given a real address on the address bus (memory mapped I/O) or they are mapped into a special area of input/output memory (isolated I/O). Figure 15.1 shows the two methods. Devices mapped into memory are accessed by reading or writing to the physical address. Isolated I/O provides ports which are gateways between the interface device and the processor. They are isolated from the system using a buffering system and are accessed by four machine code instructions. The IN instruction inputs a byte, or a word, and the OUT instruction outputs a byte, or a word. A Pascal compiler interprets the equivalent high-level functions and produces machine code which uses these instructions.

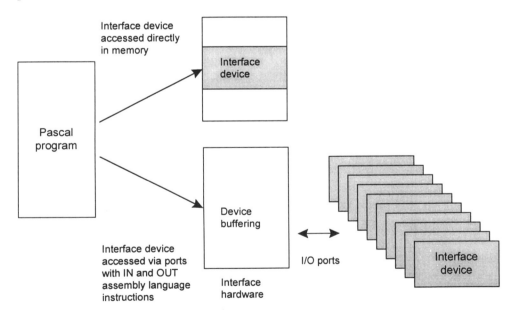

Figure 15.1 Memory mapping or isolated interfacing

15.2 Interfacing with memory

The 80X86 processor interfaces with memory through a bus controller, as shown in Figure 15.2. This device interprets the microprocessor signals and generates the required memory signals. Two main output lines differentiate between a read or a write operation ($R/\overline{W}$) and between direct and isolated memory access ($M/\overline{IO}$). The $R/\overline{W}$ line is low when data is being written to memory and high when data is being read. When $M/\overline{IO}$ is high, direct memory access is selected and when low, the isolated memory is selected.

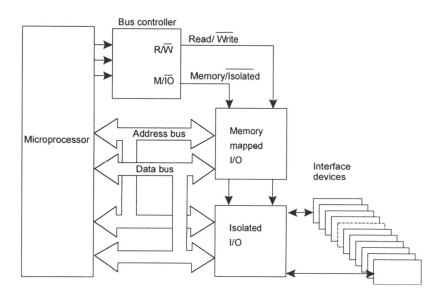

Figure 15.2   Access memory mapped and isolated I/O

15.3 Memory mapped I/O

Interface devices can map directly onto the system address and data bus. In a PC-compatible system the address bus is 20 bits wide, from address 00000h to FFFFFh (1 MB). If the PC is being used in an enhanced mode (such as with Microsoft Windows) it can access the area of memory above the 1 MB. If it uses 16-bit software (such as Microsoft Windows 3.1) then it can address up to 16 MB of physical memory, from 000000h to FFFFFFh. If it uses 32-bit software (such as Microsoft Windows 95) then the software can address up to 4 GB of physical memory, from 00000000h to FFFFFFFFh. Table 15.1 and Figure 15.3 gives a typical memory allocation.

Table 15.1 Memory allocation for a PC

Address	Device
00000h-00FFFh	Interrupt vectors
00400h-0047Fh	ROM BIOS RAM
00600h-9FFFFh	Program memory
A0000h-AFFFFh	EGA/VGA graphics
B0000h-BFFFFh	EGA/VGA graphics
C0000h-C7FFFh	EGA/VGA graphics

15.4 Isolated I/O

Devices are not normally connected directly onto the address and data bus of the computer because they may use part of the memory that a program uses or they could cause a hardware fault. On modern PCs only the graphics adaptor is mapped directly into memory, the rest communicate through a specially reserved area of memory, known as isolated I/O memory.

Isolated I/O uses 16-bit addressing from 0000h to FFFFh, thus up to 64 KB of memory can be mapped. Microsoft Windows 95 can display the isolated I/O memory map by selecting Control Panel → System → Device Manager, then selecting Properties. From the computer properties window the Input/output (I/O) option is selected. Figure 15.4 shows an example for a computer in the range from 0000h to 0064h and Figure 15.5 shows from 0378h to 03FFh.

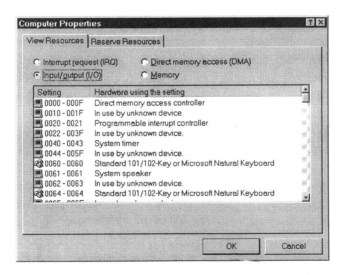

Figure 15.3 Example I/O memory map from 0000h to 0064h

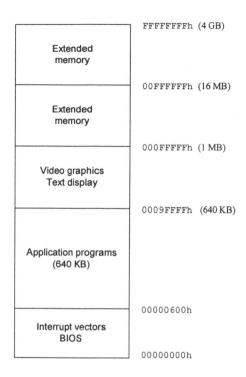

Figure 15.4 Typical PC memory map

It can be seen from Figure 15.5 that the keyboard maps into address 0060h and 0064h, the speaker maps to address 0061h and the system timer between 0040h and 0043h. Table 15.2 shows the typical uses of the isolated memory area.

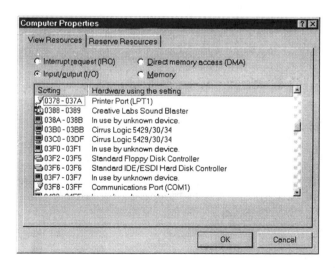

Figure 15.5 Example I/O memory map from 0378h to 03FFh

Table 15.2 Typical isolated I/O memory map

Address	Device
000h–01Fh	DMA controller
020h–021h	Programmable interrupt controller
040h–05Fh	Counter/Timer
060h–07Fh	Digital I/O
080h–09Fh	DMA controller
0A0h–0BFh	NMI reset
0C0h–0DFh	DMA controller
0E0h–0FFh	Math coprocessor
170h–178h	Hard disk (Secondary IDE drive or CD-ROM drive)
1F0h–1F8h	Hard disk (Primary IDE drive)
200h–20Fh	Game I/O adapter
210h–217h	Expansion unit
278h–27Fh	Second parallel port (LPT2:)
2F8h–2FFh	Second serial port (COM2:)
300h–31Fh	Prototype card
378h–37Fh	Primary parallel port (LPT1:)
380h–38Ch	SDLC interface
3A0h–3AFh	Primary binary synchronous port
3B0h–3BFh	Graphics adapter
3C0h–3DFh	Graphics adapter
3F0h–3F7h	Floppy disk controller
3F8h–3FFh	Primary serial port (COM1:)

15.4.1 Inputting a byte from an I/O port

The assembly language command to input a byte is:

```
IN AL,DX
```

where DX is the Data Register which contains the address of the input port. The 8-bit value loaded from this address is put into the register AL.

For Turbo Pascal the equivalent is accessed via the port[] array. Its general syntax is as follows:

```
value:=port[PORTADDRESS];
```

where PORTADDRESS is the address of the input port and value the 8-bit value at this address. To gain access to this function the statement uses dos requires to be placed near the top of the program.

15.4.2 Inputting a word from a port

The assembly language command to input a word is:

```
IN AX,DX
```

where DX is the Data Register which contains the address of the input port. The 16-bit value loaded from this address is put into the register AX.

For Turbo Pascal the equivalent is accessed via the portw[] array. Its general syntax is as follows:

```
value:=portw[PORTADDRESS];
```

where PORTADDRESS is the address of the input port and value is the 16-bit value at this address. To gain access to this function the statement uses dos requires to be placed near the top of the program.

15.4.3 Outputting a byte to an I/O port

The assembly language command to output a byte is:

```
OUT DX,AL
```

where DX is the Data Register which contains the address of the output port. The 8-bit value sent to this address is stored in register AL.

For Turbo Pascal the equivalent is accessed via the port[] array. Its general syntax is as follows:

```
port[PORTADDRESS]:=value;
```

where PORTADDRESS is the address of the output port and value is the 8-bit value to be sent to that address. To gain access to this function the statement uses dos requires to be placed near the top of the program.

15.4.4 Outputting a word

The assembly language command to input a byte is:

```
OUT DX,AX
```

where DX is the Data Register which contains the address of the output port. The 16-bit value sent to this address is stored in register AX.

For Turbo Pascal the equivalent is accessed via the port[] array. Its general syntax is as follows:

```
portw[PORTADDRESS]:=value;
```

where PORTADDRESS is the address of the output port and value is the 16-bit value to be sent to that address. To gain access to this function the statement uses dos requires to be placed near the top of the program.

The following two sections discuss how Turbo Pascal uses the input and output ports.

16 RS-232

16.1 Introduction

RS-232 is one of the most widely used techniques used to interface external equipment to computers. It uses serial communications where one bit is sent along a line, at a time. This differs from parallel communications which sends one or more bytes, at a time. The main advantage that serial communications has over parallel communications is that a single wire is needed to transmit and another to receive. RS-232 is a de facto standard that most computer and instrumentation companies comply with. It was standardized in 1962 by the Electronics Industries Association (EIA). Unfortunately this standard only allows short cable runs with low bit rates. The standard RS-232 only allows a bit rate of 19 600 bps for a maximum distance of 20 metres. New serial communications standards, such as RS-422 and RS-449, allow very long cable runs and high bit rates. For example, RS-422 allows a bit rate of up to 10 Mbps over distances up to 1 mile, using twisted-pair, coaxial cable or optical fibres. The new standards can also be used to create computer networks. This chapter introduces the RS-232 standard and gives simple programs which can be used to transmit and receive using RS-232. The following chapter shows how Turbo Pascal can be used to transmit data through the parallel port.

16.2 Electrical characteristics

16.2.1 Line voltages

The electrical characteristics of RS-232 define the minimum and maximum voltages of a logic '1' and '0'. A logic '1' ranges from –3 V to –25 V, but will typically be around –12 V. A logical '0' ranges from 3 V to 25 V, but will typically be around +12 V. Any voltage between –3 V and +3 V has an indeterminate logical state. If no pulses are present on the line the voltage level is equivalent to a high level, that is –12 V. A voltage level of 0 V at the receiver is interpreted as a line break or a short circuit. Figure 16.1 shows an example transmission.

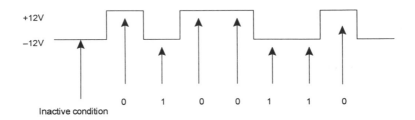

Figure 16.1   RS-232 voltage levels

16.2.2 DB25S connector

The DB25S connector is a 25-pin D-type connector and gives full RS-232 functionality. Figure 16.2 shows the pin number assignment. A DCE (the terminating cable) connector has a male outer casing with female connection pins. The DTE (the computer) has a female outer casing with male connecting pins. There are three main signal types: control, data and ground. Table 16.1 lists the main connections. Control lines are active HIGH, that is they are HIGH when the signal is active and LOW when inactive.

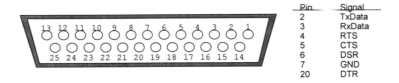

Pin	Signal
2	TxData
3	RxData
4	RTS
5	CTS
6	DSR
7	GND
20	DTR

Figure 16.2   RS-232 DB25S connector

16.2.3 DB9S Connector

The 25-pin connector is the standard for RS-232 connections but as electronic equipment becomes smaller there is a need for smaller connectors. For this purpose most PCs now use a reduced function 9-pin D-type connector rather than the full function 25-way D-type. As with the 25-pin connector the DCE (the terminating cable) connector has a male outer casing with female connection pins. The DTE (the computer) has a female outer casing with male connecting pins. Figure 16.3 shows the main connections.

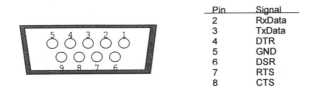

Pin	Signal
2	RxData
3	TxData
4	DTR
5	GND
6	DSR
7	RTS
8	CTS

Figure 16.3   RS-232 DB9S Interface

Table 16.1 Main pin connections used in 25-pin connector

Pin	Name	Abbreviation	Functionality
1	Frame Ground	FG	This ground normally connects the outer sheath of the cable and to earth ground
2	Transmit Data	TD	Data is sent from the DTE (computer or terminal) to a DCE via TD
3	Receive Data	RD	Data is sent from the DCE to a DTE (computer or terminal) via RD
4	Request To Send	RTS	DTE sets this active when it is ready to transmit data
5	Clear To Send	CTS	DCE sets this active to inform the DTE that it is ready to receive data
6	Data Set Ready	DSR	Similar functionality to CTS but activated by the DTE when it is ready to receive data
7	Signal Ground	SG	All signals are referenced to the signal ground (GND)
20	Data Terminal Ready	DTR	Similar functionality to RTS but activated by the DCE when it wishes to transmit data

16.2.4 PC connectors

All PCs have at least one serial communications port. The primary port is named COM1: and the secondary is COM2:. There are two types of connectors used in RS-232 communications, these are the 25- and 9-way D-type. Most modern PCs use either a 9-pin connector for the primary (COM1:) serial port and a 25-pin for a secondary serial port (COM2:), or they use two 9-pin connectors for serial ports. The serial port can be differentiated from the parallel port in that the 25-pin parallel port (LPT1:) is a 25-pin female connector on the PC and a male connector on the cable. The 25-pin serial connector is a male on the PC and a female on the cable. The different connector types can cause problems in connecting devices. Thus a 25-to-9 pin adapter is a useful attachment, especially to connect a serial mouse to a 25-pin connector.

16.3 Frame format

RS-232 uses asynchronous communications which has a start-stop data format. Each character is transmitted one at a time with a delay between them. This delay is called the inactive time and is set at a logic level high (-12 V) as shown in Figure 16.4. The transmitter sends a start bit to inform the receiver that a character is to be sent in the following bit transmission. This start bit is always a '0'. Next, 5, 6 or 7 data bits are sent as a 7-bit ASCII character, followed by a parity bit and finally either 1, 1.5 or 2 stop bits. Figure 16.4 shows a frame format and an example transmission of the character 'A', using odd parity. The rate of transmission is set by the timing of a single bit. Both the transmitter and receiver need to be set to the same bit-time interval. An internal clock on both sets this interval. These only have to be roughly synchronized and approximately at the same rate as data is transmitted in relatively short bursts.

Error control is data added to transmitted data in order to detect or correct an error in transmission. RS-232 uses a simple technique known as parity to provide a degree of error detection.

A parity bit is added to transmitted data to make the number of 1s sent either even (even parity) or odd (odd parity). A single parity bit can only detect an odd number of errors, that is, 1, 3, 5, and so on. If there is an even number of bits in error then the parity bit will be correct and no error will be detected. This type of error coding is not normally used on its own where there is the possibility of several bits being in error.

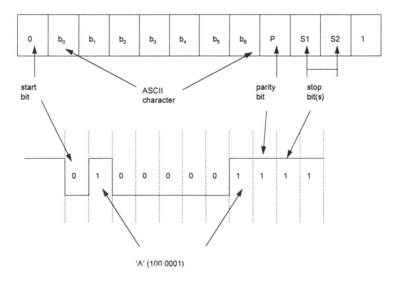

Figure 16.4 RS-232 frame format

Baud rate

One of the main parameters which specify RS-232 communications is the rate of transmission at which data is transmitted and received. It is important that the transmitter and receiver operate at, roughly, the same speed.

For asynchronous transmission the start and stop bits are added in addition to the 7 ASCII character bits and the parity. Thus a total of 10 bits are required to transmit a single character. With 2 stop bits, a total of 11 bits are required. If 10 characters are sent every second and if 11 bits are used for each character, then the transmission rate is 110 bits per second (bps). Table 16.2 lists how the bit rate relates to the characters sent per second (assuming 10 transmitted bits per character). The bit rate is measured in bits per second (bps).

	Bits
ASCII character	7
Start bit	1
Stop bit	2
Total	10

Table 16.2 Bits per second related to characters sent per second

Speed(bps)	Characters/second
300	30
1200	120
2400	240

In addition to the bit rate, another term used to describe the transmission speed is the baud rate. The bit rate refers to the actual rate at which bits are transmitted, whereas the baud rate relates to the rate at which signalling elements, used to represent bits, are transmitted. Since one signalling element encodes one bit, the two rates are then identical. Only in modems does the bit rate differ from the baud rate.

16.4 Communications between two nodes

RS-232 is intended to be a standard but not all manufacturers abide by it. Some implement the full specification while others implement just a partial specification. This is mainly because not every device requires the full functionality of RS-232, for example a modem requires many more control lines than a serial mouse.

The rate at which data is transmitted and the speed at which the transmitter and receiver can transmit/receive the data dictates whether data handshaking is required.

16.4.1 Handshaking

In the transmission of data there can be either no handshaking, hardware handshaking or software handshaking. If no handshaking is used then the receiver must be able to read the received characters before the transmitter sends another. The receiver may buffer the received character and store it in a special memory location before it is read. This memory location is named the receiver buffer. Typically, it may only hold a single character. If it is not emptied before another character is received then any character previously in the buffer will be overwritten. An example of this is illustrated in Figure 16.5. In this case the receiver has read the first two characters successfully from the receiver buffer, but it did not read the third character as the fourth transmitted character has overwritten it in the receiver buffer. If this condition occurs then some form of handshaking must be used to stop the transmitter sending characters before the receiver has had time to service the received characters.

Software handshaking involves sending special control characters. These include the DC1-DC4 control characters. Hardware handshaking involves the transmitter asking the receiver if it is ready to receive data. If the receiver buffer is empty it will inform the transmitter that it is ready to receive data. Once the data is transmitted and loaded into the receiver buffer the transmitter is informed not to transmit any more characters until the character in the receiver buffer has been read. The main hardware handshaking lines used for this purpose are:

- CTS – Clear To Send.
- RTS – Ready To Send.
- DTR – Data Terminal Ready.
- DSR – Data Set Ready.

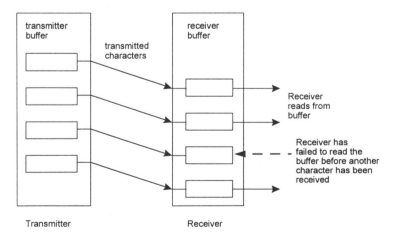

Figure 16.5 Transmission and reception of characters

16.4.2 RS-232 set-up

Windows 95/NT allows the serial port setting to be set by selecting Control Panel → System → Device Manager → Ports (COM and LPT) → Port Settings. The settings of the communications port (the IRQ and the port address) can be changed by selecting Control Panel → System → Device Manager → Ports (COM and LPT) → Resources for IRQ and Addresses. Figure 16.6 shows example parameters and settings. The selectable baud rates are typically 110, 300, 600, 1200, 2400, 4800, 9600 and 19 200 baud for an 8250-based device. With a 16650 compatible UART speed also gives enhanced speeds of 38400, 57600, 115200, 230400, 460800 and 921600 baud. Notice that the flow control can either be set to software handshaking (Xon/Xoff), hardware handshaking or none.

The parity bit can either be set to none, odd, even, mark or space. A mark in the parity option sets the parity bit to a '1' and a space sets it to a '0'.

In this case COM1: is set at 9600 baud, 8 data bits, no parity, 1 stop bit and no parity checking.

16.4.3 Simple no-handshaking communications

In this form of communication it is assumed that the receiver can read the received data from the receiver buffer before another character is received. Data is sent from a TD pin connection of the transmitter and is received in the RD pin connection at the receiver. When a DTE (such as a computer) connects to another DTE, then the transmit line (TD) on one is connected to the receive (RD) of the other and vice versa. Figure 16.7 shows the connections between the nodes.

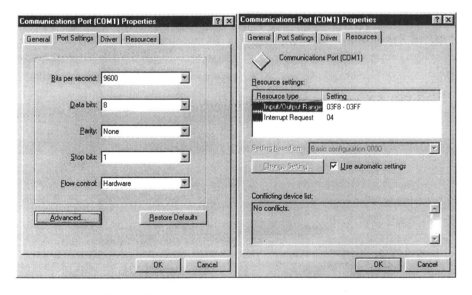

Figure 16.6   Changing port setting and parameters

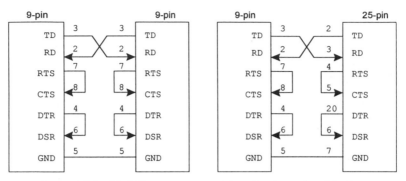

Figure 16.7   RS-232 connections with no hardware handshaking

16.4.4 Software handshaking

There are two ASCII characters that start and stop communications. These are X-ON ($\wedge$S , Cntrl-S or ASCII 11) and X-OFF ($\wedge$Q, Cntrl-Q or ASCII 13). When the transmitter receives an X-OFF character it ceases communications until an X-ON character is sent. This type of handshaking is normally used when the transmitter and receiver can process data relatively quickly. Normally, the receiver will also have a large buffer for the incoming characters. When this buffer is full it transmits an X-OFF. After it has read from the buffer the X-ON is transmitted, see Figure 16.8.

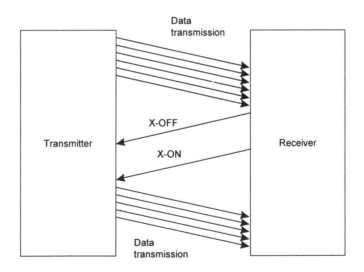

Figure 16.8   Software handshaking using X-ON and X-OFF

16.4.5 Hardware handshaking

Hardware handshaking stops characters in the receiver buffer from being overwritten. The control lines used are all active HIGH. When a node wishes

172   *Mastering Pascal*

to transmit data it asserts the RTS line active (that is, HIGH). It then monitors the CTS line until it goes active (that is, HIGH). If the CTS line at the transmitter stays inactive then the receiver is busy and cannot receive data, at the present. When the receiver reads from its buffer the RTS line will automatically go active indicating to the transmitter that it is now ready to receive a character.

Receiving data is similar to the transmission of data, but the lines DSR and DTR are used instead of RTS and CTS. When the DCE wishes to transmit to the DTE the DSR input to the receiver will become active. If the receiver cannot receive the character it will set the DTR line inactive. When it is clear to receive it sets the DTR line active and the remote node then transmits the character. The DTR line will be set inactive until the character has been processed.

16.4.6 Two-way communications with handshaking

For full handshaking of the data between two nodes the RTS and CTS lines are crossed over (as are the DTR and DSR lines). This allows for full remote node feedback (see Figure 16.9).

16.5 Programming RS-232

Normally, serial transmission is achieved via the RS-232 standard. Although 25 lines are defined usually only a few are used. Data is sent along the TD line and received by the RD line with a common ground return. The other lines used for handshaking are RTS (Ready to Send) which is an output signal to indicate that data is ready to be transmitted and CTS (Clear to Send), which is an input indicating that the remote equipment is ready to receive data.

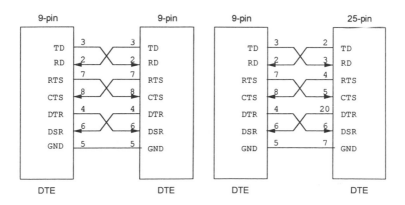

Figure 16.9 RS-232 communications with handshaking

The 8250 IC is commonly used in serial communications. It can either be mounted onto the motherboard of the PC or fitted to an I/O card. This section discusses how it is programmed.

16.5.1 Programming the serial device

The main registers used in RS-232 communications are the Line Control Register (LCR), the Line Status Register (LSR) and the Transmit and Receive buffers (see Figure 16.10). The Transmit and Receive buffers share the same addresses.

The base address of the primary port (COM1:) is normally set at 3F8h and the secondary port (COM2:) at 2F8h. A standard PC can support up to four COM ports.

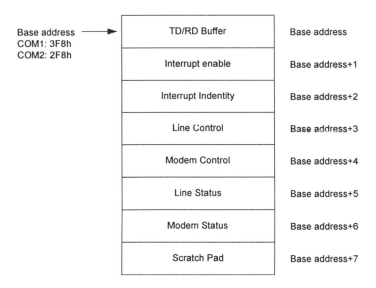

Figure 16.10 Serial communication registers

16.5.2 Line Status Register (LSR)

The LSR determines the status of the transmitter and receiver buffers. It can only be read from, and all the bits are automatically set by hardware. The bit definitions are given in Figure 16.11. When an error occurs in the transmission of a character one (or several) of the error bits is (are) set to a '1'.

One danger when transmitting data is that a new character can be written to the transmitter buffer before the previous character has been sent. This over-writes the contents of the character being transmitted. To avoid this the status bit S_6 is tested to determine if there is still a character in the buffer. If there is then it is set to a '1', else the transmitter buffer is empty.

To send a character:

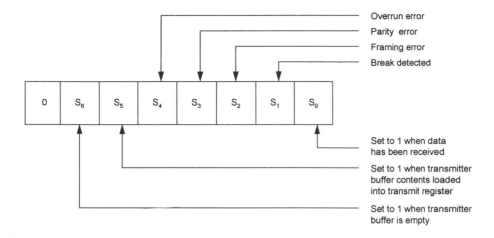

Figure 16.11 Line Status Register

> *Test Bit 6 until set;*
> *Send character;*

A typical Pascal routine is:

```
repeat
   status := port[LSR] and $40;
until (status=$40);
```

When receiving data the S_0 bit is tested to determine if there is a bit in the receiver buffer. To receive a character:

> *Test Bit 0 until set;*
> *Read character;*

A typical Pascal routine is:

```
repeat
    status := port[LSR] and $01;
until (status=$01);
```

Figure 16.12 shows how the LSR is tested for the transmission and reception of characters.

16.5.3 Line Control Register (LCR)

The LCR sets up the communications parameters. These include the number of bits per character, the parity and the number of stop bits. It can be written to or read from and has a similar function to that of the control registers used in the PPI and PTC. The bit definitions are given in Figure 16.13.

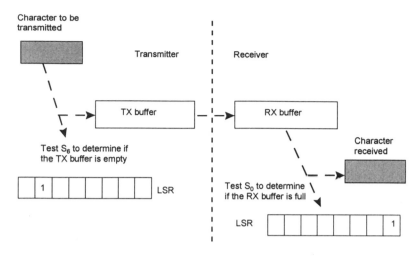

Figure 16.12 Testing of the LSR for the transmission and reception of characters

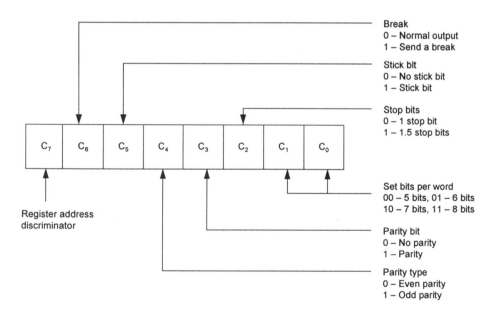

Figure 16.13 Line Control Register

The msb, C_7, must to be set to a '0' in order to access the transmitter and receiver buffers, else if it is set to a '1' the baud rate divider is set up. The baud rate is set by loading an appropriate 16-bit divisor into the addresses of transmitter/receiver buffer address and the next address. The value loaded depends on the crystal frequency connected to the IC. Table 16.3 shows divisors for a crystal frequency is 1.8432 MHz. In general the divisor, N, is related to the baud rate by:

$$Baud\ rate = \frac{Clock\ frequency}{16 \times N}$$

For example, for 1.8432 MHz and 9600 baud $N = 1.8432 \times 10^6/(9600 \times 16) = 12$ (000Ch).

Table 16.3 baud rate divisors

baud rate	Divisor (value loaded into Tx/Rx buffer)
110	0417h
300	0180h
600	00C0h
1200	0060h
1800	0040h
2400	0030h
4800	0018h
9600	000Ch
19200	0006h

16.5.4 Register addresses

The addresses of the main registers are given in Table 16.4. To load the baud rate divisor, first the LCR bit 7 is set to a '1', then the LSB is loaded into divisor LSB and the MSB into the divisor MSB register. Finally, bit 7 is set back to a '0'. For example, for 9600 baud, COM1 and 1.8432 MHz clock then 0Ch is loaded in 3F8h and 00h into 3F9h.

When bit 7 is set at a '0' then a read from base address reads from the RD buffer and a write operation writes to the TD buffer. An example of this is shown in Figure 16.14.

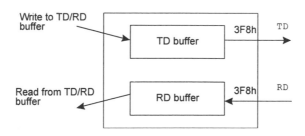

Figure 16.14 Read and write from TD/RD buffer

Table 16.4 Serial communications addresses

Primary	Secondary	Register	Bit 7 of LCR
3F8h	2F8h	TD buffer	'0'
3F8h	2F8h	RD buffer	'0'
3F8h	2F8h	Divisor LSB	'1'
3F9h	2F9h	Divisor MSB	'1'
3FBh	2FBh	Line Control Register	
3FDh	2FDh	Line Status Register	

16.6 RS-232 programs

Figure 16.15 shows the main RS-232 connection for 9- and 25-pin connections without hardware handshaking. The loopback connections are used to test the RS-232 hardware and the software, while the null modem connections are used to transmit characters between two computers. Program 16.1 uses a loop back on the TD/RD lines so that a character sent by the computer will automatically be received into the receiver buffer. This set up is useful in testing the transmit and receive routines. The character to be sent is entered via the keyboard. A *CNTRL-D* (^D) keystroke exits the program.

Program 16.2 can be used as a sender program (send.c) and Program 16.3 can be used as a receiver program (receive.c). With these program the null modem connections shown in Figure 16.15 are used.

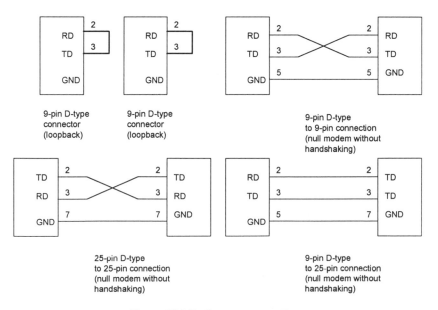

Figure 16.15 System connections

Program 16.1

```pascal
program prog16_1(input,output);
(*    This program transmits a character from COM1: and receives    *)
(*    it via this port. The TD is connected to RD.                  *)
uses crt;
const    TXDATA  =    $3F8;   LSR     =    $3FD;
         LCR     =    $3FB;   CNTRLD  =    #4;
var      inchar, outchar:char;

procedure setup_serial;
begin
   port[LCR] := $80;  (* set up bit 7 to a 1                         *)
   port[TXDATA] := $0C;
   port[TXDATA+1] := $00;
   (* load TxRegister with 12, crystal frequency is 1.8432 MHz      *)
   port[LCR] := $0A
   (* Bit pattern loaded is 00001010b, from msb to lsb these are:   *)
   (* Access TD/RD buffer, normal output, no stick bit              *)
   (* even parity, parity on, 1 stop bit, 7 data bits               *)
end;

procedure send_character(ch:char);
var       status:byte;
begin
   repeat
      status := port[LSR] and $40;
   until (status=$40);
      (*repeat until bit Tx buffer is empty                         *)
   port[TXDATA] := ord(ch); (*send ASCII code                       *)
end;

function  get_character:char;
var       status,inbyte:byte;
begin

   repeat
      status := port[LSR] and $01;
   until (status=$01);
   inbyte := port[TXDATA];
   get_character:= chr(inbyte);
end;

begin
   setup_serial;

   repeat
      outchar:=readkey;
      send_character(outchar);
      inchar:=get_character;
      writeln('Character received was ',inchar);
   until (outchar=CNTRLD);

end.
```

📋 **Program 16.2**

```
program prog16_2(input,output);
(* sender.pas                                                  *)

uses crt;

const
     TXDATA =  $3F8;   LSR  = $3FD;   LCR  = $3FB;

var   outchar:char;

procedure  setup_serial;
begin

   port[LCR]  := port[LCR] or $80;
     (* set up bit 7 to a 1                                    *)
   port[TXDATA]  := $0C;
   port[TXDATA+1]  := $00;
     (* load TxRegister with 12                                *)
     (* crystal frequency is 1.8432MHz                         *)
   port[LCR]  := port[LCR] and $7F
     (* set up bit 7 to a 0                                    *)
     (* bit 7 must be a 0 to access TxBuff or RxBuff           *)
     (* serial port has been set up                            *)
end;

procedure  send_character(ch:char);
var           status:byte;
begin

   repeat
     status := port[LSR] and $40;
   until (status=$40);
   (*repeat until bit Tx buffer is empty              *)

   port[TXDATA]  := ord(ch); (*send ASCII code        *)
end;

begin
   setup_serial;
   repeat
     outchar:=readkey;
     send_character(outchar);
   until (outchar=#4);
end.
```

📋 **Program 16.3**

```
program prog16_3(input,output);
(* receive.pas                                      *)

uses crt;

const
     TXDATA =$3F8;   LSR  = $3FD;   LCR  = $3FB;
```

```
var   inchar:char;

procedure  setup_serial;
begin

   port[LCR]  := port[LCR]  or $80;
      (* set up bit 7 to a 1                                 *)
   port[TXDATA]  := $0C;
   port[TXDATA+1]  := $00;
      (* load TxRegister with 12                             *)
      (* crystal frequency is 1.8432MHz                      *)
   port[LCR]  := port[LCR]  and $7F
      (* set up bit 7 to a 0                                 *)
      (* bit 7 must be a 0 to access TxBuff or RxBuff        *)
      (* serial port has been set up                         *)
end;

function   get_character:char;
var        status,inbyte:byte;
begin

   repeat
      status := port[LSR] and $01;
   until (status=$01);

   inbyte := port[TXDATA];

   get_character:= chr(inbyte);

end;

begin
   setup_serial;

   repeat
      inchar:=get_character;
      write(inchar);
   until (inchar=#4);
end.
```

16.7 Exercises

16.7.1 Write a program that continuously sends the character 'A' to the serial line. Observe the output on an oscilloscope and identify the bit pattern and the baud rate.

16.7.2 Write a program that continuously sends the characters from 'A' to 'Z' to the serial line. Observe the output on an oscilloscope.

16.7.3 Complete Table 16.5 to give the actual time to send 1000 characters for the given baud rates. Compare these values with estimated values.

Table 16.5 baud rate divisors

baud rate	Time to send 1000 characters (sec)
110	
300	
600	
1200	
2400	
4800	
9600	
19200	

Note that approximately 10 bits are used for each character thus 960 characters/sec will be transmitted at 9600 baud.

16.7.4 Modify Program 16.1 so that the program prompts the user for the baud rate when the program is started. A sample run is shown in Test run 16.1.

Test run 16.1
```
Enter baud rate required:
1   110
2   150
3   300
4   600
5   1200
6   2400
7   4800
8   9600
>> 8
RS232 transmission set to 9600 baud
```

16.7.5 One problem with Programs 16.2 and 16.3 is that when the return key is pressed only one character is sent. The received character will be a carriage return which returns the cursor back to the start of a line and not to the next line. Modify the receiver program so that a line feed will be generated automatically when a carriage return is received. Note a carriage return is an ASCII 13 and line feed is a 10.

16.7.6 Modify the get_character() routine so that it returns an error flag if it detects an error or if there is a time-out. Table 16.6 lists the error flags and the returned error value. If a character is not received within 10 seconds an error message should be displayed.

Test the routine by connecting two PCs together and set the transmitter with differing RS-232 parameters.

Table 16.6 Error returns from get_character()

Error condition	Error flag return	Notes
Parity error	−1	
Overrun error	−2	
Framing error	−3	
Break detected	−4	
Time-out	−5	get_character() should time-out if no characters are received within 10 seconds.

17 Parallel Port

17.1 Introduction

This chapter discusses parallel communications. The Centronics printer interface transmits 8 bits of data at a time to an external device, normally a printer. A 25-pin D-type connector is used to connect to the PC and a 36-pin Centronics interface connector normally connects to the printer. This interface is not normally used for other types of interfacing as the standard interface only transmits data over the data lines in one direction, that is, from the PC to the external device. Some interface devices overcome this problem by using four of the input handshaking lines to input data and then multiplexing using an output handshaking line to multiplex them to produce eight output bits.

As technology has improved there is a great need for a bi-directional parallel port to connect to devices such as tape backup drives, CD-ROMs, and so on. The Centronic interface unfortunately lacks speeds (150 kbps), has limited length of lines (2 m) and very few computer manufacturers complied with an electrical standard.

Thus, in 1991, several manufacturers (including IBM and Texas Instruments) formed a group called NPA (National Printing Alliance). Their original objective was to develop a standard for control printers over a network. To achieve this a bi-directional standard was developed which was compatible with existing software. This standard was submitted to the IEEE so that they could standardize it. The committee that the IEEE set up was known as the IEEE 1284 committee and the standard they produced is known as the IEEE 1284-1994 Standard (as it was released in 1994).

With this standard all parallel ports use a bi-directional link in either a compatible, nibble or byte mode. These modes are relatively slow as the software must monitor the handshaking lines (up to 100 kbps). To allow high-speed the EPP (Enhanced Parallel Port) and ECP (Extended Capabilities Port Protocol) modes which allow high-speed data transfer using automatic hardware handshaking. In addition to the previous three modes, EPP and ECP are being implemented on the latest I/O controllers by most of the Super I/O chip manufacturers. These modes use hardware to assist in the data transfer. For example, in EPP mode, a byte of data can be transferred to the peripheral by a simple OUT instruction. The I/O controller handles all the handshaking and data transfer to the peripheral.

17.2 PC connections

Figure 17.1 shows the pin connections on the PC connector. The data lines (D0–D7) output data from the PC and each of the data lines has an associated ground line (GND).

17.3 Data handshaking

The main handshaking lines are $\overline{\text{ACK}}$, BUSY and $\overline{\text{STROBE}}$. Initially the computer places the data on the data bus, then it sets the $\overline{\text{STROBE}}$ line low to inform the external device that the data on the data bus is valid. When the external device has read the data it sets the $\overline{\text{ACK}}$ lines low to acknowledge that it has read the data. The PC then waits for the printer to set the BUSY line inactive, that is, low. Figure 17.2 shows a typical handshaking operation and Table 17.1 outlines the definitions of the pins.

The parallel interface can be accessed either by direct reads to and writes from the I/O memory addresses or from a program which uses the BIOS printer interrupt. This interrupt allows a program either to get the status of the printer or to write a character to it. Table 17.2 outlines the interrupt calls.

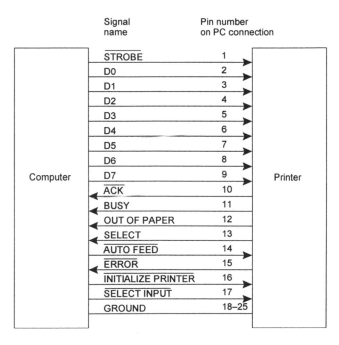

Figure 17.1 Centronics parallel interface showing pin numbers on PC connector

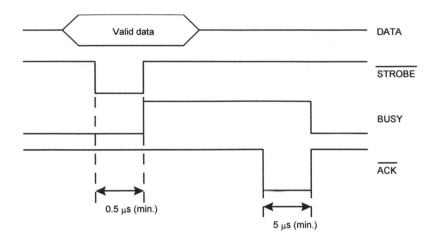

Figure 17.2 Data handshaking with the Centronics parallel printer interface

17.3.1 BIOS printer

Program 17.1 uses the BIOS printer interrupt to test the status of the printer and output characters to the printer.

Table 17.1 Signal definitions

Signal	In/out	Description
STROBE	Out	Indicates that valid data is on the data lines (active low)
AUTO FEED	Out	Instructs the printer to insert a line feed for every carriage return (active low)
SELECT INPUT	Out	Indicates to the printer that it is selected (active low)
INIT	Out	Resets the printer
ACK	In	Indicate that the last character was received (active low)
BUSY	In	Indicates that the printer is busy and thus cannot accept data
OUT OF PAPER	In	Out of paper
SELECT	In	Indicates that the printer is on-line and connected
ERROR	In	Indicates that an error exists (active low)

Table 17.2 BIOS printer interrupt

Description	Input registers	Output registers

Initialize printer port	AH = 01h
	DX = printer number (00h-02h)
		AH = printer status
		  bit 7: not busy
		  bit 6: acknowledge
		  bit 5: out of paper
		  bit 4: selected
		  bit 3: I/O error
		  bit 2: unused
		  bit 1: unused
		  bit 0: timeout

Write character to printer	AH = 00h AL = character to write DX = printer number (00h-02h)	AH = printer status
Get printer status	AH = 02h DX = printer number (00h-02h)	AH = printer status

Program 17.1

```
program prog17_1(input,output);

uses DOS, CRT;

const PRINTERR=-1;

var status:integer;
    ch:char;

function init_printer:integer;
var   inregs:registers;
begin
    inregs.ah:=$01;        (* initialize printer  *)
    inregs.dx:=0;          (* LPT1:               *)
    intr($17,inregs);
    if ((inregs.ah and $20)=$20) then
    begin
       writeln('Out of paper');
       init_printer:=PRINTERR;
    end
    else if ((inregs.ah and $08)=$08) then
    begin
       writeln('I/O error');
       init_printer:=PRINTERR;
    end
    else if ((inregs.ah and $01)=$01) then
    begin
    writeln('Printer timeout');
       init_printer:=PRINTERR;
    end;
    init_printer:=0;
```

```
end;

procedure print_character(ch:char);
var inregs:registers;
begin

   inregs.ah:=$00; (* print character *)
   inregs.dx:=0; (* LPT1: *)
   inregs.al:=ord(ch);

   intr($17,inregs);
end;

begin
   status:=init_printer;
   if (status=PRINTERR) then exit;

   repeat
      write('Enter character to output to printer ');
      ch:=readkey;
      print_character(ch);
   until (ch=#4); (* repeat until Ctrl-D pressed *)
end.
```

17.4 I/O addressing

17.4.1 Addresses

The printer port has three I/O addresses assigned for the data, status and control ports. These addresses are normally assigned to:

Printer	Data register	Status register	Control register
LPT1	378h	379h	37ah
LPT2	278h	279h	27ah

The DOS debug program be used to display the base addresses for the serial
and parallel ports by displaying the 32 memory location starting at
0040:0008. For example:

```
-d 40:00
0040:0000   F8 03 F8 02 00 00 00 00-78 03 00 00 00 00 29 02
```

The first four 16-bit addresses gives the serial communications ports. In this
case there are two COM ports at address 03F8h (COM1) and 02F8h (for
COM2). The next four 16-bit addresses gives the parallel port addressees. In
this case there is two parallel ports. One at 0378h (LPT1) and one at 0229h
(LPT4).

17.4.2 Output lines

Figure 17.3 shows the bit definitions of the registers. The Data port register links to the output lines. Writing a 1 to the bit position in the port sets the output high, while a 0 sets the corresponding output line to a low. Thus to output the binary value 1010 1010b (AAh) to the parallel port data then using Turbo Pascal:

```
port[0x378]:=$AA;
```

The output data lines are each capable of sourcing 2.6 mA and sinking 24 mA, it is thus essential that the external device does not try to pull these lines to ground.

The Control port also contains five output lines, of which the lower four bits are $\overline{\text{STROBE}}$, $\overline{\text{AUTO FEED}}$, INIT and $\overline{\text{SELECT INPUT}}$, as illustrated in Figure 17.3. These lines can be used as either control lines or as data outputs. With the data line a 1 in the register gives an output high, while the lines in the Control port have inverted logic. Thus a 1 to a bit in the register causes an output low.

Program 17.2 outputs the binary pattern 0101 0101b (55h) to the data lines and sets $\overline{\text{SELECT INPUT}}$=0, INIT=1, $\overline{\text{AUTO FEED}}$=1, and $\overline{\text{STROBE}}$=0, the value of the Data port will be 55h and the value written to the Control port will be XXXX 1101 (where X represents don't care). The value for the control output lines must be invert, so that the $\overline{\text{STROBE}}$ line will be set to a 1 so that it will be output as a LOW.

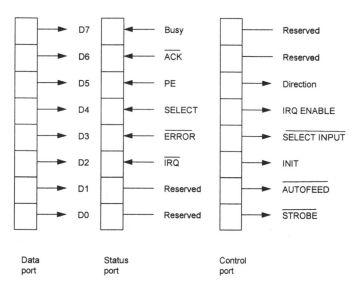

Figure 17.3 Port Assignments

📋 **Program 17.2**

```
program prog17_2(input,output);

const   DATA=$378;
        STATUS=DATA+1;
        CONTROL=DATA+2;

var out1,out2:integer;
begin

    out1 := $55;            (* 0101 0101                           *)
    port[DATA]:=out1;
    out2 := $0D;            (* 0000 1101                           *)
    port[CONTROL]:= out2;   (* STROBE=LOW, AUTOFEED=HIGH, etc *)
end.
```

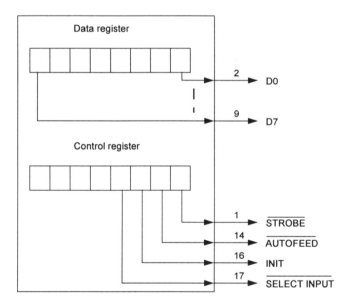

Figure 17.4 Output lines

The setting of the output value (in this case, out2) looks slightly confusing as the output is the inverse of the logical setting (that is, a 1 sets the output low). An alternative method is to exclusive-OR (EX-OR) the output value with $B which will invert the 1st, 2nd and 4th least significant bits ($\overline{\text{SELECT INPUT}}$=0, $\overline{\text{AUTO FEED}}$=1, and $\overline{\text{STROBE}}$=0), while leaving the 3rd least significant bit (INIT) untouched. Thus the following will achieve the same as the previous program:

```
out2 := $06;                      (* 0000 0110                           *)
port[CONTROL]:= out2 xor 0xb; (* STROBE=LOW, AUTOFEED=HIGH, etc *)
```

If the 5th bit on the control register (IRQ Enable) is written as 1 then the output on this line will go from a high to a low which will cause the processor to be interrupted.

The control lines are driven by open collector drivers pulled to +5 Vdc through 4.7 kΩ resistors. Each can sink approximately 7 mA and maintain 0.8 V down-level.

17.4.3 Inputs

There are five inputs from the parallel port (BUSY, $\overline{\text{ACK}}$, PE, SELECT and $\overline{\text{ERROR}}$). The status of these lines can be found by simply reading the upper 5 bits of the Status register, as illustrated in Figure 17.5.

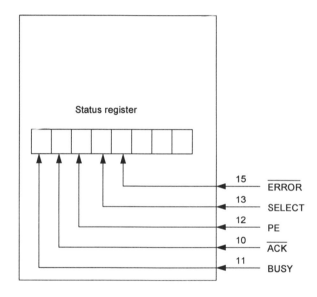

Figure 17.5   Input lines

Unfortunately, the BUSY line has an inverted status. Thus when a LOW is present on BUSY, the bit will actually be read as a 1. For example Program 17.3 reads the bits from the status register, inverts the BUSY bit and then shifts the bits three places to the right so that the 5 inputs bit are in the 5 least significant bits.

🗁 **Program 17.3**
```
program prog17_3(input,output);

const  DATA=$378;
       STATUS=DATA+1;

var    in1:integer;
begin
```

```
    in1 := port[STATUS];  (* read from status register         *)
    in1 := in1 xor $80;   (* invert  BUSY bit                  *)
    in1 := in1 shr 3;     (* move bits so that the inputs are  *)
                          (* the least  significant bits       *)
    writeln('Status bits are ',in1);
end.
```

17.4.4 Electrical interfacing

The output lines can be used to drive LEDs. Figure 17.6 shows an example circuit where a LOW output will cause the LED to be ON while a HIGH causes the output to be OFF. For an input an open push button causes a HIGH input on the input.

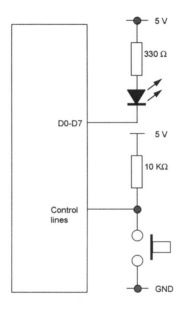

Figure 17.6 Interfacing to inputs and outputs

17.4.5 Simple example

Program 17.4 uses a push button connected to pin 11 (BUSY). When the button is open then the input to BUSY will be a HIGH and the most significant bit in the status register will thus be a 0 (as the BUSY signal is inverted). When the button is closed then this bit will be a 1. This is tested with:

```
if (in1 and $80)=$80) then
```

When this condition is TRUE (that is, when the button is closed) then the output data lines (D0–D7) will flash on and off with a delay of 1 second between flashes. An output of all 1s to the data lines causes the LEDs to be off, and all 0s cause the LEDs to be on.

192   *Mastering Pascal*

```
program prog17_4(input,output);
(* Flash LEDs on and off when the push button connected to BUSY   *)
(* is closed                                                      *)

uses CRT;

const  DATA=$378;        STATUS=DATA+1;          CONTROL=DATA+2;

var in1:integer;
begin

   repeat
     in1:= port[STATUS];

     if ((in1 and $80)= $80)  then
                       (* if switch closed this is TRUE  *)
     begin
        port[DATA]:=$00;     (* LEDs on   *)
        delay(1000);
        port[DATA]:= $ff;    (* LEDs off  *)
        delay(1000);
     end
     else
        port[DATA]:=$01; (* switch open *)
   until keypressed;
end.
```

17.5 Exercises

17.5.1 Write a program that sends a 'walking-ones' code to the parallel port. The delay between changes should be one second. A 'walking-ones' code is as follows:

> 00000001
> 00000010
> 00000100
> 00001000
>   :   :
> 10000000
> 00000001
> 00000010
> and so on.

Hint: Use a repeat...until loop with either the shift left operators (shl) or output the values $01, $02, $04, $08, $10, $20, $40, $80, $01, $02, and so on. An outline of the program is given next:

```
repeat
   i:=1;
   repeat
      port[$378]:=i;
      i:=i shl 1;
      delay(1000);
   until (i=$100);
until (keypressed);
```

17.5.2   Write separate programs which output the patterns in (a) and (b). The sequences are as follows:

(a)   00000001   (b)   10000001
        00000010   01000010
        00000100   00100100
        00001000   00011000
        00010000   00100100
        00100000   01000010
        01000000   10000001
        10000000   01000010
        01000000   00100100
        00100000   00011000
        00010000   00100100
          ::   and so on.
        00000001
        00000010
        and so on.

An outline of a program for (a) is given next:

```
repeat
   i:=1;
   repeat
      port[$378]:=i;
      i:=i shl 1;
      delay(1000);
      until (i=$100);
   repeat
      i:=i shr 1;
      port[$378]:=i;
      delay(1000);
   until (i=$1);
until (keypressed);
```

17.5.3   Write separate programs which output the following sequences:

(a)   1010 1010   (b)   1111 1111
        0101 0101   0000 0000
        1010 1010   1111 1111
        0101 0101   0000 0000
        and so on.   and so on.

(c)
```
0000 0001
0000 0011
0000 1111
0001 1111
0011 1111
0111 1111
1111 1111
0000 0001
0000 0011
0000 0111
0000 1111
0001 1111
```
and so on.

(d)
```
0000 0001
0000 0011
0000 0111
0000 1111
0001 1111
0011 1111
0111 1111
1111 1111
0111 1111
0011 1111
0001 1111
0000 1111
```
and so on.

(e)   The inverse of (d) above.

17.5.4   Write a program that reads a byte from parallel port and display the equivalent ASCII code to the screen. Table 17.3 shows some examples.

Table 17.3 Conversions

Character	Binary	Hex	Decimal
'0'	0011 0000b	30h	48
'1'	0011 0001b	31h	49
	.	.	.
	.	.	.
	.	.	.
'?'	0011 1111b	3Fh	63
'@'	0100 0000b	40h	64
'A'	0100 0001b	41h	65
'B'	0100 0010b	42h	66
	.	.	.
	.	.	.
	.	.	.
'a'	0110 0001b	61h	97
'b'	0110 0010b	62h	98
	and so on.		

17.5.5   Binary coded decimal (BCD) is used mainly in decimal displays and is equivalent to the decimal system where a 4-bit code represents each decimal number. The first 4 bits represent the units, the next 4 the tens, and so on. Write a program that outputs to the parallel a BCD sequence with a one-second delay between changes. A sample BCD table is given in Table 17.4. The output should count from 0 to 99.

Table 17.4 BCD conversion

Digit	BCD
00	00000000
01	00000001
02	00000010
03	00000011
04	00000100
05	00000101
06	00000110
07	00000111
08	00001000
09	00001001
10	00010000
11	00010001
.	.
.	.
.	.
97	10010111
98	10011000
99	10011001

Hint: One possible implementation is to use two variables to represent the units and tens. These would then be used in a nested loop. The resultant output value will then be (tens shl 4)+units. An outline of the loop code is given next.

```
for ten:=0 to 9 do
   for units:=0 to 9 do
   begin

   end;
```

18 Hardware Interrupts

18.1 Introduction

Computer systems either use polling or interrupt-driven software to service external equipment. With polling the computer continually monitors a status line and waits for it to become active. While an interrupt-driven device sends an interrupt request to the computer, which is then serviced by an interrupt service routine (ISR). Interrupt-driven devices are normally better in that the computer is thus free to do other things while polling slows the system down as it must continually monitor the external device. Polling can also cause problems in that a device may be ready to send data and the computer is not watching the status line at that point. Figure 18.1 illustrates polling and interrupt-driven devices.

The generation of an interrupt can occur by hardware or software, as illustrated in Figure 18.2. If a device wishes to interrupt the processor it informs the programmable interrupt controller (PIC). The PIC then decides whether it should interrupt the processor. If there is a processor interrupt then the processor reads the PIC to determine which device caused the interrupt. Then, depending on the device that caused the interrupt, a call to an ISR is made. The ISR then communicates with the device and processes any data. When it has finished the program execution returns to the original program.

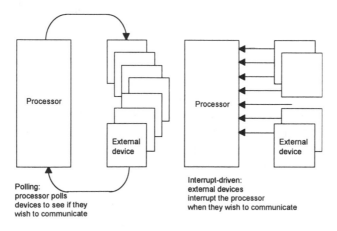

Figure 18.1 Polling or interrupt-driven communications

197

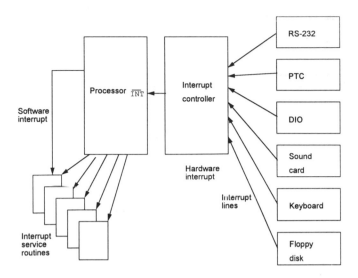

Figure 18.2 Interrupt handling

A software interrupt causes the program to interrupt its execution and goes to an interrupt service routine. Typical software interrupts include reading a key from the keyboard, outputting text to the screen and reading the current date and time.

18.2 Hardware interrupts

Hardware interrupts allow external devices to gain the attention of the processor. Depending on the type of interrupt the processor leaves the current program and goes to a special program called an interrupt service routine (ISR). This program communicates with the device and processes any data. After it has completed its task then program execution returns to the program that was running before the interrupt occurred. Examples of interrupts include the processing of keys from a keyboard and data from a sound card.

As previously mentioned, a device informs the processor that it wants to interrupt it by setting an interrupt line on the PC. Then, depending on the device that caused the interrupt, a call to an ISR is made. Each PIC allow access to eight interrupt request lines. Most PCs use two PICs which gives access to 16 interrupt lines.

18.3 Interrupt vectors

Each device that requires to be 'interrupt-driven' is assigned an IRQ (interrupt request) line. Each IRQ is active high. The first eight (IRQ0–IRQ7) map into interrupts 8 to 15 (08h–0Fh) and the next eight (IRQ8–IRQ15) into interrupts 112 to 119 (70h–77h). Table 18.1 outlines the usage of each of these interrupts. When IRQ0 is made active the ISR corresponds to interrupt vector 8. IRQ0 normally connects to the system timer, the keyboard to IRQ1, and so on. The standard set up of these interrupts is illustrated in Figure 18.3. The system timer interrupts the processor 18.2 times per second and is used to update the system time. When the keyboard has data it interrupts the processor with the IRQ1 line.

Data received from serial ports interrupts the processor with IRQ3 and IRQ4 and the parallel ports use IRQ5 and IRQ7. If one of the parallel, or serial ports does not exist then the IRQ line normally assigned to it can be used by another device. It is typical for interrupt-driven I/O cards, such as a sound card, to have a programmable IRQ line which is mapped to an IRQ line that is not being used.

Note that several devices can use the same interrupt line. A typical example is COM1: and COM3: sharing IRQ4 and COM2: and COM4: sharing IRQ3. If they do share then the ISR must be able to poll the shared devices to determine which of them caused the interrupt. If two different types of device (such as a sound card and a serial port) use the same IRQ line then there may be a contention problem as the ISR may not be able to communicate with different types of interfaces.

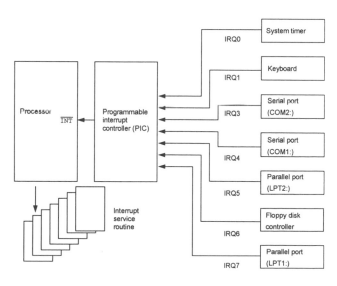

Figure 18.3 Standard usage of IRQ lines

Table 18.1 Interrupt handling

Interrupt	Name	Generated by
08 (08h)	System timer	IRQ0
09 (09h)	Keyboard	IRQ1
10 (0Ah)	Reserved	IRQ2
11 (0Bh)	Serial communications (COM2:)	IRQ3
12 (0Ch)	Serial communications (COM1:)	IRQ4
13 (0Dh)	Parallel port (LPT2:)	IRQ5
14 (0Eh)	Floppy disk controller	IRQ6
15 (0Fh)	Parallel printer (LPT1:)	IRQ7
112 (70h)	Real-time clock	IRQ8
113 (71h)	Redirection of IRQ2	IRQ9
114 (72h)	Reserved	IRQ10
115 (73h)	Reserved	IRQ11
116 (74h)	Reserved	IRQ12
117 (75h)	Math co-processor	IRQ13
118 (76h)	Hard disk controller	IRQ14
119 (77h)	Reserved	IRQ15

Microsoft Windows 95 contains a useful program which determines the usage of the system interrupts. It is selected from Control Panel by selecting System→ Device Manager→ Properties. Figure 18.4 shows a sample window. In this case it can be seen that the system timer uses IRQ0, the keyboard uses IRQ1, the PIC uses IRQ2, and so on. Notice that a Sound Blaster is using IRQ5. This interupt is normally reserved for the secondary printer port. If there is no printer connected then IRQ5 can be used by another device. Some devices can have their I/O address and interrupt line changed. An example is given in Figure 18.5. In this case the IRQ line is set to IRQ7 and the base address is 378h.

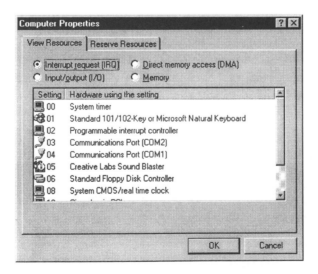

Figure 18.4 Standard usage of IRQ lines

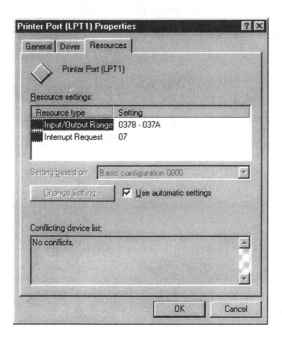

Figure 18.5   Standard set up of IRQ lines

18.3.1 IRQ0: System timer

The system timer uses IRQ0 to interrupt the processor 18.2 times per second and is used to keep the time-of-day clock updated.

18.3.2 IRQ1: Keyboard data ready

The keyboard uses IRQ1 to signal to the processor that data is ready to be received from the keyboard. This data is normally a scan code, but the interrupt handler performs differently for the following special keystrokes:

- *Ctrl-Break* invokes interrupt 1Bh.
- *SysRq* invokes interrupt 15h/AH=85h.
- *Ctrl-Alt-Del* performs hard or soft reboot.
- *Shift-PrtSc* invokes interrupt 05h.

18.3.3 IRQ2: Redirection of IRQ9

The BIOS redirects the interrupt for IRQ9 back here.

18.3.4 IRQ3: Secondary serial port (COM2:)

The secondary serial port (COM2:) uses IRQ3 to interrupt the processor. Typically, COM3: to COM8: also use it, although COM3: may use IRQ4.

18.3.5 IRQ4: Primary serial port (COM1:)

The primary serial port (COM1:) uses IRQ4 to interrupt the processor. Typically, COM3: also uses it.

18.3.6 IRQ5: Secondary parallel port (LPT2:)

On older PCs the IRQ5 line was used by the fixed disk. On new systems the secondary parallel port uses it. Typically, it is used by a sound card on PCs which have no secondary parallel port connected.

18.3.7 IRQ6: Floppy disk controller

The floppy disk controller activates the IRQ6 line on completion of a disk operation.

18.3.8 IRQ7: Primary parallel port (LPT1:)

Printers (or other parallel devices) activate the IRQ7 line when they become active. As with IRQ5 it may be used by another device, if there are no other devices connected to this line.

18.3.9 IRQ9

Redirected to IRQ2 service routine.

18.4 Programmable interrupt controller (PIC)

The PC uses the 8259 IC to control hardware-generated interrupts. It is known as a programmable interrupt controller and has eight input interrupt request lines and an output line to interrupt the processor. Originally, PCs only had one PIC and eight IRQ lines (IRQ0-IRQ7). Modern PCs can use up to 15 IRQ lines which are set up by connecting a secondary PIC interrupt request output line to the IRQ2 line of the primary PIC. The interrupt lines on the secondary PIC are then assigned IRQ lines of IRQ8 to IRQ15. This set up is shown in Figure 18.7. When an interrupt occurs on any of these lines it is sensed by the processor on the IRQ2 line. The processor then interrogrates the primary and secondary PIC for the interrupt line which caused the interrupt.

The primary and secondary PICs are programmed via port addresses 20h and 21h, as given in Table 18.2.

The operation of the PIC is programmed using registers. The IRQ input lines are either configured as level-sensitive or edge-triggered interrupt. With edge-triggered interrupts a change from a low to a high on the IRQ line causes the interrupt. A level-sensitive interrupt occurs when the IRQ line is high. Most devices generate edge-triggered interrupts.

Table 18.2 Interrupt port addresses

Port address	Name	Description
20h	Interrupt control port (ICR)	Controls interrupts and signifies the end of an interrupt
21h	Interrupt mask register (IMR)	Used to enable and disable interrupt lines

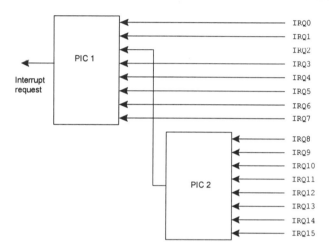

Figure 18.6 PC PIC connections

In the IMR an interrupt line is enabled by setting the assigned bit to a 0 (zero). This allows the interrupt line to interrupt the processor. Figure 18.7 shows the bit definitions of the IMR. For example, if bit 0 is set to a 0 then the system timer on IRQ0 is enabled.

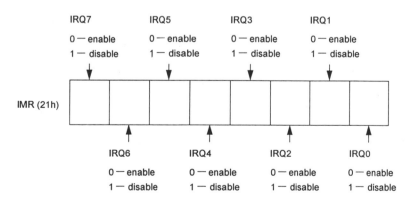

Figure 18.7 Interrupt mask register bit definitions

In the example code given next the lines IRQ0, IRQ1 and IRQ6 are allowed to interrupt the processor, whereas, IRQ2, IRQ3, IRQ4 and IRQ7 are disabled.

```
port[$21]:=$BC; (* 1011 1100 enable disk (bit 6),
           keyboard (1) and timer (0) interrupts   *)
```

When an interrupt occurs all other interrupts are disabled and no other device can interrupt the processor. Interrupts are enabled again by setting the EOI bit on the interrupt control port, as shown in Figure 18.8.

The following code enables interrupts.:

```
port[$20]:=$20; (* EOI command  *)
```

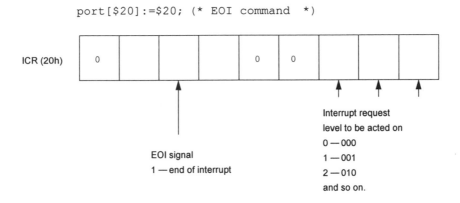

Figure 18.8 Interrupt control register bit definitions

18.5 Interrupt-driven RS-232

Program 18.1 is a simple interrupt-driven DOS-based RS-232 program which is writen for Turbo Pascal. If possible connect two PCs together with a cable which swaps the TX and RX lines, as shown in Figure 16.15 (in Chapter 16). Each of the computers should be able to transmit and receive concurrently. A description of this program is given in the next section.

Program 18.1
```
program rs232(input,output);

uses dos,crt;

const ESC=$1B;
      RSBUFSIZE=100;            (* RS232 buffer size            *)
```

```
          COM1BASE=$3F8;            (* Base port address for COM1   *)
          TXDATA=COM1BASE;          (* Transmit register            *)
          RXR=COM1BASE;             (* Receive register             *)
          IER=(COM1BASE+1);         (* Interrupt Enable             *)
          IIR=(COM1BASE+2);         (* Interrupt ID                 *)
          LCR=(COM1BASE+3);         (* Line control                 *)
          MCR=(COM1BASE+4);         (* Modem control                *)
          LSR=(COM1BASE+5);         (* Line Status                  *)

(* Addresses of the 8259 Programmable Interrupt Controller (PIC). *)

          IMR=$21;     (* Interrupt Mask Register port   *)
          ICR=$20;     (* Interrupt Control Port         *)

(* An end of interrupt needs to be sent to the Control Port of *)
(* the 8259 when a hardware interrupt ends.                     *)
          EOI=$20;                      (* End Of Interrupt        *)

var   buffer:string[RSBUFSIZE];
      startbuf,endbuf:integer;
      oldint:pointer;
      ch:char;
      done,empty:boolean;

procedure rs_interrupt;interrupt;
begin
   if ((port[IIR] and $07) = $04) then
   begin
      buffer[endbuf] := chr(port[RXR]);
      endbuf:=endbuf+1;
      if (endbuf = RSBUFSIZE) then endbuf:=0;
   end;

   (* Set end of interrupt flag *)
   port[ICR]:= EOI;
end;

procedure  setup_serial;
begin

   port[LCR] := port[LCR] or $80;
      (* set up bit 7 to a 1                                    *)
   port[TXDATA] := $0C;
   port[TXDATA+1] := $00;
      (* load TxRegister with 12                                *)
      (* crystal frequency is 1.8432MHz                         *)
   port[LCR] := $0A
      (* Bit pattern is 00001010b, from msb to lsb these are: *)
      (* Access TD/RD buffer, normal output, no stick bit      *)
      (* even parity, parity on, 1 stop bit, 7 data bits       *)
end;

procedure  send_character(ch:char);
var        status:byte;
begin

   repeat
     status := port[LSR] and $40;
```

```pascal
     until (status=$40);
        (*repeat until bit Tx buffer is empty                  *)

     port[TXDATA] := ord(ch); (*send ASCII code               *)
end;

function      get_character:char;
var           status,inbyte:byte;
begin

   repeat
      status := port[LSR] and $01;
   until (status=$01);

   inbyte := port[TXDATA];

   get_character:= chr(inbyte);

end;

function get_buffer(ch:char):boolean;
(* return a TRUE if buffer has characters *)
begin
   if (startbuf = endbuf) then
           get_buffer:=FALSE
        else
        begin
           ch := buffer[startbuf];
           startbuf:=startbuf+1;
           if (startbuf = RSBUFSIZE) then startbuf := 0;
           get_buffer := TRUE;
        end;
end;

procedure set_vectors;
begin
     getintvec($0C,oldint);  (* save the old interrupt vector  *)
     setintvec($0C,addr(rs_interrupt));
                        (* install the new interrupt handler *)
end;

(* Uninstall interrupt vectors before exiting the program *)
procedure reset_vectors;
begin
     setintvec($0C, oldint);
end;

procedure disable_interrupts;
var ch:integer;
begin
     ch := port[IMR] or $10; (* disable IRQ4 interrupt *)
     port[IMR]:= ch;
     port[IER]:= 0;
end;

procedure enable_interrupts;
var ch:integer;
begin
```

```
   (* initialize rs232 port   *)
   ch := port[MCR] or $08;
   port[MCR]:= ch;
   (* enable interrupts for IRQ4   *)
   port[IER]:=$01;
   ch := port[IMR] and $ef;
   port[IMR]:= ch;
end;

begin
     done   := FALSE;
     startbuf:=0; endbuf:=0;

     setup_serial;
     set_vectors; (* set new interrupt vectors and store old ones*)
     enable_interrupts;

     writeln('Terminal emulator, press [ESC] to quit\n');
     repeat
        if (keypressed) then
        begin
           ch:=readkey;
           if (ch=char(ESC)) then done:=TRUE
           else send_character(ch);
        end;
           (* empty RS232 buffer   *)
        empty:=FALSE;
        repeat
           if (get_buffer(ch)=TRUE) then write(ch)
           else empty:=TRUE;
        until (empty=TRUE);
     until (done=TRUE);
     disable_interrupts;
     reset_vectors;
end.
```

18.5.1 Description of program

The initial part of the program sets up the required RS-232 parameters. It uses
bioscom() to set COM1: with the parameters of 1200 bps, 1 stop bit, even
parity and 7 data bits.

```
procedure  setup_serial;
begin

   port[LCR] := port[LCR] or $80;
      (* set up bit 7 to a 1                                    *)
   port[TXDATA] := $0C;
   port[TXDATA+1] := $00;
      (* load TxRegister with 12                                *)
      (* crystal frequency is 1.8432MHz                         *)
   port[LCR] := $0A
      (* Bit pattern is 00001010b, from msb to lsb these are:*)
      (* Access TD/RD buffer, normal output, no stick bit      *)
      (* even parity, parity on, 1 stop bit, 7 data bits       *)
end;
```

After the serial port has been initialized the interrupt service routine for the IRQ4 line is set to point to a new 'user-defined' service routine. The primary serial port COM1: sets the IRQ4 line active when it receives a character. The interrupt associated with IRQ4 is 0Ch (12). The getintvec procedure gets the ISR address for this interrupt, which is then stored in the variable oldint so that at the end of the program it can be restored. Finally, in the set_vectors procedure, the interrupt assigns a new 'user-defined' ISR (in this case it is the procedure rs_interrupt).

```
procedure set_vectors;
begin
    getintvec($0C,oldint);   (* save the old interrupt vector   *)
    setintvec($0C,addr(rs_interrupt));
                     (* install the new interrupt handler *)
end;
```

At the end of the program the ISR is restored with the following code.

```
procedure reset_vectors;
begin
    setintvec($0C, oldint);
end;
```

The COM1: port is initialized for interrupts with the code given next. The statement:

```
    ch := port[MCR] or $08;
    port[MCR]:= ch;
```

resets the RS-232 port by setting bit 3 for the modem control register (MCR) to a 1. Some RS-232 ports require this bit to be set. The interrupt enable register (IER) enables interrupts on a port. Its address is offset by 1 from the base address of the port (that is, 3F9h for COM1:). If the least significant bit of this register is set to a 1 then interrupts are enabled, else they are disabled.

To enable the IRQ4 line on the PIC, bit 5 of the IMR (interrupt mask register) is to be set to a 0 (zero). The statement:

```
    ch := port[IMR] and $ef;
    port[IMR]:= ch;
```

achieves this as it bitwise ANDs all the bits, except for bit 4, with a 1. This is because any bit which is ANDed with a 0 results in a 0.

```
procedure enable_interrupts;
var ch:integer;
begin
    (* initialize rs232 port   *)
    ch := port[MCR] or $08;
```

```
    port[MCR]:= ch;
    (* enable interrupts for IRQ4    *)
    port[IER]:=$01;
    ch := port[IMR] and $ef;
    port[IMR]:= ch;
end;
```

At the end of the program the function `disable_interrupts` sets IER register to all 0s. This disables interrupts on the COM1: port. Bit 4 of the IMR is also set to a 1 which disables IRQ4 interrupts.

```
procedure disable_interrupts;
var ch:integer;
begin
    ch := port[IMR] or $10;  (* disable IRQ4 interrupt *)
    port[IMR]:= ch;
    port[IER]:= 0;
end;
```

The ISR for the IRQ4 function is set to `rs_interrupt`. When it is called, the Interrupt Status Register (this is named IIR to avoid confusion with the interrupt service routine) is tested to determine if a character has been received. Its address is offset by 2 from the base address of the port (that is, 3FAh for COM1:). The first three bits give the status of the interrupt. A 000b indicates that there are no interrupts pending, a 100b that data has been received, or a 111b that an error or break has occurred. The statement if ((port[IIR] and $07) = $04) tests if data has been received. If this statement is true then data has been received and the character is then read from the receiver buffer array with the statement buffer[endbuf] := chr(port[RXR]);. The end of the buffer variable (endbuf) is then incremented by 1.

At the end of this ISR the end of interrupt flag is set in the interrupt control register with the statement port[ICR]:= EOI;. The startbuf and endbuf variables are global, thus all parts of the program have access to them.

```
procedure rs_interrupt;interrupt;
begin
   if ((port[IIR] and $07) = $04) then
   begin
     buffer[endbuf] := chr(port[RXR]);
     endbuf:=endbuf+1;
     if (endbuf = RSBUFSIZE) then endbuf:=0;
   end;

   (* Set end of interrupt flag *)
   port[ICR]:= EOI;
end;
```

The get_buffer function is given next. It is called from the main program and it tests the variables startbuf and endbuf. If they are equal then it returns a FALSE to the main program. This indicates that there are no characters in the buffer. If there are characters in the buffer then the function returns the character pointed to by the startbuf variable. This variable is then incremented. The difference between startbuf and endbuf gives the number of characters in the buffer. Note that when startbuf or endbuf reach the end of the buffer (RSBUFSIZE) they are set back to the first character, that is, element 0.

```
function get_buffer(ch:char):boolean;
(* return a TRUE if buffer has characters *)
begin
   if (startbuf = endbuf) then
            get_buffer:=FALSE
        else
        begin
           ch := buffer[startbuf];
           startbuf:=startbuf+1;
           if (startbuf = RSBUFSIZE) then startbuf := 0;
           get_buffer := TRUE;
        end;
end;
```

The get_character and send_character procedures are similar to those developed in Chapter 16. For completeness these are listed next.

```
procedure  send_character(ch:char);
var        status:byte;
begin

   repeat
      status := port[LSR] and $40;
   until (status=$40);
      (*repeat until bit Tx buffer is empty          *)

   port[TXDATA] := ord(ch); (*send ASCII code          *)
end;

function    get_character:char;
var         status,inbyte:byte;
begin

   repeat
      status := port[LSR] and $01;
   until (status=$01);

   inbyte := port[TXDATA];

   get_character:= chr(inbyte);

end;
```

The main program calls the initialization and the de-initialization functions. It also contains a loop which continues until the Esc key is pressed. Within this loop the keyboard is tested to determine if a key has been pressed. If it has then the `readkey` function is called. This function returns a key from the keyboard and displays it to the screen. Once read into the variable `ch` it is tested to determine if it is the Esc key. If it is then the program exits the loop, else it transmits the entered character using the `send_character` function. Next the `get_buffer` function is called. If there are no characters in the buffer then a FALSE value is returned, else the character at the start of the buffer is returned and displayed to the screen using `write`.

```
begin
      done   := FALSE;
      startbuf:=0; endbuf:=0;

      setup_serial;
      set_vectors; (* set new interrupt vectors and store old ones *)
      enable_interrupts;

      writeln('Terminal emulator, press [ESC] to quit\n');
      repeat
         if (keypressed) then
         begin
            ch:=readkey;
            if (ch=char(ESC)) then done:=TRUE
            else send_character(ch);
         end;
            (* empty RS232 buffer   *)
         empty:=FALSE;
         repeat
            if (get_buffer(ch)=TRUE) then write(ch)
            else empty:=TRUE;
         until (empty=TRUE);
      until (done=TRUE);
      disable_interrupts;
      reset_vectors;
end.
```

18.6 Exercices

18.6.1 Modify Program 18.1 so that a new-line character is displayed properly (Remember a new-line is represented by both a LF and a CR characters (which are #10 and #13). Thus if one of these are received then use a `writeln` to force a new-line.

18.6.2 Prove that Program 18.1 is a true multi-tasking system by inserting a delay in the main loop, as shown next. The program should be able to buffer all received characters and display them to the screen when the sleep delay is over.

```
repeat
   delay(10000);
      (*go to sleep for 10 seconds, real-time system *)
      (* will buffer all received characters          *)
   if (keypressed) then
   begin
      ch:=readkey;
      if (ch=char(ESC)) then done:=TRUE
      else send_character(ch);
   end;
      etc.
```

18.6.3   Modify Program 18.1 so that the transmitted characters are displayed in the top half of the screen and then received in the bottom half of the screen.

18.6.4   Modify Program 18.1 so that it communicates via COM2: (if the PC has one).

19 Date and Time

19.1 Introduction

Many programs require to either set or get the current date or time. The PC has a system timer which uses interrupt line IRQ0 to interrupt the processor 18.2 times per second. This is then used to update the time of day. Figure 19.1 shows an example usage of interrupts in a PC. Notice that IRQ0 is set to the system timer.

Turbo Pascal uses BIOS to get and set the current time. The main procedures used are:

- **GetTime**. Gets the current system time.
- **SetTime**. Sets the current system time.
- **GetDate**. Gets the current system date.
- **SetDate**. Sets the current system date.
- **SetFTime**. Sets the date and time a file was last written.
- **GetFTime**. Sets the date and time a file was last written.

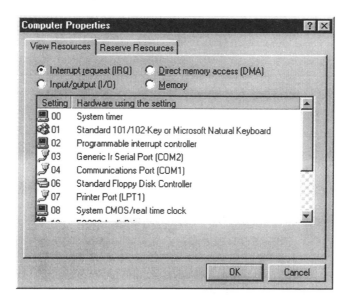

Figure 19.1 Interrupt listing

213

19.2 Time

The procedures uses to get and set the time are `GetTime` and `SetTime`.

19.2.1 GetTime

The `GetTime` procedure returns the current time set in the operating system. Its syntax is:

```
procedure GetTime(var Hour, Minute, Second,  Sec100 : Word);
```

and uses the DOS unit. A typical conversion is from hours, minutes and seconds to seconds. This is achieved with:

```
newtime:=60*60*hr+60*min+sec;
```

The variables `hr`, `min` and `sec` will be declared with the `word` data type and the `newtime` variable as a `longint`. To convert to 100th of seconds then:

```
newtime:=100*(60*60*hr+60*min+sec)+sec100;
```

An example program using `GetTime` is given in Section 19.7.

19.2.2 SetTime

The `SetTime` procedure sets the current time in the operating system. Its syntax is:

```
procedure SetTime(Hour, Minute, Second,  Sec100 : Word);
```

19.3 Date

The procedures uses to get and set the date are `GetDate` and `SetDate`.

19.3.1 GetDate

The `GetDate` procedure returns the current date set in the operating system.

```
procedure GetDate(var Year, Month, Day,  DayOfWeek : Word);
```

19.3.2 SetDate

The `SetDate` procedure sets the current date in the operating system. Its syntax is:

```
procedure SetDate(Year, Month, Day : Word);
```

19.4 DateTime record

The `DateTime` data type is used with `UnpackTime` and `PackTime` procedures to examine and construct 4-byte, packed date-and-time values. Its syntax is:

```
type
  DateTime = record
                Year,Month,Day,Hour,
                Min,Sec: Word;
  end;
```

19.5 Packing Time

The procedures uses to pack and unpack the date and time are `PackTime` and `UnpackTime`.

19.5.1 PackTime

The `PackTime` procedure converts a `DateTime` record into a 4-byte, packed date-and-time `Longint` used by `SetFTime`.

```
procedure PackTime(var T : DateTime;  var Time : Longint);
```

19.5.2 UnpackTime

The `UnpackTime` procedure converts a 4-byte, packed date-and-time `Longint` returned by `GetFTime` into an unpacked `DateTime` record. Its syntax is:

```
procedure UnpackTime(Time : Longint; var T : DateTime);
```

19.6 File Time

The procedures used to get and set a file's time are `GetFTime` and `SetFTime`.

19.6.1 SetFTime

The `SetFTime` procedure sets the date and time a file was last written. Its syntax is:

```
procedure SetFTime(var F; Time : Longint);
```

19.6.2 GetFTime

The GetFTime procedure returns the date and time a file was last written. Its syntax is:

```
procedure GetFTime(var F;  var Time : Longint);
```

19.7 Examples

Typically in a program the amount of time an event took is required. Program 19.1 gets the time that the program is started and determines the number of seconds and puts the value in oldtime. It then uses the repeat...until loop to wait for the user to press a key. The new time is then taken and the number of seconds is put into the newtime variable.

Program 19.1

```
program prog19_1(input,output);

uses dos,crt;

var     hr,min,sec,sec100:word;
        oldtime,newtime:longint;
begin
     gettime(hr,min,sec,sec100);
     oldtime:=60*60*hr+60*min+sec;
     writeln('Timing... Press any key to finish');

     repeat
          (* Dummy loop, wait for keypress *)
     until keypressed;

     gettime(hr,min,sec,sec100);
     newtime:=60*60*hr+60*min+sec;
     writeln('Number of seconds: ',newtime-oldtime);
end.
```

Program 19.2 is similar to Program 19.1 but the time is calculated in 100th of seconds.

Program 19.2

```
program prog19_2(input,output);

uses dos,crt;

var     hr,min,sec,sec100:word;
        oldtime,newtime:longint;
begin
```

```
gettime(hr,min,sec,sec100);
oldtime:=100*(60*60*hr+60*min+sec)+sec100;
writeln('Timing... Press any key to finish');

repeat
        (* Dummy loop, wait for keypress *)
until keypressed;

gettime(hr,min,sec,sec100);
newtime:=100*(60*60*hr+60*min+sec)+sec100;
writeln('Number of 100th seconds: ',newtime-oldtime);
end.
```

A problem with the two previous programs is that they do not take the date into account. Thus if the date changes then the number of seconds will be taken as a negative value. Thus the `PackTime` procedure can be used to convert the date and time into a `longint`. Program 19.3 shows how this can be achieved. It fills up the `Datetime` record using `GetTime` and `GetDate`.

Program 19.3

```
program prog19_3(input,output);

uses dos,crt;

var     hr,min,sec,sec100,year,month,day,dweek:word;
        t:datetime;
        oldtime,newtime:longint;
begin

        getdate(year,month,day,dweek);
        gettime(hr,min,sec,sec100);

        t.hour:=hr;t.min:=min;t.sec:=sec;
        t.year:=year;t.month:=month;t.day:=day;

        packtime(t,oldtime);
        writeln('Number of seconds: ',oldtime);
        repeat

        until keypressed;

        getdate(year,month,day,dweek);
        gettime(hr,min,sec,sec100);

        t.hour:=hr;t.min:=min;t.sec:=sec;
        t.year:=year;t.month:=month;t.day:=day;

        packtime(t,newtime);
        writeln('Number of seconds: ',2*(newtime-oldtime));
end.
```

Program 19.4 is similar to Program 19.3 but the time conversion has been implemented using a function (`getsecond`).

```
program prog19_4(input,output);

uses dos,crt;

var newtime,oldtime:longint;

function getsecond:longint;
var      hr,min,sec,sec100,year,month,day,dweek:word;
         t:datetime;
         now:longint;
begin
     getdate(year,month,day,dweek);
     gettime(hr,min,sec,sec100);

     t.hour:=hr;t.min:=min;t.sec:=sec;
     t.year:=year;t.month:=month;t.day:=day;

     packtime(t,now);
     getsecond:=now;
end;

begin

     oldtime:=getsecond;

     repeat

     until keypressed;

     newtime:=getsecond;

     writeln('Number of seconds: ',2*(newtime-oldtime));

end.
```

19.8 Counting timer ticks

As previously mentioned the IRQ0 interrupt is used to interrupt the processor 18.2 times per second. This generates a software interrupt 1Ch. Program 19.5 redirects this interrupt so that it will call the routine my_interrupt 18.2 times a second. This routine is used to increment a counter value (count). This value when divided by 18.2 will thus give the number of seconds which have passed (as the counter value is set to zero at the start of the program).

Program 19.5

```
program prog19_5(input,output);
uses DOS,CRT;

var      count, oldcount,newcount,time:longint;
```

```
        old_int:pointer;

procedure my_interrupt;interrupt;
begin
   count:=count+1;
end;


begin
     count:=0;
     writeln('Press any key to exit');
     getintvec($1C,old_int); (* save the old interrupt vector  *)
     setintvec($1C,addr(my_interrupt));
                       (* install the new interrupt handler *)

     repeat
        (* dummy loop *)
     until keypressed;

     time:=10*count div 182;
     writeln('number of seconds is ',time);

     (* set the old interrupt handler back *)
     setintvec($1c, old_int);
end.
```

19.9 Exercises

19.9.1   Write a program which displays a message 'TICK' every 15 seconds. Hint: use the mod operator to determine if the number of seconds is divisible by 15. For example:

```
if ((seconds mod 15)=0) then
   writeln('TICK');
```

Repeat this program for an interval of 1 minute.

19.9.2   Write a program which displays the current time at the top left-hand corner of the screen. Hint: either clear the screen for every update (clrscr), or use the gotoxy() function.

19.9.3   Enter Program 19.5 and thus prove that IRQ0 is interrupting the computer 18.2 per second.

20 System Commands

20.1 Introduction

An operating system allows the user to access the hardware in an easy-to-use manner. It accepts commands from the keyboard and displays them to the monitor. The two most popular operating systems are DOS and Microsoft Windows. The Disk Operating System, or DOS, gained its name from its original purpose of providing a controller for the computer to access its disk drives. The language of DOS consists of a set of commands which are entered directly by the user and interpreted to perform file management tasks, program execution and system configuration. DOS is a non multi-tasking operating system in that it can only run one program at a time, whereas Windows 95 and NT are multi-tasking.

The main functions of an operating system are to run programs, copy and remove files, create directories, move within a directory structure and to list files.

20.2 System calls

Turbo Pascal allows access to systems calls. The main calls and parameters are:

- **Exec**. Executes a child program.
- **ChDir**. Changes the current directory.
- **MkDir**. Creates a new directory.
- **RmDir**. Removes a directory.
- **FindFirst**. This finds the first file in a directory that matches the file specification.
- **FindNext**. Finds the next file in a directory that matches the file specification.
- **ParamCount**. Counts the number of parameters in the command line.
- **ParamStr**. Identifies each of the parameters in the command line.
- **DiskFree**. Determines the amount of free space on a disk drive.
- **DiskSpace**. Determine the amount of space on a disk drive.

20.2.1 Exec

A program can call the operating system in a number of ways. One method is to use exec, which accepts a command string which gets passed to the operating system. One disadvantage of exec is that the control of the program is given over to an operating system program. The program has little control over this called program until it returns from the operating system. Its syntax is:

```
Exec(ExecPath, CmdLine);
```

where ExecPath is the full pathname for the executable program and CmdLine is command line parameters to be passed to the program. For example:

```
Exec('c:\turbo\myprog1.exe', '');
Exec('c:\windows\command\edit.exe', 'text.txt');
```

In order to run a DOS command (such as COPY, DIR, MKDIR, and so on) then the COMMAND.COM program must be run. The command line passed to COMMAND.COM is the DOS command with a /C preceding it. For example:

```
Exec(GetEnv('COMSPEC'), '/C dir');
Exec(GetEnv('COMSPEC'), '/C copy file1.txt file2.txt');
```

where GetEnv gets the pathname for the COMMAND.COM program.

Program 20.1 copies one file to another, using the DOS COPY command.

Program 20.1

```
program prog20_1(input,output);
uses dos;

var str,file1,file2:string;

begin
   write('Enter file which is to be copied >>');
   readln(file1);

   write('Enter file which is to be copied to >>');
   readln(file2);

   str:='/C copy'+' '+file1+' '+file2;
   SwapVectors;
   Exec(GetEnv('COMSPEC'), str);
   SwapVectors;
   if (DosError<>0) then
      writeln(DosError);
end.
```

20.2.2 DOSError

If any of the system commands fail then the `DosError` contains a value which is not zero. The valid values are:

0.	No errors.	2.	File not found
3.	Path not found	5.	Access denied
6.	Invalid handle	8.	Not enough memory
10.	Invalid environment	11.	Invalid format
18.	No more files		

20.2.3 Chdir

The `ChDir` procedure changes the current directory. Its syntax is:

```
procedure ChDir(s : string);
```

Program 20.2 uses the `chdir` function to change the current directory and uses the procedures `FindFirst` and `FindNext` (see Section 20.2.7) to list the contents of the directory. An error occurs when the `IOResult` value is not zero.

Program 20.2

```
program prog20_2(input,output);
uses dos;

var directory:string;
    dirinfo:searchrec;

begin
   repeat
      write('Enter a directory');
      readln(directory);

      if (directory='exit') then

      else
      begin
         {$I-}   (* I/O checking switch off *)
         chdir(directory);
         if (IOResult<>0) then
            writeln('Pathname not found')
         else
         begin
            writeln('Contents of this directory are:-');
            FindFirst('*.*', Anyfile, DirInfo);
            while DosError = 0 do
            begin
               writeln(DirInfo.Name);
               FindNext(DirInfo);
            end;
         end;
      end;
```

```
      end;
   until (directory='exit');
end.
```

The compiler directive {$I-} stops the program from checking I/O checking and giving an error. This then allows the program to check the error and continue as necessary.

20.2.4 MkDir

The MkDir procedure creates a new directory. Its syntax is:

```
procedure MkDir(s : string);
```

Program 20.3 shows how a directory can be created within a program.

📋 **Program 20.3**
```
program prog20_3(input,output);
uses dos;

var directory:string;

begin
   write('Enter a directory ');
   readln(directory);

   mkdir(directory);
   if (IOResult<>0) then
      writeln('Cannot make directory')
   else
      writeln('Directory created');
end.
```

20.2.5 RmDir

The RmDir procedure removes an empty subdirectory. Its syntax is:

```
procedure RmDir(s : string);
```

Program 20.4 shows an example.

📋 **Program 20.4**
```
program prog20_4(input,output);
uses dos;

var directory:string;

begin
   write('Enter a directory ');
   readln(directory);

   rmdir(directory);
```

```
      if (IOResult<>0) then
         writeln('Cannot remove directory')
      else
         writeln('Directory removed');
end.
```

20.2.6 GetDir

The GetDir procedure returns the current directory of a specified drive.

```
procedure GetDir(drive : Byte; var s : string);
```

Program 20.5 gives an example program.

⬜ **Program 20.5**
```
program prog20_5(input,output);
uses dos;

var directory:string;
begin
   GetDir(0,directory); { 0 = Current drive }
   WriteLn('Current drive and directory: ',  s);
end.
```

20.2.7 FindFirst and FindNext

The FindFirst procedure searches the specified (or current) directory for the first entry matching the specified file name and set of attributes. Its syntax is:

```
procedure FindFirst(Path : string;  Attr : Word;
                        var S : SearchRec);
```

where Attrib can be:

```
   VolumeID   = $08;
   Directory  = $10;
   Archive    = $20;
   AnyFile    = $3F;
```

The FindNext procedure returns the next entry that matches the name and attributes specified in an earlier call to FindFirst. Its syntax is:

```
procedure FindNext(var S : SearchRec);
```

The SearchRec data type is defined as:

```
   type
      SearchRec = record
                  Fill: array[1..21] of Byte;
                  Attr: Byte;
```

```
              Time: Longint;
              Size: Longint;
              Name: string[12];
     end;
```

Program 20.6 shows an example of how a directories contents can be listed.

Program 20.6

```
program prog20_6(input,output);
uses dos;

var directory:string;
    dirinfo:searchrec;
    t:datetime;

begin
     FindFirst('*.*', Anyfile, DirInfo);
     while DosError = 0 do
     begin
          write(DirInfo.Name:15,' ');

          if (DirInfo.Attr=$20) then write('File     ')
          else if (DirInfo.Attr=$10) then write('Directory');

          unpacktime(DirInfo.Time,T);
          write(T.hour:2,':',T.min:2,' ');
          write(T.day:2,'/',T.month:2,'/',T.year:2, ' ');
          writeln(DirInfo.Size:10);
          FindNext(DirInfo);
     end;
end.
```

An extract from a sample run is shown next.

```
          . Directory18:39  9/ 4/1997          0
         .. Directory18:39  9/ 4/1997          0
  P_CH0.BAK File     10:44 25/10/1997       2392
  P20_1.BAK File     11:10 25/10/1997        889
       TEMP Directory11: 8 25/10/1997          0
  P20_2.PAS File     11: 8 25/10/1997        259
  P20_3.PAS File     11:29 25/10/1997        663
  P20_4.PAS File     11:32 25/10/1997        114
  P20_5.BAK File     11:42 25/10/1997        299
  P_CH0.PAS File     11:51 25/10/1997       3729
 P20_1I.PAS File     13:32 25/10/1997        810
 P20_1I.BAK File     13:30 25/10/1997        830
  P20_7.PAS File     14: 9 25/10/1997        560
  P20_7.BAK File     14: 9 25/10/1997        560
  P20_3.EXE File     11:29 25/10/1997       3504
  P20_4.EXE File     11:32 25/10/1997       2576
  P20_7.EXE File     14:10 25/10/1997       3072
```

20.3 Passing arguments

Programs can get some parameters from the command line. These are called command line parameters. For example:

```
prog1 10 20 /w
```

has a program name of prog1 and has three command line parameters of '10', '20' and '/w'. Each of these parameters is in the form of a string, thus numeric values must be converted using the procedure `val`.

The number of parameters in the command line is defined by `Param-Count` and the command line parameters with `ParamStr(index)`. Program 20.7 shows a sample program which displays all the command line options. Note in the Turbo Pascal environment, command line options can be added with `Options→Parameters`.

Program 20.7
```
program temp;
var i:word;
begin
   for i:=0 to paramcount do
      writeln('Parameter ',I,' is ',paramstr(i));
end.
```

A sample run of this program is given in Test run 20.1. The command line prompt is shown as a greater than symbol (>). The program name is stored in `paramstr[0]` and the rest of the arguments are stored in `paramstr[1]` to `argv[paramcount]`. All command line arguments are treated as strings. If the program is to operate on them numerically then they must be converted using a string conversion function (such as `val()`).

Test run 20.1
```
> arg1 list 100 4.31 -f
Parameter 0 is C:\TURBO\ARG1.EXE
Parameter 1 is 100
Parameter 2 is 4.31
Parameter 3 is -f
```

Program 20.8 determines the sine of an angle, where the angle is entered through the command line parameter list. If the user runs the program with the wrong number of command line parameters then the program displays a help screen. Test run 20.2 shows a sample run. In this case the file is named `sine.pas` and the executable program is named `sine.exe`.

📋 **Program 20.8**

```
var value,result:real;
    code:integer;
begin
   if (paramcount<>1) then
   begin
     writeln('Program to determine sine of a value');
     writeln('Format for data is: ');
     writeln('sine VALUE');
     exit;
   end;

   val(paramstr(1),value,code);

   result:=sin(value);
   writeln('Sine of value is ',result:8:3);
end.
```

A sample run is given in Test run 20.2.

💻 **Test run 20.2**

```
C:\SRC\ARGS> sine
Program to determine sine of a value
Format for data is:
sine VALUE

C:\SRC\ARGS> sine 10
Sine of value is    -0.544
```

20.3.1 DiskSize

The DiskSize function returns the total size in bytes of a specified disk drive. Its syntax is:

```
function DiskSize(Drive: Byte) : Longint;
```

📋 **Program 20.9**

```
program prog20_9(input,output);
uses Dos;
begin
    writeln(DiskSize(0) div 1024,'kB capacity');
end.
```

20.3.2 DiskFree

The DiskFree function returns the number of free bytes of a specified disk drive.

```
function DiskFree(Drive: Byte) : Longint;
```

```
program prog20_10(input,output);
uses Dos;
begin
    writeln(DiskFree(0) div 1024, 'kB free');
end.
```

20.4 Exercises

20.4.1 Write a program which reads a data file containing floating point values and print the average, maximum and minimum values. The name of the file is passed to the program via the command line arguments. A sample run is shown in Test run 20.3.

⌨ **Test run 20.3**
```
> getaver in.dat
The average value is 43.41
The maximum found is 100.34 and minimum is -4.00
>
```

20.4.2 Write a program for the mathematical functions TAN, COS, SIN, and EXP. The program should receive the value via the command line arguments. Test run 20.4 shows a sample run.

⌨ **Test run 20.4**
```
> TAN 1.2
The tan of 1.2 is 2.572
> SIN 1.2
The sin of 1.2 is 0.932
```

20.4.3 Modify the program in 20.4.2 so that the user can specify whether the value is in degrees (/d) or radians (/r) or ask for help (/?). Test run 20.5 shows a sample run.

⌨ **Test run 20.5**
```
> TAN 56.0 /d
The tan of 56.0 degrees is 1.482
> SIN 1.2 /r
The sin of 1.2 radians is 0.932
> SIN /?
FORMAT: SIN VALUE [EXTENSION]
This is a program which will determine the
Sine of a value, where value is in degrees (/d)
or radians (/r). /? will print this page
```

20.4.4 Modify some programs from previous chapters so that the user can prompt for help on the program using / ? in the command line. Test run 20.6 shows a sample run.

⌨ **Test run 20.6**
```
C:> RESON_LC /?
FORMAT: RESON_LC R C F [EXTENSION]
This is a program which will determine the
resonant frequency of a parallel RLC circuit
/? will print this page
C:>
```

20.4.5 Write a program with command line arguments which will determine a preferred value for a resistor. Test run 20.7 shows a sample run.

⌨ **Test run 20.7**
```
C:> R_VALUE 1.43 K
Nearest value is 1.4K
C:>
```

---

21 Introduction to Delphi

21.1 Introduction

Microsoft Windows has become the de facto PC operating system. All versions up to, and including, Windows 3.11 used DOS as the core operating system. New versions of Windows, such as Windows NT and Windows 95 do not use DOS and can thus use the full capabilities of memory and of the processor. The most popular programming languages for Windows programming are:

- Microsoft Visual Basic.
- Microsoft Visual C++ and Borland C++.
- Delphi (which is available from Borland).

Visual Basic has the advantage over the other languages in that it is relatively easy to use and to program, although the development packages which are used with C++ and Delphi make constructing the user interface relatively easy. Figure 21.1 shows a sample Borland Delphi Version 1 screen. Other versions of Delphi, such as Version 2–3 are similar in their approach.

21.2 Event-driven programming

Traditional methods of programming involve writing a program which flows from one part to the next in a linear manner. Most programs are designed using a top-down structured design, where the task is split into a number of submodules, these are then called when they are required. This means that it is relatively difficult to interrupt the operation of a certain part of a program to do another activity, such as updating the graphics display.

Delphi uses standard Pascal and can also used object-oriented Pascal (OOP). In general it is:

- **Event-driven**. Where the execution of a program is not predefined and its execution is triggered by events, such as a mouse click, a keyboard press, and so on.

- **Designed from the user interface outwards**. The program is typically designed by first developing the user interface and then coded to respond to events within the interface.

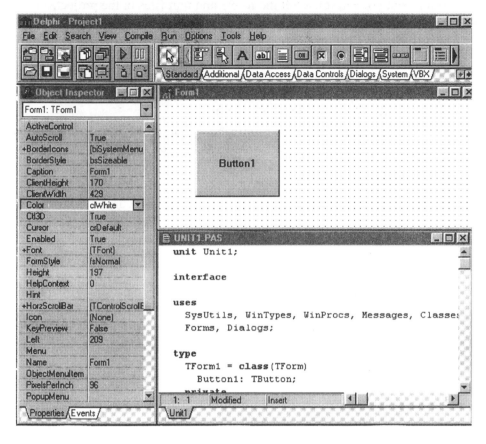

Figure 21.1   Delphi user interface

21.3 Delphi files

A listing of a sample directory which contains Delphi files is:

```
PROJECT1  DPR           161  21/10/97  21:16  project1.dpr
UNIT1     DFM           172  21/10/97  21:17  UNIT1.DFM
PROJECT1  OPT           284  21/10/97  21:18  PROJECT1.opt
UNIT1     PAS           344  21/10/97  21:17  unit1.pas
PROJECT1  RES           794  21/10/97  21:18  PROJECT1.RES
UNIT1     DCU         1,648  21/10/97  21:30  UNIT1.DCU
PROJECT1  EXE       190,208  21/10/97  21:30  PROJECT1.EXE
```

The files are:

- **Project files** (.DPR). A project file is initially generated when the user starts a new project (File→New Project). This file controls a Delphi application and is saved with a .DPR extension. There can only be one .DPR file for each project. It lists all the forms and unit files in the project.
- **Unit files** (.PAS). These store the source code for the form files (.DFM). These source code files contain Pascal coded event handlers that specify how the form and its components are to operate. Delphi keeps the binary and source code files synchronized as you create and modify the form. When a new form is added to an application then Delphi creates the associated unit file and adds it in the Project file.
- **Graphical Form file** (.DFM). These are binary files which contain the design properties of each form contained in the project. One .DFM file is generated along with the corresponding .PAS file for each form the project contains.
- **Project options file** (.OPT). This file contains the current settings for Project Options. It is automatically generated when the project is first saved and then updated for all subsequent changes to project settings.
- **Compiler resource file** (.RES). This is a binary file which contains the application icons and other outside resources used by the project.
- **Unit object code** (.DCU). These files contained compiled unit files (.PAS).

21.4 Other terms

Visual Basic uses a number of other terms to describe design procedure, these are:

- **Components**. The Delphi interface contains a window with component objects which are pasted onto a form. These components can be simple text, menus, spreadsheet grids, radio buttons, and so on. Each component has a set of properties that defines their operation, such as their colour, the font size, whether it can be resized, and so on. Some components, such as command buttons, menus, and so on, normally have code attached to them, but simple controls, such as text and a graphics image can simply exist on a form with no associated code. Example components are: TRadioButton (Windows radio button), TButton (push button control) and TListBox (Windows list box).
- **Forms**. A form forms the anchor for all parts of a Delphi program. Initially it is a blank window and the user pastes controls onto it to create the required user interface. Code is then associated with events on the form, such

as responding to a button press or a slider control, although some control elements do not have associated code. A program can have one or more forms, each of which displays and handles data in different ways. Whether you are adding components to the form, editing properties, or coding in the form unit, you are editing the form.

21.5 Main screen

The main screen in Delphi contains a menu form, main form, project windows and object window.

21.5.1 Menu bar

The menu bar and tool bar appear in a single, floating window, as shown in Figure 21.2. The menu bar contains options for file manipulation (File), editing (Edit), searching the program (Search), viewing options (View), compiling the program (Compile), running the program (Run), setting options (Options), running tools (Tools) and getting help (Help). These can either be selected with the mouse, using the function key F10 and then selecting the option with the arrow keys and pressing return or use the hot key. The hot key is Alt and the underlined character, thus Alt-F selects the File menu, Alt-S selects the Search menu, and so on.

Figure 21.2 Delphi menu bar, speedbar and component palette

21.5.2 Speedbar

The toolbar contains shortcut buttons for commonly used menu items, the most used buttons are:

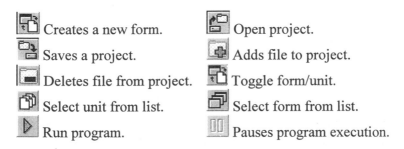

Creates a new form.   Open project.

Saves a project.   Adds file to project.

Deletes file from project.   Toggle form/unit.

Select unit from list.   Select form from list.

Run program.   Pauses program execution.

21.5.3 Component palette

The component palette contains a number of icons which are arranged in libraries, such as: Standard, Additional, Data Access, Data Controls, Dialogs, System, VBX and Samples. A virtual component library (VCL) is made up of objects, most of which are also components. Using the objects and components of VCL allows code to be quickly generated for the standard objects. These objects contain both code and data, where the data is stored in the properties of the objects and the code is made from methods that act upon the property values.

Programs in Delphi are normally written in the following order:

1. Select a component from the component palette and then add it to a form.
2. Modify the component's property values using the Object Inspector.
3. Add events that can occur when the program is run using an event handler.

The component palette contains the icons for components. These include:

- **Pointer**. The pointer does not draw any components and is used to resize or move a component once it has been put on a form. When a component is added to a form then the pointer is automatically selected.

- **Main Menu**. This allows the creation of a menu system for the form. It differs from a Popup menu in that Popup menus do not have a menu bar, and typically do not appear until the user right-clicks in the form (Component name: TMainMenu).

- **Label**. This adds text to a form which cannot be edited. The Edit or Memo components can be used when the text is required to be edited (Component name: TLabel).

- **Popup menu**. This provides a form or other component with a menu that appears independently of any main menu in the form. Typically this is used when the user right-clicks the mouse button (Component name: TPopupMenu)

- **Edit**. This is used to read or write a single line of text. The Edit component does not recognize end-of-line characters, whereas the Memo component does (Component name: TEdit).

- **Memo**. This is used to read or write multiple lines of text, whether entered by the user or with the program (Component name: TMemo).

- **CheckBox**. This is used to create a check box, which can either be on or off. It is used when the user can select none, one or more options. This differs from radio buttons in that they only allow one choice at a time (Component name: TCheckBox).

- **RadioButton**. This is used to create a display of a number of options of which only one can be chosen (Component name: TRadioButton).

- **Button**. This is used to provide command buttons (Component name: TButton).

- **ListBox**. This is used to display a scrollable list of items that users can select but cannot directly modify. This differs from the ComboBox component which has a Text property to enable users to enter their own items (Component name: TListBox).

- **ComboBox**. This is used to combine the functionality of a list box and an edit box and enables users to select from a predefined list or to enter their own text (Component name: TComboBox).

- **ScrollBar**. (horizontal scroll bar). This is used to either to scroll up and down through a list of text or graphical information or to indicate the current position on a scale (Component name: TScrollBar)

- **GroupBox**. This is used as a container for other components within a form, such as radio buttons or check boxes. These components can then be modified as a single unit.

- **RadioGroup**. This is used to group radio buttons on a form (Component name: TRadioGroup).

- **Image**. This is used to place graphical images on a form. Delphi supports the following formats: bitmaps (.BMP), metafiles (.WMF) and icons (.ICO).

- **Shape**. This is used to display graphical shapes on a form.

21.5.4 Project window

A project contains all the elements of the application, such as forms, units and resources. New projects are initiated by selecting File→New Project. This then generates a new project file which is maintained through the development of the project. A project file has a .DPR extension and there can only be one .DPR file for each project. An example project file is:

```
program Project1         {Details};
uses
  Forms,
  Unit1 in 'UNIT1.PAS' {Form1}; {Details}

{$R *.RES}               {Details}
```

```
begin
   Application.CreateForm(TForm, Form1);   {Details}
   Application.Run(Form1);                 {Details }
end.
```

Each time a new form or unit is created they are added to the project (with the uses clausc).

The Project window displays the forms and units used in the currently active project, as shown in Figure 21.3. This window is displayed by selecting View→Project Manager. Within this window the following can be achieved:

- Use View Code to open a Code window for an existing form.
- Use View Form to open an existing form.
- Use Remove or Add to remove or add code to a project.

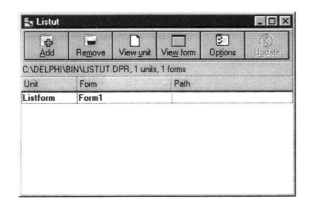

Figure 21.3   Delphi project manager window

21.5.5   Form window

The Form window, as shown in Figure 21.4, creates application windows and dialog boxes. A new form is automatically created when a new project is initiated, otherwise it is initiated with File→New Form. Figure 21.5 shows the form options when the New Form is selected.

Each form has a Control-menu box, Minimize and Maximize buttons, and a title bar, and can be moved and resized.

21.6 Object Inspector

The Object Inspector window displays the properties of the currently selected form or component. It allows properties such as the colour, font type and size of text, background colour of a form, type of graphic image, and so on, to be changcd.

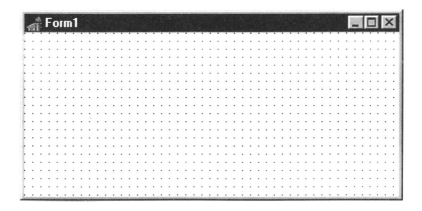

Figure 21.4 Delphi Form window

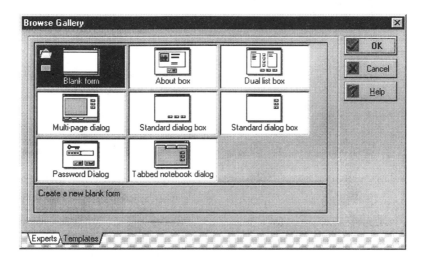

Figure 21.5 Delphi New Form window

First, the object to be changed is selected and the Object Inspector should then show its properties (if it does not then it can be viewed by selecting Object Inspector or by pressing F11). The Object Inspector window is closed by double-clicking on the Control-menu box. Figure 21.6 shows an example Object Inspector window. The Object selector is a pull-down menu which displays the active component (in this case, Button1) and its type (in this case, Tbutton). A Property column shows all the properties associated with the selected component (in this case, it includes Caption, Cursor, Default, and so on). The Value column displays the values of the properties (in this case it includes Start, crDefault, False, and so on).

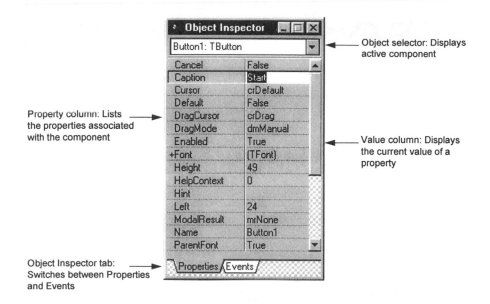

Object selector: Displays active component

Property column: Lists the properties associated with the component

Value column: Displays the current value of a property

Object Inspector tab: Switches between Properties and Events

Figure 21.6 Object Inspector window

The Object select displays the name and type of the object in the form:

Object name : *Object type*

The Object Inspector window also contains two pages (which are selected by selecting one of the Object Inspector tabs), these are:

- **Events list**. The Events page displays the events of the form or component that is currently selected. The event handler column allows, by double clicking on the column element, an event handler to be added. After the name has been selected then the Code Editor is displayed so that code can be added to the event.
- **Properties list**. This properties page displays the properties of an object (form or component) and their current settings. To change a properties setting then the properties name is selected and the new setting is either typed or selected from a menu. Properties that have predefined settings (such as a range of colours or true/false) display the list of settings by clicking the down arrow at the right of the settings box (▼), or they can be cycled through by double-clicking the property name in the left column. In Figure 21.8 the Caption property for a Button has been set to 'Press Me'. A ⬚ in the second column indicates either the selection of colours from a palette or the selection of picture files through a dialog box or another record structure for the property (such as options property). It can be seen from Figure 21.7 that the event, in this case, includes OnClick and OnDragDrop.

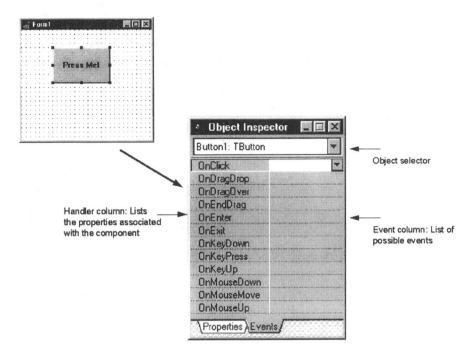

Figure 21.7   Events window

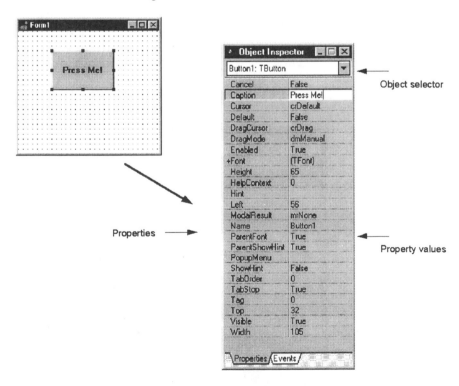

Figure 21.8   Properties window

Figure 21.9 shows an example form with a number of objects. It can be seen that the Object selector now displays the different objects in the form, such as: Button1, Button2, Button3, CheckBox1, ComboBox1, DirectoryListBox1, and so on.

Figure 21.10 shows an example of colour settings. Note that the colour appears as a name (clSilver, clRed, and so on), or by double-clicking on the Color property value, a colour palette is displayed, as also illustrated in Figure 21.10.

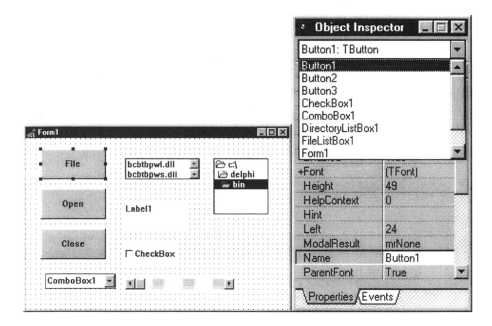

Figure 21.9 Example list of controls

21.7 Exercises

21.7.1 Place a Button on a form and display its properties. Note all of the properties and, with the help of the help manual, identify the functions of the properties. Note that help on a property can be found by highlighting the property and pressing F1.

21.7.2 For a Button identify the events that are associated with it.

21.7.3 Conduct the following:

(i) Add a Button to a form.

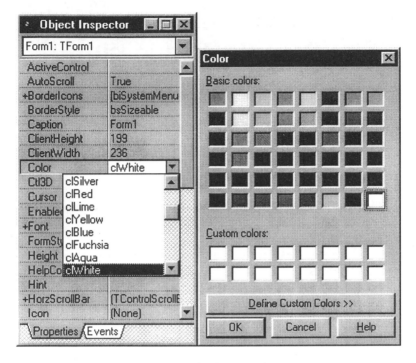

Figure 21.10 Setting colour

(ii) Change the Caption on the CommandButton to 'EXIT'.

(iii) Change the Font on the CommandButton to 'Times Roman' and the font size to 16.

(iv) Resize the Button so that the text fits comfortably into the button.

(iv) Change the background colour of the form to yellow.

(v) Change the Caption name of the form to 'My Application'.

21.7.4 Develop the form given in Figure 21.11.

21.7.5 Explain why, in the previous exercise, that a radio button is used for the age option and a check box is used to select the choices of Show Graphics and Play Sounds. Which of the following would be radio buttons or check boxes:

(i) Items on a shopping list.

(ii) Selection of a horse to win a race.

(iii) Selection of paint colour on a new car.

(iv) Selection of several modules on a course.

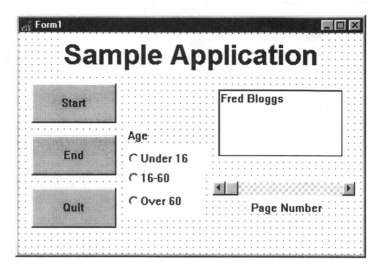

Figure 21.11 Exercise

22 Delphi Input/Output

22.1 Introduction

This chapter shows the real power of Delphi. This comes from using the full power of Microsoft Windows, especially when using 32-bit operating systems such as Windows 3.1 with Win32s, Windows 95 and Windows NT. These use Win32 which provides a standard programming model to allow a Windows program to run as a full 32-bit program. It also gives access to a great deal of advanced Windows functions (known as APIs – Application Programming Interface). Win32 has the following advantages:

- A 32-bit programming model for Windows 3.x that shares binary compatibility with Windows NT and Windows 95.
- The ability to produce an application program which can be used with Windows NT, Windows 95, and Windows 3.1x.
- Full OLE (object linking and embedding) support, including 16-bit/32-bit interoperability. OLE allows application programs to share data where an OLE server provides information for an OLE client.
- Improved performance with 32-bit operations.
- Access to a large amount of Win32 APIs (application programming interface) for Windows NT and Windows 95 (such as Windows, Menus, Resources, Memory Management, Graphics, File Compression, and so on).
- Win32 semantics for the application programming interface (API).

Win32s is an operating system extension that allows Win32 applications for Windows NT and Windows 95 to run on Windows version 3.1x. At the heart of Win32s is a virtual device driver (VxD) and a number of dynamic-link libraries (DLLs). These extend Windows 3.1x to support Win32-based applications. On Windows NT and Windows 95 there is no need to distribute extra files, while Windows 3.x requires the installation of the Win32 files.

22.1.1 Win32 APIs

There are a great deal of extra APIs that can be used with Win32, these can be classified with:

- Windows operations (creating windows, scrolling bars, menus, dialog boxes, and so on).
- Graphics functions (painting, drawing, colours, palettes and so on).
- OLE and DDE (dynamic data exchange).
- TrueType fonts.
- Common dialogs.
- Network support (NetBios and Windows sockets 1.1 APIs).
- Multimedia support (sound APIs).
- File compression.
- Support for help files, bitmaps, icons and metafiles.
- Multiple document interface (MDI).

These Windows APIs are defined through the WinProcs unit.

22.2 Running Pascal programs

Delphi enhances Pascal in that it allows the use of components to enter and display data in a program. Delphi is also event driven. Functions and procedures in Pascal such as `Readln` and `Writeln` can also be supported. When a new project is standard the initial unit template that is created is of the form:

☐ **Program 22.1**
```
unit Unit1;

interface

uses
   SysUtils, WinTypes, WinProcs, Messages, Classes, Graphics,
             Controls,
   Forms, Dialogs;

type
  TForm1 = class(TForm)
  private
    { Private declarations }
  public
    { Public declarations }
  end;

var
  Form1: TForm1;

implementation

{$R *.DFM}
end.
```

Functions such as `Readln`, `Writeln`, `KeyPressed`, `ReadKey` are defined in the `WinCrt` unit. Thus to use this the `WinCrt` unit must be added to the `uses` list. The example given next shows how they can be used (bold text highlights the changes from the standard template):

📋 **Program 22.2**

```
unit Unit1;

interface

uses
    WinCrt, SysUtils, WinTypes, WinProcs, Messages, Classes, Graphics,
            Controls, Forms, Dialogs;

type
  TForm1 = class(TForm)
  private
    { Private declarations }
  public
    { Public declarations }
  end;

var
  Form1: TForm1;
  voltage,current,resistance:real;
  ch:char;

implementation

{$R *.DFM}
begin

     writeln('Enter a voltage');
     readln(voltage);
     writeln('Enter a current');
     readln(current);
     resistance:=voltage/current;
     writeln('Resistance is',resistance:8:2);

     writeln('Press any key to exit');
     ch:=readkey;
end.
```

Programs which use the functions in the `WinCrt` unit run within a separate window. A sample run of this program is shown in Figure 22.1

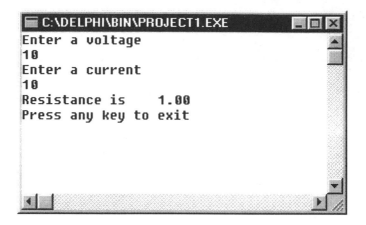

Figure 22.1   Program run with readln and writeln

22.3 Message and dialog boxes

22.3.1 ShowMessage

The ShowMessage procedure displays a message box with an OK button. The Msg parameter is the message string that appears within the message box. The name of your application's executable file appears as the caption of the message box. It is defined in the Dialogs unit and its syntax is:

```
procedure ShowMessage(const Msg: string);
```

Program 22.3 shows a simple example where the ShowMessage procedure is used to display the message 'Hello, Goodbye'. Figure 22.2 shows a sample run.

📋 **Program 22.3**
```
unit Unit1;

interface

uses
  SysUtils, WinTypes, WinProcs, Messages, Classes, Graphics,
    Controls, Forms, Dialogs;

type
  TForm1 = class(TForm)
  private
    { Private declarations }
  public
```

```
    { Public declarations }
  end;

var
  Form1: TForm1;

implementation

{$R *.DFM}
begin
    ShowMessage('Hello, Goodbye');
end.
```

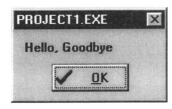

Figure 22.2   Sample run with ShowMessage procedure

22.3.2 *Message Box*

The MessageBox function displays a message in a dialog box with specified buttons and then waits for the user to select a button. The value returned indicates the chosen button. The basic format is:

```
function MessageBox(Text, Caption: PChar; Flags: Word): Integer;
```

where:

Text   Is a string of characters which is the message to be displayed.

Caption   Is a string of characters which is the title of the dialog box.

Flags   A numeric value that is the sum of values that specifies the number, the type of buttons to display, the icon style and the default button. Table 22.1 outlines these values and if it is omitted then the default value for buttons is 0.

Table 22.1 defines the button settings. The values from 0 to 5 define the type of the button to be displayed. For example, a value of 5 will have two buttons, which are Retry and Cancel. The values 16, 32, 48 and 64 identify the icon to be displayed. For example, a value of 32 will display a question bubble. The values 0, 256 and 512 define which button is the default. Each of these values can be added together to create the required set of buttons, icons and default button. For example, to create a dialog box with the OK and Cancel buttons, a Critical icon and the Cancel button to be the default, then the setting would be:

```
setting = 1 + 16 + 256
```

which is 273. Note that to aid documentation in the program then the predefined constant values can be used, so for the previous example:

```
setting = MB_OKCANCEL + MB_ICONHAND + MB_DEFBUTTON2
```

Table 22.1 Button settings

Constant	Value	Description
MB_OK	0	Display OK button only
MB_OKCANCEL	1	Display OK and Cancel buttons. See example 1 in Figure 22.3
MB_ABORTRETRYIGNORE	2	Display Abort, Retry, and Ignore buttons. See example 2 in Figure 22.3
MB_YESNOCANCEL	3	Display Yes, No, and Cancel buttons. See example 3 in Figure 22.3
MB_YESNO	4	Display Yes and No buttons. See example 4 in Figure 22.3
MB_RETRYCANCEL	5	Display Retry and Cancel buttons. See example 5 in Figure 22.3.
MB_ICONHAND	16	Display Critical Message icon. See example 1 in Figure 22.4
MB_ICONQUESTION	32	Display Warning Query icon. See example 2 in Figure 22.4
MB_ICONEXCLAMATION	48	Display Warning Message icon. See example 3 in Figure 22.4
MB_ICONINFORMATION	64	Display Information Message icon. See example 4 in Figure 22.4
MB_DEFBUTTON1	0	First button is default
MB_DEFBUTTON2	256	Second button is default
MB_DEFBUTTON3	512	Third button is default

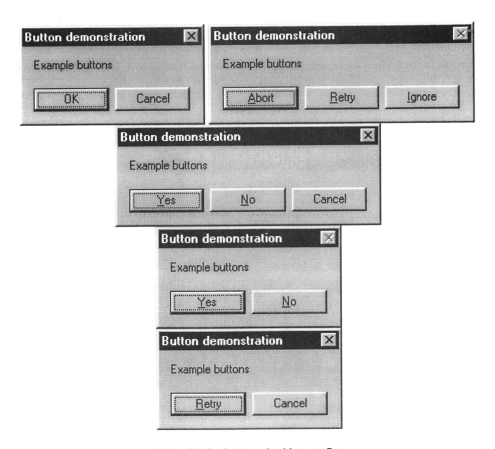

Figure 22.3 Buttons for MessageBox

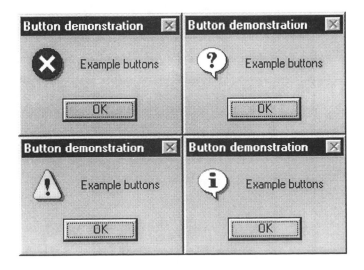

Figure 22.4 Icons for MessageBox

The `MessageBox` function returns a value depending on the button pressed; these return values are outlined in Table 22.2. For example, if the user presses the OK button then the return value will be 1. If the dialog box has a Cancel button then the user pressing ESC has the same effect as choosing Cancel.

Table 22.2 MessageBox return values

Constant	Value	Button chosen
IDOK	1	OK
IDCANCEL	2	Cancel
IDABORT	3	Abort
IDRETRY	4	Retry
IDIGNORE	5	Ignore
IDYES	6	Yes
IDNO	7	No

Program 22.4 gives an example of a program which displays a dialog box with Yes and No buttons, and a question mark icon (the highlighted text shows the parts that have been added to the default unit text). The response will thus either be a 6 (if the Yes button is selected) or a 7 (if the No button is selected). Figure 22.5 shows a sample run.

Program 22.4

```
unit Unit1;

interface

uses
   SysUtils, WinTypes, WinProcs, Messages, Classes, Graphics,
      Controls, Forms, Dialogs;

type
  TForm1 = class(TForm)
  private
    { Private declarations }
  public
    { Public declarations }
  end;

var
  Form1: TForm1;
  response:integer;
  style:integer;

implementation

{$R *.DFM}
begin

    style:=MB_YESNO + MB_ICONQUESTION;
```

```
response:=Application.MessageBox('Press a button',
                       'Button demonstration',style);
if (response=IDYES) then
    Application.MessageBox('Yes','Result',MB_ICONEXCLAMATION)
else
    Application.MessageBox('No','Result',MB_ICONEXCLAMATION);
end.
```

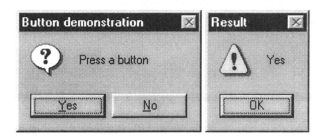

Figure 22.5 Example run

22.3.3 Message Dialog

The MessageDlg function displays a message dialog box in the centre of the screen. The message box displays the value of the Msg string constant. Its syntax is:

```
function MessageDlg(const Msg: string; AType: TMsgDlgType;
    AButtons: TMsgDlgButtons;   HelpCtx: Longint): Word;
```

Atype   Determines the type of message box that appears. These are the possible values as defined in Table 22.3.

Abuttons Determines which buttons appear in the message box. The buttons that are to be displayed are included in brackets. These are defined in Table 22.4. For example to show the buttons Yes, No and OK then [mbYes, mbNo, mbOK] is used.

HelpCtx   Determines which Help screen is available for the message box.

Table 22.3 Atype values

Value	Meaning
mtWarning	Message box containing a yellow exclamation point symbol
mtError	Message box containing a red stop sign
mtInformation	Message box containing a blue 'i'
mtConfirmation	Message box containing a green question mark
mtCustom	No bitmap

Table 22.4 Abutton values

Value	Button type	
mbYes	Yes	Green check mark and the text 'Yes'
mbNo	No	Red circle and slash mark through the circle and the text 'No'
mbOK	OK	Green check mark and the text 'OK'
mbCancel	Cancel	Red X and the text 'Cancel'
mbHelp	Help	Cyan question mark and the text 'Help'
mbAbort	Abort	Red check mark and the text 'Abort'
mbRetry	Retry	Two green circular arrows and the text 'Retry'
mbIgnore	Ignore	Green man walking away and the text 'Ignore'
mbAll	All	Green double check marks and the text 'All'

The function returns the value of the button the user selected. Valid return values are:

```
mrNone      mrOk        mrCancel     mrAbort
mrRetry     mrIgnore    mrYes        mrNo
mrAbort     mrRetry     mrIgnore     mrAll
```

As an example, place a button on a form, as shown in Figure 22.6. Change the caption on the button's properties so that it is 'Exit'. Next, either select the events tab from the Object Inspector or double click on the button. The screen in Figure 22.7 shows the unit window. Into here the code can be added. In this case the added code (which is highlighted) is:

```
procedure TForm1.Button1Click(Sender: TObject);
begin

  if MessageDlg('Do you wish to exit?', mtInformation,
          [mbYes, mbNo], 0) = mrYes then
  begin
    MessageDlg('Exiting program', mtInformation, [mbOk], 0);
    Close;
  end;
end;

end.
```

Figure 22.9 shows a sample run. It can be seen that the dialog box has two buttons, Yes and No. If the selected button is Yes then another dialog is shown with the message 'Exiting program'.

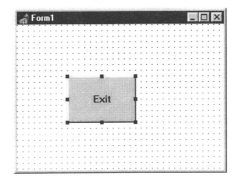

Figure 22.6 Example button

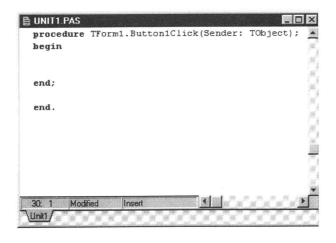

Figure 22.7 Unit window

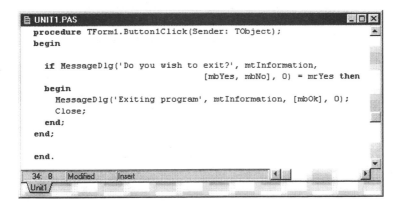

Figure 22.8 Addition of code

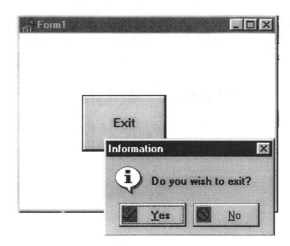

Figure 22.9 Sample run

22.4.1 Input Box

The InputBox function prompts the user either to input text or to choose a button. A value is then returned from the contents of the text box. Its syntax is:

```
function InputBox(const ACaption, APrompt,
                  ADefault: string): string;
```

where

ACaption   String of text which is displayed in the dialog box.

APrompt   Text that prompts the user to enter input in the edit box.

ADefault   String which is displayed in the text box and is the default response if no other input is provided. If this field is omitted then the text box is initially empty.

The InputBox function has a Cancel and an OK button. If the user chooses the OK button then the string in the edit box is the value returned, else the default value is return. The program thus does not know if the user has pressed the OK or the Cancel buttons (this is overcome with the InputQuery function).

Program 22.5 displays an input dialog box when the user clicks the button on the form. The input dialog box includes a prompt string and a default string. The string the user enters in the dialog box is stored in the Input-String variable. Figure 22.10 shows an example run.

Program 22.5

```
unit Unit1;

interface

uses
   SysUtils, WinTypes, WinProcs, Messages, Classes, Graphics,
   Controls, Forms, Dialogs, StdCtrls;

type
  TForm1 = class(TForm)
    Button1: TButton;
    procedure Button1Click(Sender: TObject);
  private
    { Private declarations }
  public
    { Public declarations }
  end;

var
  Form1: TForm1;

implementation

{$R *.DFM}

procedure TForm1.Button1Click(Sender: TObject);
var instr:string;
begin

  instr:=InputBox('Enter a value','Value','10');
  close;
end;

end.
```

22.4.2 Input Query

The InputQuery function is similar to InputBox but the button pressed is returned through the function header. Its syntax is:

```
function InputQuery(const ACaption, APrompt: string;
     var Value: string): Boolean;
```

A TRUE return indicates that the OK button was pressed, else a FALSE is returned. The entered string is returned from the Value string.

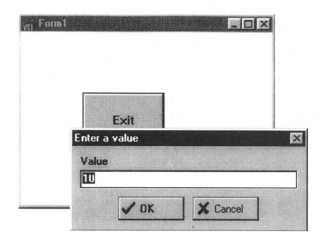

Figure 22.10 Example run

22.5.1 Write a Delphi program using the `MessageDialog` function which displays the following dialog boxes:

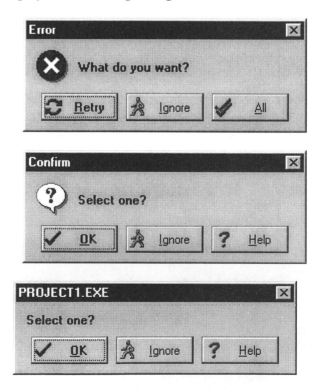

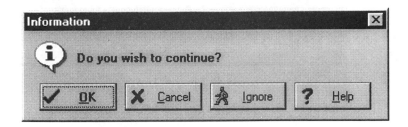

22.5.2 Using Pascal programs written in previous programs, modify them so that they run within Delphi.

22.5.3 Write a Delphi program in which the user enters their name and the program displays it in a dialog box, which asks the user if entered name is correct. Sample input and dialog boxes are shown next.

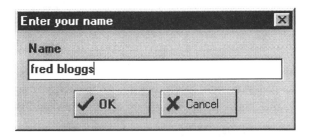

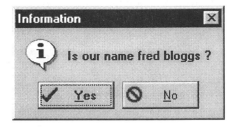

An outline of the code is given next.

```
var
  Form1: TForm1;
  instr:string;

implementation
begin

{$R *.DFM}

  instr:=InputBox('Enter your name','Name','fred');
  MessageDlg('Is our name '+instr+' ?', mtInformation,
                                    [mbYes, mbNo], 0)

end.
```

23 Delphi Forms

23.1 Introduction

This chapter discusses how forms are constructed and how code is associated
with the form.

23.2 Setting properties

Each object has a set of properties associated with it. For example, the Label
component in Figure 23.1 has an object name of Label1. This object has a
number of associated properties, such as Align, Alignment, AutoSize, Caption, and so on. These properties can be changed within the program by using
the dot notation. For example, to change the font to 'Courier New', the text
displayed in the object 'Help:' and the colour of the text is cBtnFace:

```
Label1.Caption := "Help:"
Label1.Text := taLeftJustify
Label1.Color := cBtnFace
```

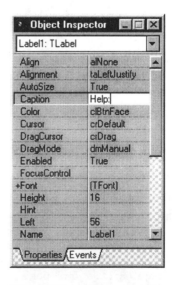

Figure 23.1   Object properties

Delphi programs are normally designed by first defining the user interface (the form) and writing the code which is associated with events and components. The best way to illustrate the process is with an example.

23.3.1 Multiple choice example

In this example the user is to design a form with a simple question and three optional examples. It should display if the answer is correct (TRUE) or wrong (FALSE). The program should continue after each selection until the user selects an exit button.

Step 1: The label component is selected **A**. Then the text 'What is the capital of France' is entered in the caption field, as shown in Figure 23.2.

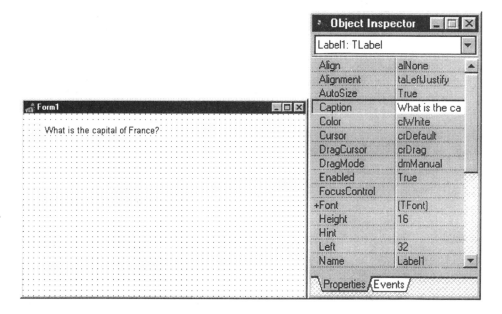

Figure 23.2   Step 1

Step 2: Next the user adds a command button by selecting the command control. The button is then added to the form and the Caption property is set to 'Edinburgh', as shown in Figure 23.3.

Step 3: Next the user adds another command button by selecting the button component. The button is then added to the form and the Caption property is set to 'Paris', as shown in Figure 23.4.

Step 4: Next the user adds another command button by selecting the command control. The button is added to the form and the Caption property is set to 'Munich', as shown in Figure 23.5.

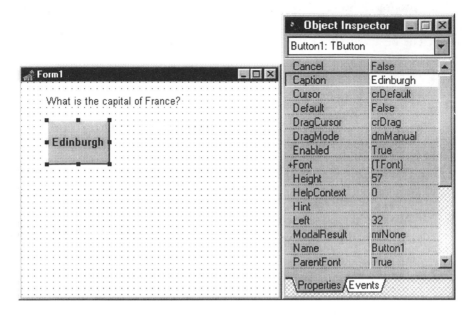

Figure 23.3 Step 2

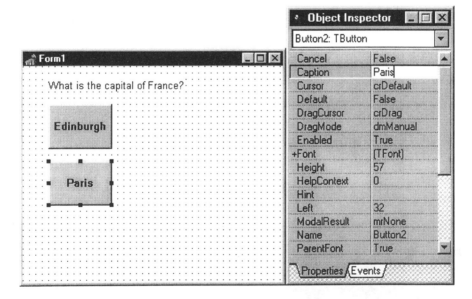

Figure 23.4 Step 3

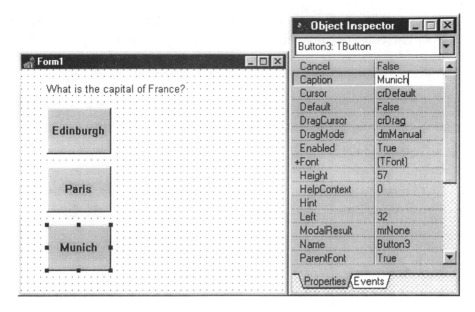

Figure 23.5   Step 4

Step 5: Next the user adds an Edit component 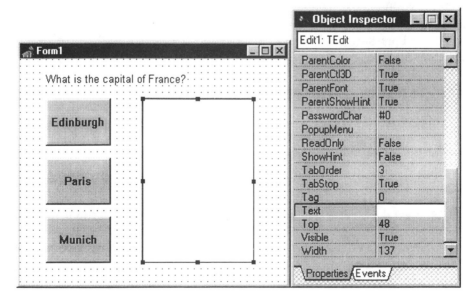. This is added to the right-hand side of the form, as shown in Figure 23.6. The Text property is then changed to have an empty field. The Edit component will be used to display text from the program.

Figure 23.6   Step 5

Step 6: Next the user adds another command button by selecting the command control. The button is added to the form and the Caption property is set to 'Exit', as shown in Figure 23.7. A character in the name can be underlined by putting an & before it. Thus '&Exit' will be displayed as 'Exit'.

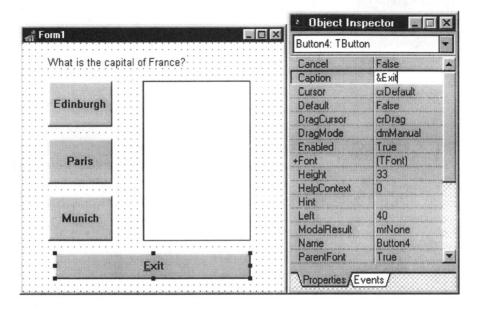

Figure 23.7   Step 6

Step 7: Next the code can be attached to each of the command buttons. This is done by either double clicking on the command button or by selecting the button and pressing the F7 key. To display to the TextBox (the object named Text1) then the text property is set with:

```
procedure TForm1.Button1Click(Sender: TObject);
begin
     edit1.text:='FALSE' ;
end;
```

which displays the string 'FALSE' to the text window. The associated code is shown in Figure 23.8.

Step 8: Next the code associated with the second command button is set, with:

```
procedure TForm1.Button2Click(Sender: TObject);
begin
     edit1.text:='TRUE';
end;
```

as shown in Figure 23.9.

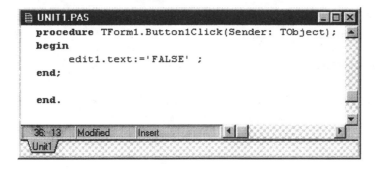

Figure 23.8 Added code

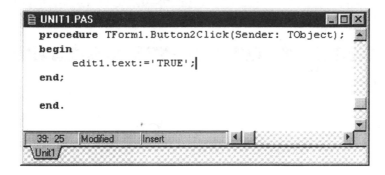

Figure 23.9 Added code

Step 9:
Next the code associated with the third command button is set, with:

```
procedure TForm1.Button3Click(Sender: TObject);
begin
     edit1.text:='FALSE';
end;
```

as shown in Figure 23.10.

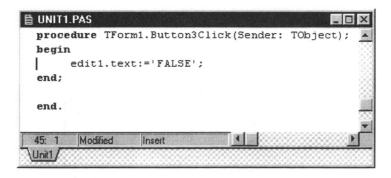

Figure 23.10 Added code

Step 10: Finally the code associated with the exit command button is set by adding the code:

```
procedure TForm1.Button4Click(Sender: TObject);
begin

  if MessageDlg('Do you wish to exit?', mtInformation,
         [mbYes, mbNo], 0) = mrYes then
    Close;
end;
```

which causes the program to end and the code is shown in Figure 23.11. The program can then be executed with Run→Run. Figure 23.12 shows a sample run.

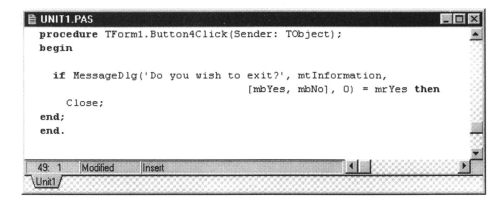

Figure 23.11   Added code

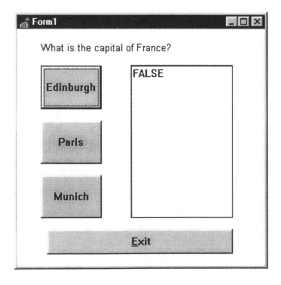

Figure 23.12   Sample test run

Next the form and the project are saved using the File→Project option. If the file has not been saved before then the user will be prompted to give the project and the form a new file name. In this case save the unit file and the project as UNIT01.PAS and PROJECT01.DPR. These are listed in Program 23.1. It can be seen that the unit file (Program 23.1) contains all the component events as procedures. The project file (Program 23.2) contains the definition for the main form (named Form1). The real strength of Delphi is that it is an aid to code development and does not try to replace it.

☐ **Program 23.1 (Unit file)**

```
unit Unit1;

interface

uses
   SysUtils, WinTypes, WinProcs, Messages, Classes, Graphics,
   Controls, Forms, Dialogs, StdCtrls;

type
  TForm1 = class(TForm)
    Label1: TLabel;
    Button1: TButton;
    Button2: TButton;
    Button3: TButton;
    Edit1: TEdit;
    Button4: TButton;
    procedure Button1Click(Sender: TObject);
    procedure Button2Click(Sender: TObject);
    procedure Button3Click(Sender: TObject);
    procedure Button4Click(Sender: TObject);
  private
    { Private declarations }
  public
    { Public declarations }
  end;

var
  Form1: TForm1;

implementation

{$R *.DFM}

procedure TForm1.Button1Click(Sender: TObject);
begin
    edit1.text:='FALSE' ;
end;

procedure TForm1.Button2Click(Sender: TObject);
begin
    edit1.text:='TRUE';
end;

procedure TForm1.Button3Click(Sender: TObject);
```

```
begin
     edit1.text:='FALSE';
end;

procedure TForm1.Button4Click(Sender: TObject);
begin

  if MessageDlg('Do you wish to exit?', mtInformation,
          [mbYes, mbNo], 0) = mrYes then
    Close;
end;
end.
```

⬚ **Program 23.2 (Project file)**
```
program Project1;

uses
  Forms,
  Unit1 in 'UNIT1.PAS' {Form1};

{$R *.RES}

begin
  Application.CreateForm(TForm1, Form1);

  Application.Run;

end.
```

23.4 Temperature conversion program

In this example the user will enter either a temperature in centigrade or Fahrenheit and the program will convert to an equivalent Fahrenheit or centigrade temperature. The steps taken, with reference to Figure 23.13, are:

1. Add a Text component and change its Caption property to 'Centigrade'.
2. Add a Text component and change its Caption property to 'Fahrenheit'.
3. Add an Edit component and put it beside the Centigrade Label. Next change its Text property to '0'.
4. Add an Edit component and put it beside the Fahrenheit Label. Next change its Text property to '32'.
5. Add a Button component and put it below the text boxes. Next change its Caption property to 'C to F'. This button will convert the value in centigrade to Fahrenheit and put the result in the Fahrenheit edit box.
6. Add a Button component and put it beside the other button. Next change its Caption property to 'F to C'. This button will convert the value in Fahrenheit to centigrade and put the result in the Centigrade edit box.

266   *Mastering Pascal*

7. Add a Button component and put it below the other buttons. Next change its Caption property to 'Exit'. This button will be used to exit from the program.

8. Select the form and change the Caption property to 'Temperature Conversion'.

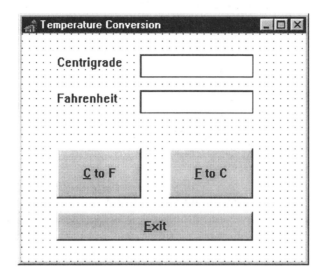

Figure 23.13 Temperature conversion form

Next the code associated with each component can be added, as follows:

1. First add code to the first command button (C to F) which will be used to convert the text from the Centigrade text box (Edit1) and display it to the Fahrenheit text box (Edit2). This is achieved with:

```
procedure TForm1.Button1Click(Sender: TObject);
var value,faren,cent:real;
    code:integer;
    outstr:string;
begin
    val(edit1.text,cent,code);
    faren := 9 / 5 * cent + 32;
    str(faren:8:3,outstr);
    edit2.text:=outstr;
end;
```

2. Next add code to the second command button (F to C) which will be used to convert the text from the Fahrenheit text box (Edit2) and display it to the Centigrade text box (Edit1). This is achieved with:

```
procedure TForm1.Button2Click(Sender: TObject);
var value,faren,cent:real;
```

```
     code:integer;
     outstr:string;
begin

     val(edit2.text,faren,code);
     cent := 5 / 9 * (faren - 32);
     str(cent:8:3,outstr);
     edit1.text:=outstr;
end;
```

3. Next add code to the third command button (Exit) which will be used to exit the program. This is achieved with:

```
procedure TForm1.Button3Click(Sender: TObject);
begin
   if MessageDlg('Do you wish to exit?', mtInformation,
          [mbYes, mbNo], 0) = mrYes then
     Close;
end;
```

A test run of the program is given in Figure 23.14.

The temperature conversion program has a weakness as the user can enter a value which is not a valid temperature value and the program will accept it. For example, if the user enters a string of characters then the program stops and displays the message shown in Figure 23.15.

To overcome this problem the value that is entered is tested to see if it is a valid numeric value, using the `Val(Str,Value,Code)` function. If the string is invalid then the index of the offending character is stored in `Code`; otherwise, `Code` is set to zero. Thus if the `Code` variable is equal to zero then there is a valid value, else an 'INVALID' text is displayed. The modified code for the two command buttons is given next and a sample run is shown in Figure 23.16.

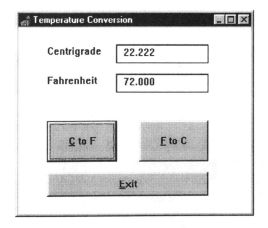

Figure 23.14 Sample run

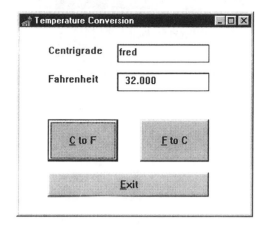

Figure 23.15 Sample run with invalid input

```
procedure TForm1.Button1Click(Sender: TObject);
var value,faren:real;
    code:integer;
    outstr:string;
begin

    val(edit1.text,value,code);

    if (code=0) then
    begin
        faren := 9 / 5 * value + 32;
        str(faren:8:3,outstr);
        edit2.text:=outstr;
    end
    else
        edit2.text:='INVALID';

end;

procedure TForm1.Button2Click(Sender: TObject);
var value,faren,cent:real;
    code:integer;
    outstr:string;
begin

    val(edit2.text,faren,code);

    if (code=0) then
    begin
        cent := 5 / 9 * (faren - 32);
        str(cent:8:3,outstr);
        edit1.text:=outstr;
    end
    else
        edit1.text:='INVALID';
end;
```

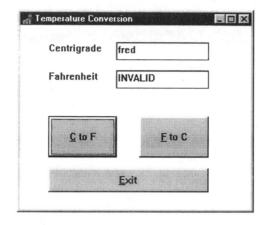

Figure 23.16 Sample run with invalid input

In this example the program calculates the roots of a quadratic equation with entered values of a, b and c. The general form of a quadratic equation is:

$$ax^2 + bx + c = 0$$

the general solution is:

$$x_{1,2} = \frac{-b \pm \sqrt{b^2 - 4ac}}{2a}$$

This leads to three types of roots, these are:

if ($b^2 > 4ac$) then there are two real roots;
else if ($b^2 = 4ac$) then there is a single root of $-b/4a$;
else if ($b^2 < 4ac$) then these are two complex roots which are:

$$x_{1,2} = -\frac{b}{2a} \pm j\frac{\sqrt{4ac - b^2}}{2a}$$

The steps taken, with reference to Figure 23.17, are:

1. Add a Label component and change its Caption property to 'a'.
2. Add a Label component and change its Caption property to 'b'.

270   *Mastering Pascal*

3. Add a Label component and change its Caption property to 'c'.
4. Add a Label component and change its Caption property to 'x1'.
5. Add a Label component and change its Caption property to 'x2'.
6. Add an Edit component and put it beside the a Label. Next change its Text property to '0' (this is the Text1 object).
7. Add an Edit component and put it beside the b Label. Next change its Text property to '0' (this is the Text2 object).
8. Add an Edit component and put it beside the c Label. Next change its Text property to '0' (this is the Text3 object).
9. Add an Edit component and put it beside the x1 Label. Next change its Text property to '0' (this is the Text4 object).
10. Add an Edit component and put it beside the x2 Label. Next change its Text property to '0' (this is the Text5 object).
11. Add a Button component and put it below the text boxes. Next change its Caption property to 'Calculate'. This command button will be used to determine the roots of the equation.
12. Add a Button component and put it beside the other button. Next change its Caption property to 'Exit'. This command button will be used to exit the program.
13. Select the form and change the Caption property to 'Quadratic Equation'.

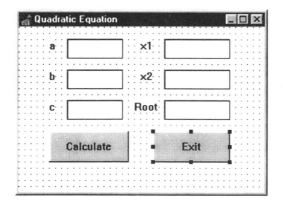

Figure 23.17   Quadratic equation form

Next the code associated with each control can be added, as follows:

1. First add code to the first command button (Calculate) which will be used to calculate the roots and display to the roots text box (Edit4 and Edit5). This is achieved with:

```
procedure TForm1.Button1Click(Sender: TObject);
var        outstr,outstr1,outstr2:string;
           a,b,c,x1,x2:real;
           code:integer;
```

```
begin
     val(edit1.text,a,code);
     val(edit2.text,b,code);
     val(edit3.text,c,code);

     if (b*b>4*a*c) then
     begin
        edit6.text:='REAL';
        x1:=(-b+sqrt(b*b-4*a*c))/(2*a);
        x2:=(-b-sqrt(b*b-4*a*c))/(2*a);
        str(x1:6:2,outstr);
        edit4.text:=outstr;
        str(x2:6:2,outstr);
        edit5.text:=outstr;
     end
     else if (b*b=4*a*c) then
     begin
        edit6.text:='SINGULAR';
        x1:=-b/(2*a);
        str(x1:6:3,outstr);
        edit4.text:=outstr;
        edit5.text:='';
     end
     else
     begin
        edit6.text:='COMPLEX';
        x1:=-b/(2*a);
        x2:=sqrt(4*a*c-b*b)/(2*a);
        str(x1:6:2,outstr1);
        str(x2:6:2,outstr2);
        outstr:=outstr1+'+j'+outstr2;
        edit4.text:=outstr;
        outstr:=outstr1+'-j'+outstr2;
        edit5.text:=outstr;
     end;
end;
```

2. Next add code to the second command button (Exit):

```
procedure TForm1.Button2Click(Sender: TObject);
begin
  if MessageDlg('Do you wish to exit?', mtInformation,
          [mbYes, mbNo], 0) = mrYes then
     Close;
end;
```

Figure 23.18 shows two sample runs.

23.6 Resistance calculation with slider controls program

An excellent method of allowing the user to input a value within a fixed range is to use a slider control. The main properties, as shown in Figure 23.19, of a scroll bar are:

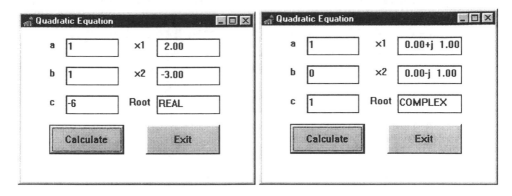

Figure 23.18 Sample runs

- Max. Which defines the maximum value of the scroll bar.
- Min. Which defines the minimum value of the scroll bar.
- Position. Which gives the current slider value.

As an example, a horizontal slider will be set up with a voltage range of 0 to 100. The value of the slider will be shown. The steps taken, with reference to Figure 23.20, are:

1. Add a Label component and change its Caption property to 'Voltage'.
2. Add a Label component and change its Caption property to '0'.
3. Add a ScrollBar component below the labels. Next change its Max property to '100' and its Min property to '0'.

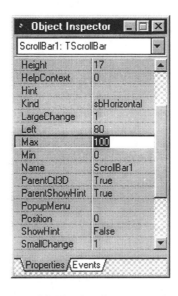

Figure 23.19 Scroll bar properties

Next the code associated with each control can be added, as follows:

1. Add code to the horizontal scroll bar which will be used to display its value to the voltage value label (Label2). This is achieved with:

```
procedure TForm1.ScrollBar1Change(Sender: TObject);
var        outstr:string;
begin
     str(ScrollBar1.position,outstr);
     label2.caption:=outstr;
end;
```

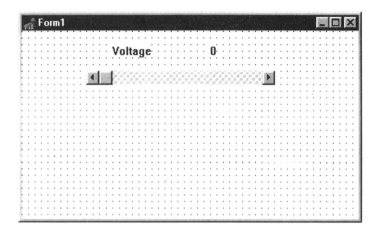

Figure 23.20   Voltage form

This will take the value from the scroll bar (ScrollBar1.Value) and display to the second label box (Label2). When the program is run then the user can move the scroll bar back and forward which causes a change in the displayed voltage value (from 0 to 100). A sample run is shown in Figure 23.21.

This project can now be enhanced by adding another slider for current and displaying the equivalent resistance (which is voltage divided by current). The steps taken, with reference to Figure 23.22, are:

1. Add a Label component and change its Caption property to 'Voltage'.
2. Add a Label component and change its Caption property to '0'.
3. Add a ScrollBar component below the labels (ScrollBar1). Next change its Max property to '100' and its Min property to '0'.
4. Add a Label component and change its Caption property to 'Current'.
5. Add a Label component and change its Caption property to '0'.
6. Add a ScrollBar component below the labels (ScrollBar2). Next change its Max property to '100' and its Min property to '0'.
7. Add a Label component and change its Caption property to 'Resistance'.
8. Add a Label component and change its Caption property to '0'.

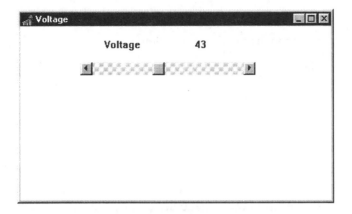

Figure 23.21   Sample run

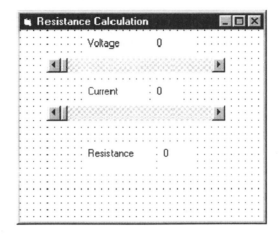

Figure 23.22   New form

Next the code associated with each control can be added, as follows:

1. Add code to the first horizontal scroll bar (ScrollBar1) which will be used to display its value to the voltage value label (Label2). The resistance label (Label6) is also updated with the result of the voltage divided by the current. This is achieved with:

```
procedure TForm1.ScrollBar1Change(Sender: TObject);
var      outstr:string;
         voltage,current,resistance:real;
begin
     voltage:=scrollbar1.position;
     str(voltage:8:2,outstr);
     label2.caption:=outstr;
     current:=scrollbar2.position/100;
     str(current:8:2,outstr);
     label4.caption:=outstr;
```

```
        if (current<>0) then
        begin
            resistance:=voltage/current;
            str(resistance:8:3,outstr);
            label6.caption:=outstr;
        end
        else
        label6.caption:='INFINITY';
    end;
```

2. Add code to the second horizontal scroll bar (ScrollBar2) which will be used to display its value to the current value label (Label4) with the value of the scroll bar divided by 100. The resistance label (Label6) is also updated with the result of the voltage divided by the current. This is achieved with:

```
procedure TForm1.ScrollBar2Change(Sender: TObject);
var        outstr:string;
           voltage,current,resistance:real;
begin
     voltage:=scrollbar1.position;
     str(voltage:8:2,outstr);
     label2.caption:=outstr;
     current:=scrollbar2.position/100;
     str(current:8:2,outstr);
     label4.caption:=outstr;
     if (current<>0) then
     begin
         resistance:=voltage/current;
         str(resistance:8:3,outstr);
         label6.caption:=outstr;
     end
     else
     label6.caption:='INFINITY';
end;
```

Figure 23.23 shows a sample run.

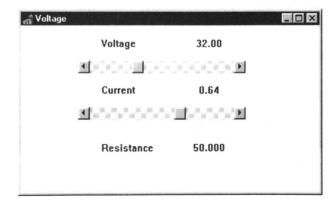

Figure 23.23   Sample run

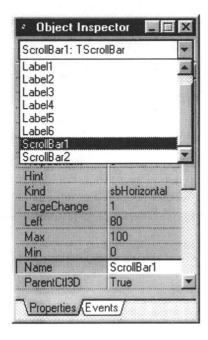

Figure 23.24 Object names

In this case an improved naming convention might be:

```
Label1          Voltage_Label
Label2          Voltage_Show
Label3          Current_Label
Label4          Current_Show
Label5          Resistance_Label
Label6          Resistance_Show
ScrollBar1      Voltage_Value
ScrollBar2      Current_Value
Form1           Resistance_Calc
```

These are set by selecting the properties of each of the objects and then changing the Name property to the required name. An example of changing the name of the form to `Resistance_Calc` is given in the left-hand side of Figure 23.25.

The right-hand side of Figure 23.25 shows the list of objects after each of their names has been changed. Notice that it is now easier to locate the required object.

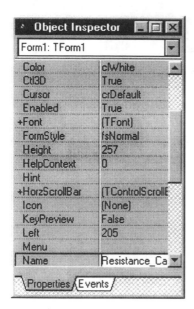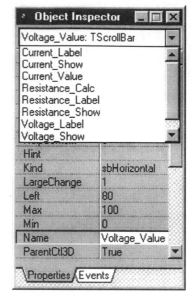

Figure 23.25 Changing the name of the form and of an object

Next the code must be modified so that the references are to the newly named objects. The code for the voltage scroll bar (`Voltage_Value`) is now:

```
procedure TResistance_Calc.Voltage_ValueChange(Sender: TObject);
var       outstr:string;
          voltage,current,resistance:real;
begin
     voltage:=voltage_value.position;
     str(voltage:8:2,outstr);
     voltage_show.caption:=outstr;
     current:=current_value.position/100;
     str(current:8:2,outstr);
     current_show.caption:=outstr;
     if (current<>0) then
     begin
        resistance:=voltage/current;
        str(resistance:8:3,outstr);
        resistance_show.caption:=outstr;
     end
     else
     resistance_show.caption:='INFINITY';
end;
```

and the code for the current scroll bar (`Current_Value`) is now:

```
procedure TResistance_Calc.Current_ValueChange(Sender: TObject);
var       outstr:string;
          voltage,current,resistance:real;
begin

     voltage:=voltage_value.position;
```

```
      str(voltage:8:2,outstr);
      voltage_show.caption:=outstr;
      current:=current_value.position/100;
      str(current:8:2,outstr);
      current_show.caption:=outstr;
      if (current<>0) then
      begin
         resistance:=voltage/current;
         str(resistance:8:3,outstr);
         resistance_show.caption:=outstr;
      end
      else
      resistance_show.caption:='INFINITY';
end;
```

23.7 Exercises

23.7.1 Write a Delphi program in which the user enters either a value in either radians or degrees and the program converts to either degrees or radians, respectively. Figure 23.26 shows a sample run.

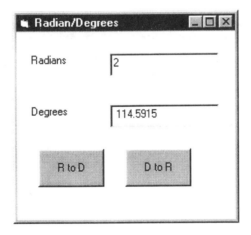

Figure 23.26 Radians to degrees conversion

23.7.2 Modify the program in Exercise 23.7.1 so that invalid entries are not accepted.

23.7.3 Modify the program in Exercise 23.7.1 so that the conversion value is automatically converted when the user enters a value (that is, there is no need for the command buttons).

23.7.4 Write separate Delphi programs with slider controls for the following formula:

(i) $F = ma$ range: m=0.01 to 1000 g, a=0.01 to 100 ms^{-2}

(ii) $V = IR$ range: I=0.1 to 100 A, V=0.1 to 100 V

23.7.5 Write a Delphi program that calculates the values of m and c for a straight line. The values of (x_1, y_1) and (x_2, y_2) should be generated with slider controls (with a range of –100 to +100 for each of the values). Figure 23.27 shows a sample design.

23.7.6 Modify the program in Exercise 23.7.5 so that a divide by zero does not occur when the difference in the x values is zero. If this is so then the program should display 'INFINITY' for the gradient. If the two co-ordinates are the same then the program should display the message 'INVALID' for the gradient.

23.7.7 Write a Delphi program which has a multiple choice option question which is repeated. The program should keep a running tally of the number of correct answers and the number of incorrect answers.

23.7.8 Complete the Exercises in Chapter 3 using Delphi.

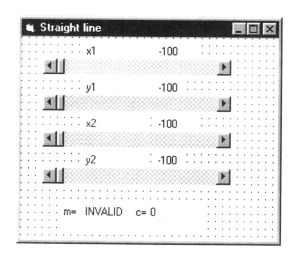

Figure 23.27 Straight line program design

Delphi Menus and Dialogs

24.1 Introduction

This chapter discusses how menus and dialog boxes are used.

24.2 Menu editor

Most Windows programs have menus in which the user selects from a range of defined pull-down menus with defined options. Delphi has an easy-to-use function called the Menu Editor which is used to create custom menus. The Menu Editor is started from the Tools Menu or from the toolbar shortcut 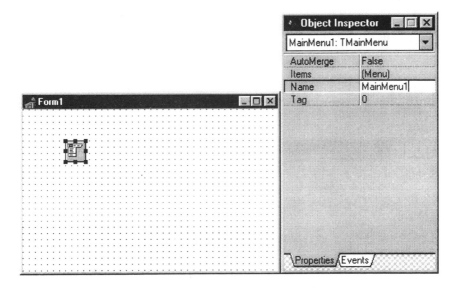.

Figure 24.1 Main menu

The menu is created and edited by double clicking on the MainMenu icon which is on the form. An example screen from the Editor is shown in Figure 24.2. The properties include:

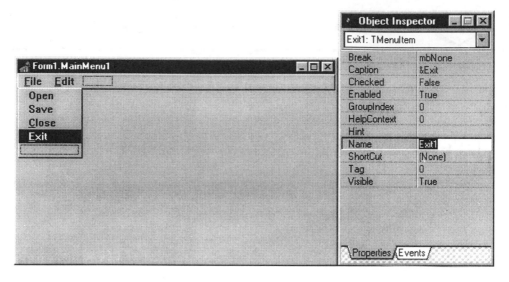

Figure 24.2 Menu option properties

- **Caption**. A text box in which the name of the menu bar or menu option is entered. Often in menus the user can select a menu option by pressing the ALT key and an assigned key (hot key). To specify the ALT-hot key, an & is inserted before the letter of the menu option. When the program is run then this letter is underlined. For example Fi&le would be displayed as File and the assigned keys would be ALT-L. A double ampersand specifies the ampersand character.
- **Name**. A text box in which the control name for the menu option is specified. This is used by the program code and is not displayed to the user when the program is run.
- **Shortcut**. A pull-down menu that can be used to specify a shortcut key (Cntrl-A to Cntrl-Z, F1 to F12, Cntrl-F1 to Cntrl-F12, Shift-F1 to Shift-F12, Shift-Cntrl-F1 to Shift-Cntrl-F12, Cntrl-Ins, Shift-Ins, Del, Shift-Del, Alt-Bkspace).
- **HelpContext**. A text box in which a unique numeric value is specified for the context ID. This value can be used to find the appropriate Help topic in the Help file.
- **Checked**. A check box which specifies if a check mark is to appear initially at the left of a menu item. It is generally used to specify if a toggled menu option is initially on or off.
- **Enabled**. A check box which specifies if the menu item is to respond to events. If it is not enabled then the menu item appears dimmed.
- **Visible**. A check box which specifies if the menu item is to appear in the menu.

24.2.1 Creating a menu system

To create a menu system the programmer adds menu options in the editor, either submenu options (by adding to a pull-down option) or main menu options (by adding to the main menu). The editor leaves spaces on each of the menu options to add and menu options are deleted by selecting the option and then pressing the delete key. A menu option is inserted using the Insert button and deleted with the Delete button.

The code associated with a menu item is defined by the menu item name. For example if a menu item has the caption of `File` then the associated code procedure (on `Tform1`) will be `TForm1.File1Click`, for `Open` it will be `TForm1.Open1Click`.

For example, to create a menu with:

```
File
   Open
   Save
   Close
   Exit
Edit
Help
About
```

1. Create a caption `&File` frrom the main menu.
2. From the `File` pull-down menu create a menu option and add a caption `&Open`.
3. From the `File` pull-down menu create a menu option and add a caption `&Save`.
4. From the `File` pull-down menu create a menu option and add a caption `&Close`.
5. From the `File` pull-down menu create a menu option and add a caption `&Exit`.
6. From the main menu create a menu option and add a caption `&Edit`.
7. Complete the menu system shown in Figure 24.3.

The associated code procedures are selected by double clicking on the menu option and are `TForm1.File1Click`, `TForm1.Open1Click` and `TForm1.Save1Click`, and so on. In Figure 24.3 the Open menu option has the Enable property set to FALSE (thus it cannot be selected by the user) and the Save option has had the Check property set to TRUE. Figure 24.4 shows a sample run.

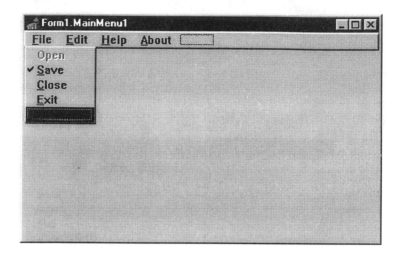

Figure 24.3   Adding a menu item

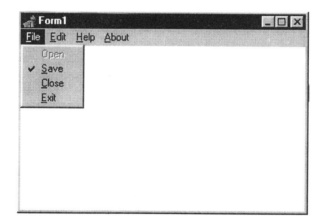

Figure 24.4   Sample run

Next a Edit box is added to the form (Edit2), as shown in Figure 24.5. The resulting objects are shown in Figure 24.6. It has the name Edit2 as the menu option Edit in the File menu has been given the name Edit1.

Next the code can be added. For example, to add code to the Exit menu button then the Exit option in the Menu Editor is double-clicked and the following code is added.

```
procedure TForm1.Exit1Click(Sender: TObject);
begin
  if MessageDlg('Do you wish to exit?', mtInformation,
         [mbYes, mbNo], 0) = mrYes then
    Close;
end;

end.
```

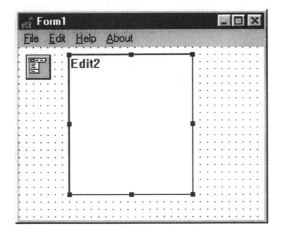

Figure 24.5 Adding edit box

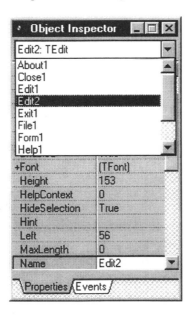

Figure 24.6 Program objects

Next the rest of the code can be added. For example in the Close option then the code could simply just add text for the Edit window, with:

```
procedure TForm1.Close1Click(Sender: TObject);
begin
     edit2.text:=edit2.text+'Close'
end;

end.
```

Figure 24.7 shows a sample run of the developed program.

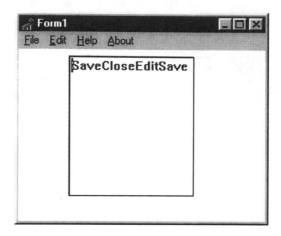

Figure 24.7 Example run

24.3 Open and close dialog boxes

The Open and Close dialog (OpenDialog and CloseDialog) boxes allow for file operations such as opening and saving files. It is basically a control between Delphi and the Microsoft Windows dynamic-link library COMMDLG.DLL. Thus this file must be in the Microsoft Windows SYSTEM directory for the common dialog control to work.

A dialog box is added to an application by first adding the CommonDialog control to a form and setting its properties. When developing the program the common dialog box is displayed as an icon on the form. A program calls the dialog with one of the following (assuming that the dialog box is named OpenDialog1):

OpenDialog1.Filter   A string which displays the filename filter. The | character is used to differentiate different files. For example the following filter enables the user to select text files or graphic files that include bitmaps and icons:

```
Text (*.txt)|*.txt | Pictures(*.bmp;*.ico)| *.bmp; *.ico
```

OpenDialog1.Filename   Returns or sets the path and filename of a selected file.

OpenDialog1.FilterIndex   Defines the default filter (with reference to the filter).

Open and Close dialog boxes are added to a form in any position, as shown in Figure 24.8. These boxes can be placed anywhere as it will not be seen on the form when the program is run. The design is shown in Figure 24.9. It includes an OpenDialog, a CloseDialog, a MainMenu and a Memo.

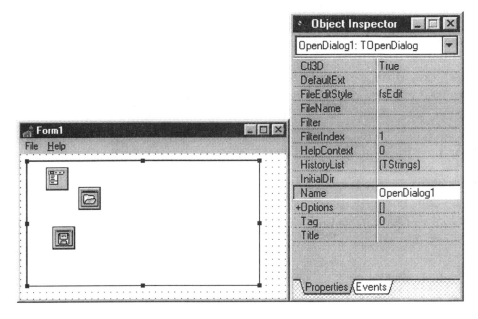

Figure 24.8 Open dialog properties

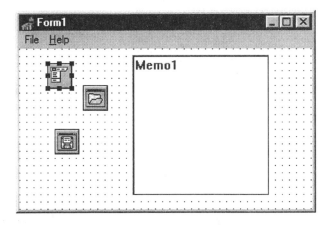

Figure 24.9 Sample design

The dialog box can be used to determine the filename of a file to be opened or saved. It is used in the next program for the Open and Save file menu options.

The code attached to the Open menu option:

```
procedure TForm1.Open1Click(Sender: TObject);
begin
  OpenDialog1.Filter :=
    'Text Files (*.txt)|*.txt| Batch Files (*.bat)|*.bat';

    if (OpenDialog1.Execute) then
    begin
        memo1.Lines.LoadfromFile(OpenDialog1.FileName);
      end;
end;
```

The TOpenDialog component creates a dialog box for the user to open a program. The Execute method is used to display the Open dialog box. If it returns a TRUE then the user has selected a file. The FileName property then stores the name of the file.

The Save option has the following code:

```
procedure TForm1.Save1Click(Sender: TObject);
begin
  SaveDialog1.Filter := OpenDialog1.Filter;
  SaveDialog1.FileName:= OpenDialog1.FileName;

    if (SaveDialog1.Execute) then
    begin
        memo1.Lines.SaveToFile(SaveDialog1.FileName);
      end;
end;
```

The SaveToFile method saves an object to the file specified in File-Name. Figure 24.10 shows a sample run and the Open dialog box. It can be seen that the default Type of File is set to "Text Files (*.txt)" and Figure 24.11 shows an example loading of a file. Figure 24.12 show the Save dialog box.

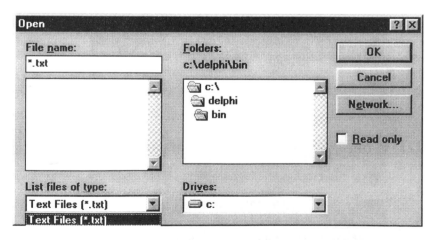

Figure 24.10 Example run

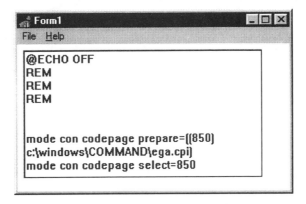

Figure 24.11 Example run

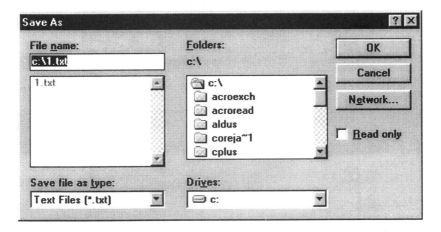

Figure 24.12 Example run

24.4 Running an application program

Delphi allows for the execution of applications with the Shell command. Its format is:

ExecProgram('*Cmd-Line*', *State*)

where

CmdLine   Is the command line for the application to be executed and must be enclosed in quotation marks. The program will search for this application in the current directory, followed by the Windows directory and the user's path.

State Specifies a value indicating in which mode the application will run. Valid values are:

0 Normal
1 Minimized
2 Maximized

The following shows an example of executing the `Calc.exe` and `Notepad.exe` programs and Figure 24.13 shows a sample run.

```
procedure TForm1.Clock1Click(Sender: TObject);
begin
     ExecProgram('c:\windows\clock.exe, 2);
end;

procedure TForm1.Calc1Click(Sender: TObject);
begin
     ExecProgram('c:\windows\calc.exe, 2);
end;
```

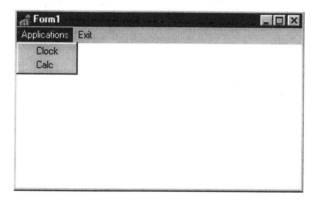

Figure 24.13 Example run

24.5 Exercises

24.5.1 Write a Delphi program with the following menu system:

```
File
    Open
    Save
    Close
Edit
    Copy
```

```
      Paste
      Select All
View
      Normal
      Full Screen
Help
```

24.5.2 Modify the menu system in Exercise 24.5.1 so that the program displays the function of the menu option.

24.5.3 Expand Program 24.5.2 and its menu system so that it runs other Windows programs. An example could be:

```
Utils
      Calculator
      Notepad
      Paint
WordProcessing
      Word
      AmiPro
Spreadsheets
      Lotus123
      Excel
      Exit
```

24.5.4 Integrate some of the programs from previous chapters into a single program with menu options. For example, the menu system could be:

```
Programs
      Temperature Conversion
      Quadratic Equation
      Straight Line
Exit
```

One possible method of implementing this program is to compile the temperature conversion, quadratic equation and straight line programs to an EXE. Then run ExeProgram from the object call.

```
ExecProgram('tempcon.exe', 1)
```

25 Delphi Events

25.1 Introduction

Delphi differs from many other programming languages in that it is event driven where the execution of a program is defined by the events that happen. This is a different approach to many programming languages which follow a defined sequence of execution and the programmer must develop routines which react to events. This chapter discusses the events that happen in Delphi.

25.2 Program events

Each object in Delphi has various events associated with it. For example, the single click on an object may cause one event but a double click causes another. The events are displayed at the right-hand side of the code window. An example is shown in Figure 25.1 which in this case shows the events: OnActivate, OnClick, OnClose, OnCreate, OnKeypress, OnKeyUp and OnKeyDown and so on. The name of the routine which contains the code for the event and object is in the form:

procedure *ObjectType.ObjectNameEvent*

where *ObjectType* is the type of the object (such as TForm1), `ObjectName` is the actual name of the object (such as Button1) and `Event` is the event (such as Click and KeyDown). For example:

```
procedure TForm1.Button1Click()
procedure TForm1.Button1KeyDown()
```

The main events that occur in Delphi include:

- **Click**. Occurs when a user performs a single click of the mouse button on the object.
- **DblClick**. Occurs when a user performs a double click of the mouse button on the object.

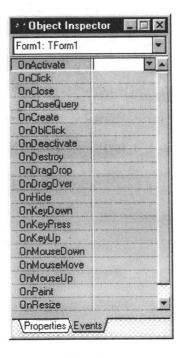

Figure 25.1 Form events

- **MouseUp**. Occurs when the user releases the mouse button.
- **MouseDown**. Occurs when the user presses the mouse button down.
- **MouseMove**. Occurs when the user moves the mouse.
- **KeyUp**. Occurs when the user releases a key.
- **KeyDown**. Occurs when the user presses a key.
- **KeyPress**. Occurs when the user presses and releases a key (the KeyDown and KeyUp events).
- **Create**. Occurs when a form is loaded.
- **DragDrop**. Occurs at the beginning and end of a drag operation of any control.
- **Resize**. Occurs when a form is first displayed or if the object size is changed.
- **Destroy**. Occurs when a form is about to be removed from the screen.

Not all controls and forms (objects) have all the events associated with them. For example a form may have the following:

```
procedure FormActivate(Sender: Tobject);

procedure FormClick(Sender: Tobject);

procedure FormClose(Sender: TObject; var Action: TCloseAction);
```

```
procedure FormCloseQuery(Sender: TObject; var CanClose: Boolean);

procedure FormCreate(Sender: Tobject);

procedure FormDblClick(Sender: Tobject);

procedure FormDeactivate(Sender: Tobject);

procedure FormDestroy(Sender: Tobject);

procedure FormDragDrop(Sender, Source: TObject; X, Y: Integer);

procedure FormDragOver(Sender, Source: TObject; X, Y: Integer;
        State: TDragState; var Accept: Boolean);

procedure FormHide(Sender: Tobject);

procedure FormKeyDown(Sender: TObject; var Key: Word;
        Shift: TShiftState);

procedure FormKeyPress(Sender: TObject; var Key: Char);

procedure FormKeyUp(Sender: TObject; var Key: Word;
        Shift: TShiftState);

procedure FormMouseDown(Sender: TObject; Button: TMouseButton;
        Shift: TShiftState; X, Y: Integer);

procedure FormMouseMove(Sender: TObject; Shift: TShiftState;
        X, Y: Integer);

procedure FormMouseUp(Sender: TObject; Button: TMouseButton;
        Shift: TShiftState; X, Y: Integer);

procedure FormPaint(Sender: Tobject);

procedure FormResize(Sender: Tobject);

procedure FormShow(Sender: TObject);
```

whereas a button (Button1) has a reduced set of routines:

```
procedure TForm1.Button1Click(Sender: TObject);

procedure TForm1.Button1KeyDown(Sender: TObject; var Key: Word;
        Shift: TShiftState);

procedure TForm1.Button1DragDrop(Sender, Source: TObject;
        X, Y: Integer);

procedure TForm1.Button1DragOver(Sender, Source: TObject;
        X, Y: Integer;  State: TDragState; var Accept: Boolean);

procedure TForm1.Button1EndDrag(Sender, Target: TObject;
        X, Y: Integer);

procedure TForm1.Button1Enter(Sender: TObject);
```

```
procedure TForm1.Button1Exit(Sender: TObject);

procedure TForm1.Button1KeyPress(Sender: TObject; var Key: Char);

procedure TForm1.Button1KeyUp(Sender: TObject; var Key: Word;
    Shift: TShiftState);

procedure TForm1.Button1MouseDown(Sender: TObject;
    Button: TMouseButton;  Shift: TShiftState; X, Y: Integer);

procedure TForm1.Button1MouseMove(Sender: TObject;
    Shift: TShiftState; X,  Y: Integer);

procedure TForm1.Button1MouseUp(Sender: TObject;
    Button: TMouseButton;  Shift: TShiftState; X, Y: Integer);
```

The parameters passed into the routine depend on the actions associated with the events. For example the Keypress event on a button causes the routine:

```
procedure TForm1.FormKeyPress(Sender: TObject; var Key: Char);

end;
```

to be called. The value of Key contains the ASCII value of the character pressed. The MouseDown event for a button has the following routine associated with it:

```
procedure TForm1.FormMouseDown(Sender: TObject;
   Button: TMouseButton;  Shift: TShiftState; X, Y: Integer);
```

where the value of Button is the value of the button press (0 for none, 1 for the left button and 2 for the right button). Shift specifies which key has been pressed, and X, Y specify the x,y co-ordinates of the mouse point. Valid values for the shift key are:

ssShift   (Shift key pressed).
ssAlt   (Alt key pressed).
ssCtrl   (Ctrl key pressed).
ssRight   (Right mouse button pressed).
ssLeft   (Left mouse button pressed).
ssMiddle   (Middle mouse button pressed).
ssDouble   (Left and right mouse buttons pressed).

and for the mouse button are:

mbRight   mbLeft   mbMiddle

25.2.1 Click

The Click event occurs when the user presses and then releases a mouse button over an object. When the object is a form the event occurs when the user clicks on a blank area or a disabled control. If the object is a control, then the event occurs when the user:

- Clicks on a control with any of the mouse buttons. When the control is a CheckBox, CommandButton, or OptionButton control then the Click event occurs only when the user clicks the left mouse button.
- Presses the ALT-*hotkey* for a control, such as pressing Alt-X for the E&xit control property name.
- Presses the Enter key when the form has a command button.
- Presses the Space key when CommandButton, OptionButton or CheckBox control has the focus.

25.2.2 Dbl Click

The Dbl Click event occurs when the user presses and releases the mouse button twice over an object. In a form it occurs when the user double clicks either on a disabled control or a blank area. On a control the event happens when the user double clicks on a component with the left mouse button.

An example form is shown in Figure 25.2. In this case an Edit box is added to the form. Then the following code is added to the form:

```
procedure TForm1.FormDblClick(Sender: TObject);
begin
     edit1.text:='MISS';
end;
```

which will display the text 'MISS' when the user clicks on any blank area in the form. The following code is added to the text box:

```
procedure TForm1.Edit1DblClick(Sender: TObject);
begin
     edit1.text:='HIT';
end;
```

which displays the text 'HIT' when the user double clicks on the text box.

25.2.3 Mouse Up, Mouse Down

The MouseUp event occurs when the user releases the mouse button and the MouseDown event occurs when the user presses a mouse button. An example format is:

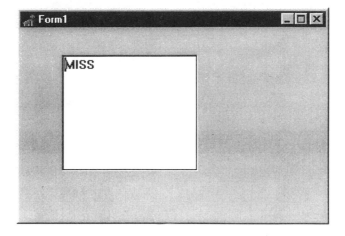

Figure 25.2 Form events

```
procedure FormMouseDown(Sender: TObject; Button: TMouseButton;
        Shift: TShiftState; X, Y: Integer);

procedure FormMouseUp(Sender: TObject; Button: TMouseButton;
        Shift: TShiftState; X, Y: Integer);
```

where

- `button` identifies which button was pressed (MouseDown) or released (MouseUp). A value of `mbRight` identifies the right mouse button, `mbLeft` identifies the left mouse button and `mbMiddle` identifies the middle mouse button.
- `shift` identifies the state of the Shift, Cntrl, and Alt keys when the button was pressed (or released). Valid values are `ssShift, ssAlt, ssCntrl, ssRight, ssLeft, ssMiddle` and `ssDouble`.
- x, y identifies the current location of the mouse pointer. The x and y values are relatively to the ScaleHeight, ScaleWidth, ScaleLeft, and ScaleTop properties of the object.

An example of code for the MouseDown event is given next and a sample run is shown in Figure 25.3.

```
procedure TForm1.Edit1MouseDown(Sender: TObject;
   Button: TMouseButton;   Shift: TShiftState; X, Y: Integer);
var outx, outy: string;
begin
     str(X:5, outx);
     str(Y:5, outy);

     If (Button = mbLeft) Then
        Edit1.Text := 'LEFT BUTTON ' + outx + ' ' + outy
```

```
      else if (Button = mbRight) then
         Edit1.Text := 'RIGHT BUTTON ' + outx + ' ' + outy
      else if (Button = mbMiddle) then
            Edit1.Text := 'MIDDLE BUTTON ' + outx + ' ' + outy
end;
```

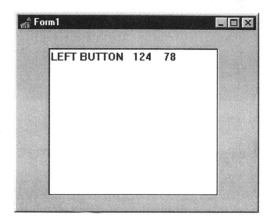

Figure 25.3 Form events

25.2.4 Mouse move

The MouseMove event occurs when the user moves the mouse. Thus it is continually being called as it moves across an object. An example format is:

```
procedure FormMouseMove(Sender: TObject; Shift: TShiftState;
      X, Y: Integer);
```

where `button`, `shift`, `x` and `y` have the same settings as the ones defined in the previous section.

An example of code for the MouseMove event is given next and a sample code is shown in Figure 25.4. Figure 25.5 shows a sample run. In this case, the x and y co-ordinate is the mouse pointer and the button pressed is displayed to the text box.

```
procedure TForm1.Edit1MouseMove(Sender: TObject;
      Shift: TShiftState; X,   Y: Integer);
var outx,outy:string;

begin
      str(x:5,outx);
      str(y:5,outy);
      edit1.Text := 'X,Y:' + outx + ' ' + outy;
end;
```

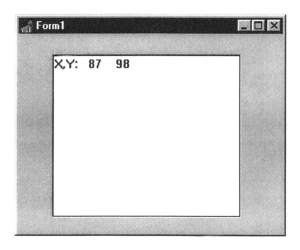

```
☐ UNIT1.PAS                                    _ ☐ ☒
 end;


 procedure TForm1.Edit1MouseMove(Sender: TObject;
     Shift: TShiftState; X,  Y: Integer);
 var outx,outy:string;
   begin
                 str(x:5,outx);
         str(y:5,outy);
         edit1.Text := 'X,Y:' + outx + ' ' + outy;
 end;


 end.

 27: 1   Modified    Insert          ◄│  │        ►
 \Unit1/
```

Figure 25.4 Sample code

```
☐ Form1                                        _ ☐ ☒

      X,Y:  87   98
```

Figure 25.5 Sample run

25.2.5 *Drag and drop*

The DragDrop event occurs at the end of a drag and drop operation of any control. An example format is:

```
procedure FormDragDrop(Sender, Source: TObject; X, Y: Integer);
```

where:

- source is the control being dragged.
- x, y specifies the current x and y co-ordinate of the mouse pointer within the target form or control. The x and y values are relative to the Height,

Width, Left, and Top properties of the object.

25.2.6 Key press

The KeyPress event occurs when the user presses and releases a key (the KeyDown and KeyUp events). An example format is:

```
procedure TForm1.Button1KeyPress(Sender: TObject; var Key: Char);
```

where `Key` specifies an ASCII character.

An example of code for the KeyPress event is given next and a sample run is shown in Figure 25.6. For this program the user can type in the blank area on the form (the grey area) and the text will be displayed in the text box.

```
procedure TForm1.Edit1KeyPress(Sender: TObject; var Key: Char);
begin
     edit1.text:='Character is ' + key;
end;
```

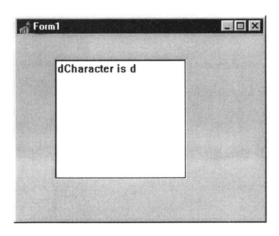

Figure 25.6 Sample run

25.2.7 Resize

The Resize event occurs when a form is first displayed or if the object size is changed. An example format is:

```
procedure FormResize(Sender: Tobject);
```

25.2.8 Close

The Close event occurs when a form is about to be removed from the screen. Then if the form is reloaded the contents of all its controls are reinitialized.

An example format is:

```
procedure FormClose(Sender: TObject; var Action: TCloseAction);
```

25.3 Exercises

25.3.1 Write a Delphi program which has a single form and a text box. The text box should show all of the events that occur with the form, that is:

Activate, Click, DblClick, DragDrop, DragOver, and so on.

Investigate when these events occur. Notice that when an event has code attached then the procedure name in the View Code pull-down menu becomes highlighted.

25.3.2 Write a Delphi program which has a single command button and a text box. The text box should show all of the events that occur with the command button, that is:

Click, KeyDown, KeyPress, KeyUp, MouseDown, MouseUp, and so on.

Investigate when these events occur.

25.3.3 Write a Delphi program in which the program displays the message 'IN TEXT AREA' when the mouse is within the text box area and 'OUT OF TEXT AREA' when it is out of the text box area.

25.3.4 Write a Delphi program which has a button. If the user presses any lower case letter then the program ends, else it should continue. A sample event which displays a message when the letter 'x' is pressed is given next:

```
procedure TForm1.Button1KeyPress(Sender: TObject;
      var Key: Char);
begin
    if (key='x') then
       label1.caption:='X pressed';
end;
```

25.3.5 Modify the program in Exercise 25.3.4 so that if the user clicks on the form (and not on the command button) the program automatically prompts the user for his/her name. This name should then appear in the command button caption property (Button1.caption).

25.3.6 Write a Delphi program which displays the message 'So long and thanks for all the fish' when the main form is unloaded. The form should be removed from the screen.

25.3.7 Write a Delphi program with a text box which displays the current keypress, including Alt-, Ctrl- and Shift- keystrokes.

25.3.8 Modify the program in Exercise 25.3.7 so that it also displays the mouse button press and the co-ordinates of the mouse.

26 Delphi Graphics

26.1 Introduction

This chapter discusses how graphics files are loaded into the program and how graphic objects can be drawn.

26.2 Loading graphics files

Delphi allows a graphics file to be loaded into a form or an image box. The standard method is:

```
Loadfromfile(graphfile)
```

Where *graphfile* specifies the name of the graphics file, if no name is given then the graphic in the form or image box is cleared. The standard graphics files supported by Delphi are:

- **BMP**. Windows bitmap file.
- **ICO**. Icon file (maximum size of 32×32 pixels).
- **RLE**. Run-length encoded files.
- **WMF**. Windows metafile files.

Normally graphics files are displayed in an image box . Thus to display the graphics file "CLOUD.BMP" to Image1 then:

```
image1.picture.loadfromfile('c:\windows\clouds.bmp');
```

The following example loads a graphics file into an image box. Figure 26.1 shows a sample form which contains an image box, a button and a dialog box.

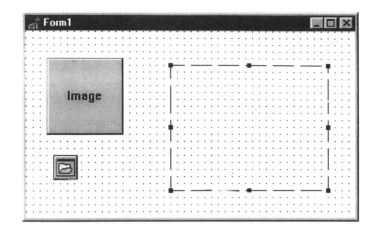

Figure 26.1 Form

The code added to the command button is as follows:

```
procedure TForm1.Button1Click(Sender: TObject);
begin
  OpenDialog1.Filter :=
    'Bmp Files (*.bmp)|*.bmp| Metafile Files (*.wmf)|*.wmf';

    if (OpenDialog1.Execute) then
    begin
      image1.picture.LoadFromFile(OpenDialog1.FileName);
    end;

end;
```

This will display a dialog box with the default file setting of *.bmp. After the user has selected a graphic then the LoadFromFile function is used to display the graphics file to the image box (Image1). Figure 26.2 shows a sample dialog box and Figure 26.3 shows a sample graphic.

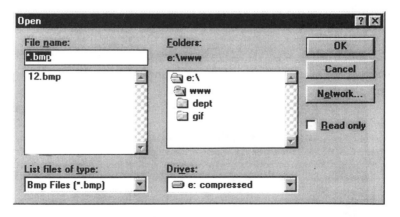

Figure 26.2 Dialog box

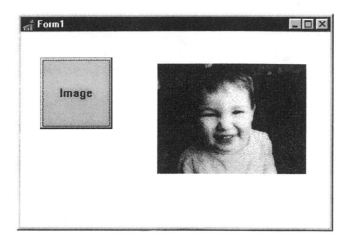

Figure 26.3   Sample graphic

| **26.3 Colours** |

26.3 Colours

Component and objects normally have a Color property which determines the background colour of a form or the colour of a component or graphics object. Table 26.1 defines the available colours.

Table 26.1   Resistor colour coding system

Value	Meaning
clBlack	Black
clMaroon	Maroon
clGreen	Green
clOlive	Olive green
clNavy	Navy blue
clPurple	Purple
clTeal	Teal
clGray	Gray
clSilver	Silver
clRed	Red
clLime	Lime green
clBlue	Blue
clFuchsia	Fuchsia
clAqua	Aqua
clWhite	White
clBackground	Current colour of your Windows background
clActiveCaption	Current colour of the title bar of the active window
clInactiveCaption	Current colour of the title bar of inactive windows

clMenu	Current background colour of menus
clWindow	Current background colour of windows
clWindowFrame	Current colour of window frames
clMenuText	Current colour of text on menus
clWindowText	Current colour of text in windows
clCaptionText	Current colour of the text on the title bar of the active window
clActiveBorder	Current border colour of the active window
clInactiveBorder	Current border colour of inactive windows
clAppWorkSpace	Current colour of the application work space
clHighlight	Current background colour of selected text
clHightlightText	Current colour of selected text
clBtnFace	Current colour of a button face
clBtnShadow	Current colour of a shadow cast by a button
clGrayText	Current colour of text that is dimmed
clBtnText	Current colour of text on a button
clInactiveCaptionText	Current colour of the text on the title bar of an inactive window
clBtnHighlight	Current colour of the highlighting on a button

For example the following will make the form background green when the form is loaded.

```
procedure TForm1.FormActivate(Sender: TObject);
begin
     form1.color:=clGreen;
end;
```

26.4 Drawing

The canvas draws the outline of the shape with its pen, then fills the interior (when applicable) with its brush and provides a graphical area on which shapes can be drawn. Delphi has a wide range of drawing functions (graphics methods); these include:

- Arc.
- Chord.
- Create.
- Destroy.
- Draw.
- Ellipse.
- FillRect.
- FloodFill.

- LineTo.
- MoveTo.
- Pie.
- Polygon.
- PolyLine.
- Rectangle.
- RoundRect.
- TextHeight.

- TextOut.
- TextRect.
- TextWidth.

26.4.1 LineTo

The LineTo graphic method draws a line to the canvas. Its standard form is:

```
canvas.LineTo (x1, y1)
```

where x1 and y1 define the end point of the line. The CurrentX and CurrentY values are set to the end of the line after a line has been drawn.

26.4.2 Rectangle

The Rectangle graphic method a draws rectangle to the canvas. Its standard form is:

```
canvas.Rectangle (x1, y1, x2, y2)
```

where (x1, y1) and (x2, y2) define the start and end of the rectangle, respectively.

The following code is added to a form and is called when the form is activated. It initially sets the co-ordinates of the form to (0,0) to (200,200) by setting the top, left, width and height properties of the form. Next a rectangle and several lines are drawn. Figure 26.4 shows the resultant form.

```
procedure TForm1.FormActivate(Sender: TObject);
begin
      form1.top:=0;             form1.left:=0;
      form1.width:=200;         form1.height:=200;
      canvas.rectangle(10,10,100,100);
      canvas.moveto(100,100);
      canvas.lineto(120,120);
      canvas.moveto(100,10);
      canvas.lineto(120,30);
      canvas.moveto(10,100);
      canvas.lineto(30,120);
      canvas.moveto(30,120);
      canvas.lineto(120,120);
      canvas.lineto(120,30);
end;
```

26.4.3 Ellipse

The Ellipse method draws an ellipse defined by a bounding rectangle on the canvas. The top-left point of the bounding rectangle is at pixel co-ordinates (x1, y1) and the bottom-right point is at (x2, y2). If the points of the rectangle form a square, a circle is drawn. Its standard form is:

```
canvas.Ellipse(x1, y1, x2, y2);
```

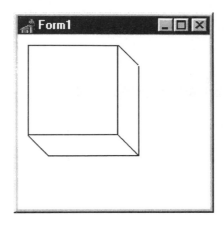

Figure 26.4   Sample graphic

26.4.4 Arc

The Arc function draws an elliptical arc. Its standard form is:

```
canvas.Arc(X1, Y1, X2, Y2, X3, Y3, X4, Y4)
```

where

X1	Defines x-co-ordinate of the upper-left corner of the bounding rectangle.
Y1	Defines y-co-ordinate of the upper-left corner of the bounding rectangle.
X2	Defines x-co-ordinate of the lower-right corner of the bounding rectangle.
Y2	Defines y-co-ordinate of the lower-right corner of the bounding rectangle.
X3	Defines x-co-ordinate of the point that defines the arc's starting point.
Y3	Defines y-co-ordinate of the point that defines the arc's starting point.
X4	Defines x-co-ordinate of the point that defines the arc's endpoint.
Y4	Defines y-co-ordinate of the point that defines the arc's endpoint.

The following code draw a number of circles (using the ellipse method), each of which is larger than the previous. Figure 26.5 shows a sample run.

```
procedure TForm1.FormActivate(Sender: TObject);
var i:integer;
begin
    form1.top:=0;           form1.left:=0;
```

308   *Mastering Pascal*

```
form1.width:=300;        form1.height:=300;
for i:=2 to 10 do
      canvas.ellipse(10*i,10*i,20*i,20*i);
end;
```

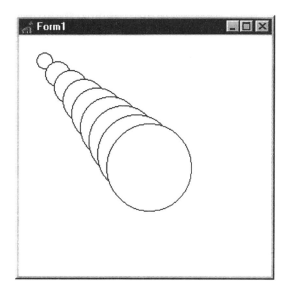

Figure 26.5 Sample run

26.4.5 Pen

A canvas object's Pen property determines the kind of pen the canvas uses for drawing lines and shape outlines. The properties that can be set are:

• Color.
• Mode.
• Style.
• Width.

The Width property returns or sets the width of lines of a graphic method. To set the line width the following is used:

```
canvas.Pen.Width = value
```

where value is defined as a number of pixels. For the style:

```
canvas.Pen.Style = value
```

where *value* is a value which corresponds to the following line styles:

psSolid   Solid line.

psDash	Line made up of a series of dashes.
psDot	Line made up of a series of dots.
psDashDot	Line made up of alternating dashes and dots.
psDashDotDot	Line made up of a series of dash-dot-dot combinations.

26.4.6 Brush

The Brush property on a canvas controls the way that fill areas are drawn. Properties associated with the Brush are Color and Style. Valid colours are defined in Table 26.1 and valid brush styles are:

```
bsSolid
bsClear
bsBDiagonal
bsFDiagonal
bsCross
bsDiagCross
bsHorizontal
bsVertical
```

The following code displays two rectangles, one has a diagonal cross and the other has a horizontal/vertical cross. Figure 26.6 show a sample run.

```
procedure TForm1.FormActivate(Sender: TObject);
var i:integer;
begin
     form1.top:=0;              form1.left:=0;
     form1.width:=200;           form1.height:=200;
     canvas.Brush.Style := bsDiagCross;
     canvas.Brush.Color := clBlack;
     canvas.Rectangle(10, 20, 100, 100);
     canvas.Brush.Style := bsCross;
     canvas.Rectangle(100, 20, 190, 100);
end;
```

26.4.7 FloodFill

The FloodFill method fills an area of the screen surface using the current brush (as specified by the Brush property). It begins at a point (x,y) and continues until it reaches the defined colour boundary. Its format is:

```
canvas.FloodFill(X, Y, Color, FillStyle);
```

where color can be any of the colours defined in Table 26.1 and Fill-Style can be:

- fsBorder, where the area is filled until the border of the defined colour is reached.
- fsSurface, where the area is filled until the defined colour is reached.

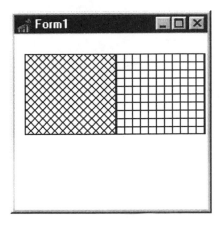

Figure 26.6   Sample run

26.4.8 Pie

The Pie method draws a section of an ellipse which is bounded by the rectangle (x1, y1) and (x2, x2). The section drawn is determined by two lines radiating from the centre of the ellipse through the points (x3, y3) and (x4, y4). Its format is:

```
canvas.Pie(x1, y1, x2, y2, x3, y3, x4, y4);
```

26.4.9 PolyLine

The PolyLine method draws a series of lines on the canvas with the current pen, connecting each of the points passed to it in points. Its format is:

```
canvas.Polyline(Points);
```

where Points is an array of (x,y) points.

The following code displays a polygon from an array of points. In this case the points are: (15, 15), (100, 40), (100, 120), and so on. Figure 26.7 shows a sample run.

```
procedure TForm1.FormActivate(Sender: TObject);
var i:integer;
begin
     form1.top:=0;            form1.left:=0;
     form1.width:=200;        form1.height:=200;
     Canvas.Pen.Color := clRed;
     Canvas.PolyLine([Point(15, 15), Point(100, 40),
        Point(100, 120),Point(140, 150),
        Point(50, 100), Point(15, 15)]);

end;
```

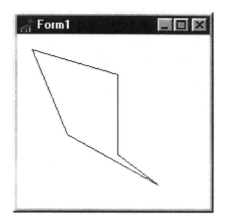

Figure 26.7   Sample run

26.4.10 Chord

The Chord method draws a line on the canvas connecting two points on the ellipse bounded by the specified rectangle. The screen pixel co-ordinates (x1, y1) and (x2, y2) define the enclosing rectangle for the chord. (x3,y3) is the starting point for the line, and (x4, y4) is the ending point. Its syntax is:

```
canvas.Chord(X1, Y1, X2, Y2, X3, Y3, X4, Y4);
```

26.4.11 FillRect

The FillRect method fills a specified rectangle on the canvas using the current brush. Its syntax is:

```
canvas.FillRect(Rect);
```

26.4.12 Clear

The Clear method clears graphics and text generated at run time from a form or image box. Its standard form is:

```
canvas.Clear
```

26.5 Exercises

26.5.1   Write a program which displays a coloured rectangle in the middle of a form. Each time the user clicks on the form the rectangle should change colour.

26.5.2   Write a Delphi program which automatically moves a rectangle from the top left-hand side of the screen to the bottom right-hand side. The program should quit once it reaches the bottom corner.

26.5.3   Write a Delphi program which randomly moves a small rectangle around the screen. If the rectangle touches any of the edges it should rebound off the edge.

26.5.4   Write a Delphi program in which the user controls the movement of a small rectangle by the arrow keys.

26.5.5   Write a Delphi program which displays a circle on the form which follows the user's mouse cursor.

26.5.6   Write separate Delphi programs which draw the following objects:

(i)   A car.
(ii)   A ship.
(iii)   A house.

Turbo Pascal Reference

The following is a list of Turbo Pascal procedures.

Append	GetIntVec	Release
Arc	GetLineSettings	RenameSetDate
Assign	GetMem	ResetSetFAttr
AssignCrt	GetPalette	RestoreCrtMode
Bar	GetTextSettings	Rewrite
Bar3D	GetTime	RmDir
BlockRead	GetVerify	RunError
BlockWrite	GetViewSettings	Sector
ChDir	GotoXY	Seek
Circle	Halt	SetActivePage
ClearDevice	HighVideo	SetAllPalette
ClearViewPort	Inc	SetAspectRatio
Close	InitGraph	SetBkColor
CloseGraph	Insert	SetCBreak
ClrEol	InsLine	SetColor
ClrScr	Intr	SetFillPattern
Dec	Keep	SetFillStyle
Delay	Line	SetFTime
Delete	LineRel	SetGraphMode
DelLine	LineTo	SetIntVec
DetectGraph	LowVideo	SetLineStyle
Dispose	Mark	SetPalette
Ellipse	MkDir	SetRGBPalette
Erase	Move	SetTextBuf
Exec	MoveTo	SetTextJustify
Exit	New	SetTextStyle
Fail	NormVideo	SetTime
FillChar	NoSound	SetUserCharSize
FillEllipse	OutText	SetVerify
FillPoly	OutTextXY	SetViewPort
FindFirst	OvrClrBuf	SetVisualPage
FindNext	OvrInit	SetWriteMode
FloodFill	OvrInitEMS	Str
Flush	OvrSetBuf	SwapVectors
FreeMem	OvrSetRetry	TextBackground
FSplit	PackTime	TextColor

GetArcCoords	PieSlice	TextMode
GetAspectRatio	PutImage	Truncate
GetCBreak	PutPixel	UnPackTime
GetDate	Randomize	Val
GetDir	Read (text)	Window
GetFAttr	Read (typed)	Write (text)
GetFillSettings	ReadLn	Write (typed)
GetFTime	Rectangle	WriteLn
GetImage		

The following is a list of Turbo Pascal functions.

Abs	GetGraphMode	ParamStr
Addr	GetMaxMode	Pi
ArcTan	GetMaxX	Pos
Chr	GetMaxY	Pred
Concat	GetModeName	Ptr
Copy	GetPaletteSize	Random
Cos	GetPixel	ReadKey
Cseg	GetX	Round
DiskFree	GetY	SeekEof
DiskSize	GraphErrorMsg	SeekEoln
DosexitCode	GraphResult	Seg
DosVersion	Hi	SetAspectRatio
Dseg	ImageSize	Sin
EnvCount	InstallUserDriver	SizeOf
EnvStr	InstallUserFont	Sound
Eof (text)	Int	SPtr
Eof (typed)	IOResult	Sqr
Eoln	KeyPressed	Sqrt
Exp	Length	SSeg
FExpand	Lo	Succ
FilePos	MaxAvail	Swap
FileSize	MemAvail	TextHeight
Frac	MsDos	TextWidth
FSearch	Odd	Trunc
GetBkColor	Ofs	TypeOf
GetColor	Ord	UpCase
GetDefaultPalette	OvrGetBuf	WhereX
GetDriverName	OvrGetRetry	WhereY
GetEnv	ParamCount	

Turbo Pascal accesses some standard procedures and functions through units, which are libraries of precompiled modules. For example, the Crt unit contains routines which access the text display. To use a unit the uses keyword must be included in a statement near the top of the program. For example, to use the `clrscr` function:

```
program test;

uses crt;

begin
   clrscr;      (* clears the screen *)
   textcolor(RED);
   textbackground(YELLOW);
   writeln('Hello');
end.
```

The listing of modules in the `crt` unit is:

AssignCrt	InsLine	TextBackground
ClrEol	KeyPressed	TextColor
ClrScr	LowVideo	TextMode
Delay	NormVideo	WhereX
DelLine	NoSound	WhereY
GotoXY	ReadKey	Window
HighVideo	Sound	

The listing of modules in the `system` unit is:

Abs	GetDir	ReadLn
Addr	GetMem	Release
Append	Halt	Rename
ArcTan	Hi	Reset
Assign	Inc	Rewrite
BlockRead	Insert	RmDir
BlockWrite	Int	Round
ChDir	IOResult	RunError
Chr	Length	Seek
Close	Ln	SeekEof
Concat	Lo	SeekEoln
Copy	Mark	Seg
Cos	MaxAvail	SetTextBuf
CSeg	MemAvail	Sin
Dec	MkDir	SizeOf
Delete	Move	Sptr
Dispose	New	Sqr
DSeg	Odd	Sqrt
Eof (text)	Ofs	Sseg
Eof (typed)	Ord	Str
Eoln	ParamCount	Succ

Erase	ParamStr	Swap
Exit	Pi	Trunc
Exp	Pos	Truncate
FilePos	Pred	UpCase
FileSize	Ptr	Val
FillChar	Random	Write (text)
Flush	Randomize	Write (typed)
Frac	Read (text)	WriteLn
FreeMem	Read (typed)	

The listing of modules in the dos unit is:

DiskFree	Fsplit	MsDos
DiskSize	GetCBreak	PackTime
DosExitCode	GetDate	SetCBreak
DosVersion	GetEnv	SetDate
EnvCount	GetFAttr	SetFAttr
EnvStr	GetFTime	SetFTime
Exec	GetIntVec	SetIntVec
Fexpand	GetTime	SetTime
FindFirst	GetVerify	SetVerify
FindNext	Intr	SwapVectors
Fsearch	Keep	UnpackTime

The listing of modules in the graph unit is:

Arc	GetMaxY	PutPixel
Bar	GetModeName	Rectangle
Bar3D	GetModeRange	RegisterBGIdriver
Circle	GetPalette	RegisterBGIfont
ClearDevice	GetPaletteSize	RestoreCrtMode
ClearViewPort	GetPixel	Sector
CloseGraph	GetTextSettings	SetActivePage
DetectGraph	GetViewSettings	SetAllPalette
Drawpoly	GetX	SetAspectRatio
Ellipse	GetY	SetBkColor
FillEllipse	GraphDefaults	SetColor
FillPoly	GraphErrorMsg	SetFillPattern
FloodFill	GraphResult	SetFillStyle
GetArcCoords	ImageSize	SetGraphBufSize
GetAspectRatio	InitGraph	SetGraphMode
GetBkColor	InstallUserDriver	SetLineStyle
GetColor	InstallUserFont	SetPalette
GetDefaultPalette	Line	SetRGBPalette
GetDriverName	LineRel	SetTextJustify

GetFillPattern	LineTo	SetTextStyle
GetFillSettings	MoveRel	SetUserCharSize
GetGraphMode	MoveTo	SetViewPort
GetImage	OutText	SetVisualPage
GetLineSettings	OutTextXY	SetWriteMode
GetMaxColor	PieSlice	TextHeight
GetMaxMode	PutImage	TextWidth
GetMaxX		

The following is a quick reference to commonly used functions.

Abs	`function Abs(x) :` `(Same type as parameter)`	Returns absolute value
ArcTan	`function ArcTan(x : real) :` `real;`	Returns the arctangent of the argument. Turbo Pascal does not have a Tan function, but tangents can be calculated using the expression Sin(x) / Cos(x)
Chr	`function Chr(x : Byte) :` `Char;`	Returns a character with a specified ordinal number

Concat	`function Concat(s1`
	`[, s2, ..., sn] : string):`
	`string;`
		Concatenates a sequence of strings

Copy	`function Copy(s : string;`
	`index : Integer;count :`
	`Integer) : string;`
		Returns a substring of a string

Cos	`function Cos(x : real) :` `real;`	Returns the cosine of the argument.
DiskFree	`function DiskFree(` `Drive: Byte) : Longint;`	Returns the number of free bytes of a specified disk drive. Unit name Dos.
DiskSize	`function DiskSize(` `Drive: Byte) : Longint;`	Returns the total size in bytes of a specified disk drive.
DosVersion	`function DosVersion : Word;`	Returns the DOS version number. The low byte of the result is the major version number, and the high byte is the minor version number. Unit name Dos.
Eof	`function Eof(var f)` `: Boolean;`	Returns the end-of-file status of a typed or untyped file.

Eoln	`function Eoln [` `(var f : text) ] : Boolean;`	Returns the end-of-line status of a file.
Exp	`function Exp(x : real) :` `real;`	Returns the exponential of the argument.
File	`function FilePos(var f) :` `Longint;`	Returns the current file position of a file.
FileSize	`function FileSize(var f) :` `Longint;`	Returns the current size of a file.
Frac	`function Frac(x : real) :` `real;`	Returns the fractional part of the argument.

Fsearch	`function FSearch(Path:`
	`PathStr;DirList:string) :`
	`PathStr;`
		Searches for a file in a list of directories by `DirList`. The directories in `DirList` must be separated by semicolons. The `PathStr` type is defined in the `Dos` unit as string [79]. Unit Name `Dos`.

Int	`function Int(x : real) :` `real;`	Returns the Integer part of the argument.
KeyPressed	`function KeyPressed :` `Boolean;`	Returns True if a key has been pressed on the keyboard, and False otherwise. Unit name `Crt`.
Length	`function Length(s : string) :` `Integer;`	Returns the dynamic length of a string.
MaxAvail	`function MaxAvail : Longint;`	Returns the size of the largest contiguous free block in the heap, corresponding to the size of the largest dynamic variable that can be allocated at that time.
MemAvail	`function MemAvail : Longint;`	Returns sum of all free blocks in the heap.
MsDos	`procedure MsDos(` `var Regs : Registers);`	Executes a DOS function call. Unit name `Dos`.
Odd	`function Odd(x : Longint) :` `Boolean;`	Tests if the argument is an odd number.

Ord	`function Ord(x) : Longint;`	Returns the ordinal number of an ordinal-type value.
SeekEoln	`function SeekEoln [ (var f : text) ]: Boolean;`	Returns the end-of-line status of a file.
Sin	`function Sin(x : real) : real;`	Returns the sine of the argument.
UpCase	`function UpCase(ch : Char) : Char;`	Converts a character to upper case.
WhereX	`function WhereX : Byte;`	Returns the x-co-ordinate of the current cursor position, relative to the current window. Unit name `Crt`.
WhereY	`function WhereY : Byte;`	Returns the y-co-ordinate of the current cursor position, relative to the current window. Unit name `Crt`.

The following is a quick reference to commonly used procedures.

Append	`procedure Append(var f : text);`	Opens an existing file for appending.
Assign	`procedure Assign(var f; name : string);`	Assigns the name of an external file to a file variable.
BlockRead	`procedure BlockRead(var f: file; var buf;count : Word [; var result: Word])`	Reads one or more records into a variable, where f is an untyped file variable, buf is any variable, count is an expression of type Word, and result is a variable of type Word.
BlockWrite	`procedure BlockWrite(var f: file;var buf; count: Word [; var result: Word])`	Writes one or more records from a variable, where f is an untyped file variable, buf is any variable, count is an expression of type Word, and result is a variable of type Word.
ChDir	`procedure ChDir(s : string);`	Changes the current directory.
Close	`procedure Close(var f);`	Closes an open file.

ClrEol	`procedure ClrEol;`	Clears all characters from the cursor position to the end of the line without moving the cursor. Unit name `Crt`.
ClrScr	`procedure ClrScr;`	Clears the active window and places the cursor in the upper left-hand corner. Unit name `Crt`.
Dec	`procedure Dec(var x` `[ ; n : Longint]);`	Decrements a variable.
Delay	`procedure Delay(MS : Word);`	Delays a specified number of milliseconds. Unit name `Crt`.

Delete	`procedure Delete(var s :`
	`string; index : Integer;`
	`count : Integer);`
		Deletes a substring from a string.

DelLine	`procedure DelLine;`	Deletes the line containing the cursor.
Erase	`procedure Erase(var f);`	Erases an external file.
Exec	`procedure Exec(Path,` `CmdLine : string);`	Executes a specified program with a specified command line. Unit name `Dos`.
Exit	`procedure Exit;`	Exits immediately from the current block. If the current block is the main program, it causes the program to terminate.
FillChar	`procedure FillChar(var x;` `count : Word; ch : Char);`	Fills a specified number of contiguous bytes with a specified value.

FindFirst	`procedure FindFirst(Path :`
	`string; Attr : Word;`
	`var S : SearchRec);`
		Searches the specified (or current) directory for the first entry matching the specified file name and set of attributes. Unit name `Dos`.

FindNext	`procedure FindNext(var S :` `SearchRec);`	Returns the next entry that matches the name and attributes specified in an earlier call to `FindFirst`. Unit name `Dos`.

Flush	procedure Flush(var f : text);	Flushes the buffer of a text file open for output.
FreeMem	procedure FreeMem(var p : pointer; size : Word);	Disposes a dynamic variable of a given size. Should not be used with Mark or Release.
GetCBreak	procedure GetCBreak(var Break: Boolean);	Returns the state of Ctrl-Break checking in DOS. Unit Name Dos.
GetDate	procedure GetDate(var Year, Month, Day, DayOfWeek : Word);	Returns the current date set in the operating system. Unit name Dos.
GetDir	procedure GetDir(d : Byte; var s : string);	Returns the current directory of a specified drive.
GetFAttr	procedure GetFAttr(var F; var Attr : Word);	Returns the attributes of a file. Unit name Dos.
GetFTime	procedure GetFTime(var F; var Time : Longint);	Returns the date and time a file was last written. Unit name Dos.
GetIntVec	procedure GetIntVec(IntNo : Byte; var Vector : pointer);	Returns the address stored in a specified interrupt vector. Unit name Dos.
GetMem	procedure GetMem(var p : pointer; size : Word);	Creates a new dynamic variable of the specified size and puts the address of the block in a pointer variable.
GetTime	procedure GetTime(var Hour, Minute, Second, Sec100 : Word);	Returns the current time set in the operating system. Unit name Dos.
GotoXY	procedure GoToXY(X, Y : Byte);	Positions the cursor. Unit name Crt.
Halt	procedure Halt [(exitcode : Word)];	Stops program execution and returns to the operating system.
HighVideo	procedure HighVideo;	Selects high intensity characters. Unit name Crt.
Inc	procedure Inc(var x [; n : Longint]);	Increments a variable.

Insert	```procedure Insert(source : string; var s : string; index : Integer);```	Inserts a substring into a string.
InsLine	```procedure InsLine;```	Inserts an empty line at the cursor position. Unit name Crt.
Intr	```procedure Intr(IntNo : Byte; var Regs : Registers);```	Executes a specified software interrupt. Unit name Dos.
Keep	```procedure Keep(ExitCode : Word);```	Keep (or Terminate Stay Resident) terminates the program and makes it stay in memory. Unit name Dos.
MkDir	```procedure MkDir(s : string);```	Creates a subdirectory.
Move	```procedure Move(var source, dest; count : Word);```	Copies a specified number of contiguous bytes from a source range to a destination range.
NoSound	```procedure NoSound;```	Turns off the internal speaker.
Randomize	```procedure Randomize;```	Initializes the built-in random generator with a random value.
Read	```procedure Read(f , v1 [, v2,...,vn]);```	Reads a file component into a variable.
ReadLn	```procedure ReadLn([var f : text;] v1 [, v2,...,vn]);```	Executes the Read procedure, then skips to the next line of the file.
Rename	```procedure Rename(var f; newname : string);```	Renames an external file.
Reset	```procedure Reset(var f [: file; recsize : Word]);```	Opens an existing file.
Rewrite	```procedure Rewrite(var f : file [;recsize : Word]);```	Creates and opens a new file.
RmDir	```procedure RmDir(s : string);```	Removes an empty subdirectory.
Seek	```procedure Seek(var f; n : Longint);```	Moves the current position of a file to a specified component.
SetCBreak	```procedure SetCBreak(Break: Boolean);```	Sets the state of Ctrl-Break checking in DOS. Unit Name Dos.
SetDate	```procedure SetDate(Year, Month, Day : Word);```	Sets the current date in the operating system. Unit name Dos.

SetFAttr	`procedure SetFAttr(var F; Attr : Word);`	Sets the attributes of a file. Unit name `Dos`.
SetFTime	`procedure SetFTime(var F; Time : Longint);`	Sets the date and time a file was last written. Unit name `Dos`.
SetIntVec	`procedure SetIntVec(IntNo : Byte; Vector : pointer);`	Sets a specified interrupt vector to a specified address. Unit name `Dos`.
SetTime	`procedure SetTime(Hour, Minute, Second, Sec100 : Word);`	Sets the current time in the operating system. Unit name `Dos`.
Str	`procedure Str(x [ : width [ : decimals ]]; var s : string);`	Converts a numeric value to the same string representation that would be output by Write.
TextColor	`procedure TextColor(Color : Byte);`	Selects the foreground character colour. Unit name `Crt`.
TextMode	`procedure TextMode(Mode : Integer);`	Selects a specific text mode. Unit name `Crt`.
Truncate	`procedure Truncate(var f);`	Truncates the file size at the current file position.
Val	`procedure Val(s : string; var v; var code : Integer);`	Converts the string value to its numeric representation, as if it were read from a text file with `Read`. s is a string-type variable; it must be a sequence of characters that form a signed whole number. v is an integer-type or real-type variable.
Window	`procedure Window(X1, Y1, X2, Y2 : Byte);`	Defines a text window on the screen. Unit name `Crt`.
Write	`procedure Write(f, v1 [, v2,...,vn ] );`	Writes a variable into a file component.
WriteLn	`procedure WriteLn( [ var f : text; ] v1 [, v2,...,vn ] );`	Executes the `Write` procedure, then outputs an end-of-line marker to the file.

B ASCII

ANSI defined a standard alphabet known as ASCII. This has since been adopted by the CCITT as a standard, known as IA5 (International Alphabet No. 5). The following tables define this alphabet in binary, as a decimal, as a hexadecimal value and as a character.

Binary	Decimal	Hex	Character	Binary	Decimal	Hex	Character
00000000	0	00	NUL	00010000	16	10	DLE
00000001	1	01	SOH	00010001	17	11	DC1
00000010	2	02	STX	00010010	18	12	DC2
00000011	3	03	ETX	00010011	19	13	DC3
00000100	4	04	EOT	00010100	20	14	DC4
00000101	5	05	ENQ	00010101	21	15	NAK
00000110	6	06	ACK	00010110	22	16	SYN
00000111	7	07	BEL	00010111	23	17	ETB
00001000	8	08	BS	00011000	24	18	CAN
00001001	9	09	HT	00011001	25	19	EM
00001010	10	0A	LF	00011010	26	1A	SUB
00001011	11	0B	VT	00011011	27	1B	ESC
00001100	12	0C	FF	00011100	28	1C	FS
00001101	13	0D	CR	00011101	29	1D	GS
00001110	14	0E	SO	00011110	30	1E	RS
00001111	15	0F	SI	00011111	31	1F	US

Binary	Decimal	Hex	Character	Binary	Decimal	Hex	Character
00100000	32	20	SPACE	00110000	48	30	0
00100001	33	21	!	00110001	49	31	1
00100010	34	22	\\	00110010	50	32	2
00100011	35	23	#	00110011	51	33	3
00100100	36	24	$	00110100	52	34	4
00100101	37	25	%	00110101	53	35	5
00100110	38	26	&	00110110	54	36	6
00100111	39	27	/	00110111	55	37	7
00101000	40	28	(	00111000	56	38	8
00101001	41	29	)	00111001	57	39	9
00101010	42	2A	*	00111010	58	3A	:
00101011	43	2B	+	00111011	59	3B	;
00101100	44	2C	,	00111100	60	3C	<
00101101	45	2D	–	00111101	61	3D	=
00101110	46	2E	.	00111110	62	3E	>
00101111	47	2F	/	00111111	63	3F	?

Binary	Decimal	Hex	Character	Binary	Decimal	Hex	Character
01000000	64	40	@	01010000	80	50	P
01000001	65	41	A	01010001	81	51	Q
01000010	66	42	B	01010010	82	52	R
01000011	67	43	C	01010011	83	53	S
01000100	68	44	D	01010100	84	54	T
01000101	69	45	E	01010101	85	55	U
01000110	70	46	F	01010110	86	56	V
01000111	71	47	G	01010111	87	57	W
01001000	72	48	H	01011000	88	58	X
01001001	73	49	I	01011001	89	59	Y
01001010	74	4A	J	01011010	90	5A	Z
01001011	75	4B	K	01011011	91	5B	[
01001100	76	4C	L	01011100	92	5C	\
01001101	77	4D	M	01011101	93	5D	]
01001110	78	4E	N	01011110	94	5E	^
01001111	79	4F	O	01011111	95	5F	_

Binary	Decimal	Hex	Character	Binary	Decimal	Hex	Character
01100000	96	60	`	01110000	112	70	p
01100001	97	61	a	01110001	113	71	q
01100010	98	62	b	01110010	114	72	r
01100011	99	63	c	01110011	115	73	s
01100100	100	64	d	01110100	116	74	t
01100101	101	65	e	01110101	117	75	u
01100110	102	66	f	01110110	118	76	v
01100111	103	67	g	01110111	119	77	w
01101000	104	68	h	01111000	120	78	x
01101001	105	69	i	01111001	121	79	y
01101010	106	6A	j	01111010	122	7A	z
01101011	107	6B	k	01111011	123	7B	{
01101100	108	6C	l	01111100	124	7C	:
01101101	109	6D	m	01111101	125	7D	}
01101110	110	6E	n	01111110	126	7E	~
01101111	111	6F	o	01111111	127	7F	DEL

The standard ASCII character set is a 7-bit character and ranges from 0 to 127. This code is rather limited as it does not contain symbols such as Greek letters, lines, and so on. For this purpose the extended ASCII code has been defined. This fits into character numbers 128 to 255. The following four tables define a typical extended ASCII character set.

Binary	Decimal	Hex	Character	Binary	Decimal	Hex	Character
10000000	128	80	ç	10010000	144	90	É
10000001	129	81	ü	10010001	145	91	æ
10000010	130	82	é	10010010	146	92	Æ
10000011	131	83	â	10010011	147	93	ô
10000100	132	84	ä	10010100	148	94	ö
10000101	133	85	à	10010101	149	95	ò
10000110	134	86	å	10010110	150	96	û
10000111	135	87	ç	10010111	151	97	ù
10001000	136	88	ê	10011000	152	98	ÿ
10001001	137	89	ë	10011001	153	99	Ö
10001010	138	8A	è	10011010	154	9A	Ü
10001011	139	8B	ï	10011011	155	9B	¢
10001100	140	8C	î	10011100	156	9C	£
10001101	141	8D	ì	10011101	157	9D	¥
10001110	142	8E	Ä	10011110	158	9E	₧
10001111	143	8F	Å	10011111	159	9F	ƒ

Binary	Decimal	Hex	Character	Binary	Decimal	Hex	Character
10100000	160	A0	á	10110000	176	B0	▓
10100001	161	A1	í	10110001	177	B1	▒
10100010	162	A2	ó	10110010	178	B2	█
10100011	163	A3	ú	10110011	179	B3	│
10100100	164	A4	ñ	10110100	180	B4	┤
10100101	165	A5	Ñ	10110101	181	B5	╡
10100110	166	A6	ª	10110110	182	B6	╢
10100111	167	A7	º	10110111	183	B7	╖
10101000	168	A8	¿	10111000	184	B8	╕
10101001	169	A9	⌐	10111001	185	B9	╣
10101010	170	AA	¬	10111010	186	BA	║
10101011	171	AB	½	10111011	187	BB	╗
10101100	172	AC	¼	10111100	188	BC	╝
10101101	173	AD	¡	10111101	189	BD	╜
10101110	174	AE	«	10111110	190	BE	╛
10101111	175	AF	»	10111111	191	BF	┐

Binary	Decimal	Hex	Character	Binary	Decimal	Hex	Character
11000000	192	C0	L	11010000	208	D0	Ⅱ
11000001	193	C1	⊥	11010001	209	D1	╤
11000010	194	C2	T	11010010	210	D2	Ⅱ
11000011	195	C3	├	11010011	211	D3	Ⅱ
11000100	196	C4	—	11010100	212	D4	╘
11000101	197	C5	+	11010101	213	D5	╒
11000110	198	C6	╞	11010110	214	D6	╓
11000111	199	C7	╟	11010111	215	D7	╫
11001000	200	C8	╚	11011000	216	D8	╪
11001001	201	C9	╔	11011001	217	D9	┘
11001010	202	CA	╩	11011010	218	DA	┌
11001011	203	CB	╦	11011011	219	DB	■
11001100	204	CC	╠	11011100	220	DC	▄
11001101	205	CD	=	11011101	221	DD	▌
11001110	206	CE	╬	11011110	222	DE	▐ `
11001111	207	CF	╧	11011111	223	DF	▀

Binary	Decimal	Hex	Character	Binary	Decimal	Hex	Character
11100000	224	E0	α	11110000	240	F0	Ξ
11100001	225	E1	ß	11110001	241	F1	±
11100010	226	E2	Γ	11110010	242	F2	≥
11100011	227	E3	π	11110011	243	F3	≤
11100100	228	E4	Σ	11110100	244	F4	⌠
11100101	229	E5	σ	11110101	245	F5	⌡
11100110	230	E6	μ	11110110	246	F6	÷
11100111	231	E7	τ	11110111	247	F7	≈
11101000	232	E8	Φ	11111000	248	F8	°
11101001	233	E9	Θ	11111001	249	F9	•
11101010	234	EA	Ω	11111010	250	FA	·
11101011	235	EB	δ	11111011	251	FB	√
11101100	236	EC	φ	11111100	252	FC	ⁿ
11101101	237	ED	φ	11111101	253	FD	²
11101110	238	EE	E	11111110	254	FE	■
11101111	239	EF	Λ	11111111	255	FF	□

Pascal character conversion examples:

```
var   ch:char;
      val:integer;

begin
      ch:= 'a';
      val:=ord(ch); (* convert to an ASCII integer *)
      writeln('ASCII value for an "A" character is ',val);
      val:=65;
      ch:=chr(val); (* convert to an ASCII character *)
      writeln('ASCII character is a 65 is ',ch);
      write('New-line character is ',#13, ' the bell is ',#7);
end.
```

Bits, Bytes and Operators

C.1 Bits and bytes

A computer operates on binary digits named bits. These can either store a '1' or a '0' (ON/ OFF). A group of 4 bits is a nibble and a group of 8 bits a byte. These 8-bits provide 256 different combinations of ON/OFF, from 00000000 to 11111111. A 16-bit field is known as a word and a 32-bit field as a long word. Binary data is stored in memories which are either permanent or non-permanent. This data is arranged as bytes and each byte has a different memory address, as illustrated in Figure C.1.

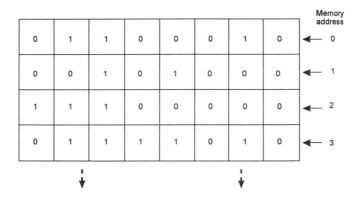

Figure C.1   Memory storage (each address holds eight bits)

C.1.1 Binary numbers

A computer operates on binary digits which use a base-2 numbering system. To determine the decimal equivalent of a binary number each column is represented by 2 raised to the power of 0, 1, 2, and so on. For example, the decimal equivalents of 1000 0001 and 0101 0011 are:

2^7	2^6	2^5	2^4	2^3	2^2	2^1	2^0	
128	64	32	16	8	4	2	1	Decimal
1	0	0	0	0	0	0	1	129
0	1	0	1	0	0	1	1	83

Thus `01001111` gives:

$(0 \times 128) + (1 \times 64) + (0 \times 32) + (0 \times 16) + (1 \times 8) + (1 \times 4) + (1 \times 2) + (1 \times 1) = 95$

The number of decimal values that a binary number can represent relates to the number of bits. For example:

- 8 bits gives 0 to $2^8 - 1$ (255) different representations;
- 16 bits gives 0 to $2^{16} - 1$ (65 535) different representations;
- 32 bits gives 0 to $2^{32} - 1$ (4 294 967 295) different representations.

The most significant bit (msb) is at the left-hand side of the binary number and the least significant bit (lsb) on the right-hand side. To convert from decimal (base-10) to binary the decimal value is divided by 2 recursively and remainder noted. The first remainder gives the least significant digit (LSD) and the last the most significant digit (MSD). For example:

```
2 | 54
    27      r 0 <<< LSD
    13      r 1
    6       r 1
    3       r 0
    1       r 1
    0       r 1 <<< MSD
```

Thus `110110` in binary is 54 decimal.

C.2 Binary arithmetic

The basic binary addition operation is given next.

$0 + 0 = 0$ $1 + 0 = 1$ $1 + 1 = 10$ $1 + 1 + 1 = 11$

This is used when adding two binary numbers together. For example:

```
  0010001
  0001111
  0100000
   11111
```

C.3 Numbers and representations

Numbers are stored in several different ways. These can be:

- Integers or floating point values.
- Single precision or double precision numbers.
- Signed or unsigned integers.

C.3.1 Negative numbers

Signed integers use a notation called 2s complement to represent negative values. In this representation the binary digits have a '1' in the most significant bit column if the number is negative, else it is a '0'. To convert a decimal value into 2s complement notation, the magnitude of the negative number is represented in binary form. Next, all the bits are inverted and a '1' is added. For example, to determine the 16-bit 2s complement of the value –65, the following steps are taken:

+65	00000000 01000001
invert	11111111 10111110
add 1	11111111 10111111

Thus, –65 is 11111111 1011111 in 16-bit 2s complement notation. Table C.1 shows that with 16 bits the range of values that can be represented in 2s complement is from –32 767 to 32 768 (that is, 65 536 values).

Table C.1   16-bit 2s complement notation

Decimal	2s complement
–32 768	10000000 00000000
–32 767	10000000 00000001
::::	::::
–2	11111111 11111110
–1	11111111 11111111
0	00000000 00000000
1	00000000 00000001
2	00000000 00000010
::::	::
32 766	01111111 11111110
32 767	01111111 11111111

When subtracting one value from another the value to be taken away is first converted into 2s complement format. This is then added to the other value and the result is in 2s complement. For example, to subtract 42 from 65, first 42 is converted into 2s complement (that is, –42) and added to the binary equivalent of 65. The result gives a carry into the sign bit and a carry-out.

```
         65           0100 0001
        -42           1101 0110
                ─────────────────
                 (1)  0001 0111
```

C.3.2 Hexadecimal and octal numbers

In assembly language binary numbers are represented with a proceeding b, for example 010101111010b and 101111101010b are binary numbers. Binary digits are often commonly represented in hexadecimal (base 16) or octal (base 8) representation. Table C.2 shows the basic conversion between decimal, binary, octal and hexadecimal numbers. In this text, hexadecimal numbers have a proceeding h. For example, 43F1h is a hexadecimal value.

To represent a binary digit as a hexadecimal value the binary digits are split into groups of four bits (starting from the least significant bit). A hexadecimal equivalent value then replaces each of the binary groups. For example, to represent 0111010111000000b the bits are split into sections of 4 to give:

Binary	0111	0101	1100	0000
Hex	7	5	C	0

Table C.2 Decimal, binary, octal and hexadecimal conversions

Decimal	Binary	Octal	Hex
0	0000	0	0
1	0001	1	1
2	0010	2	2
3	0011	3	3
4	0100	4	4
5	0101	5	5
6	0110	6	6
7	0111	7	7
8	1000	10	8
9	1001	11	9
10	1010	12	A
11	1011	13	B
12	1100	14	C
13	1101	15	D
14	1110	16	E
15	1111	17	F

Thus, 75C0h represents the binary number 0111010111000000b. To convert from decimal to hexadecimal the decimal value is divided by 16 recursively and each remainder noted. The first remainder gives the least significant digit and the final remainder the most significant digit. For example, the following shows the hexadecimal equivalent of the decimal number 1103:

```
16 │ 1103
       68   r F   <<< LSD (least significant digit)
        4   r 4
        0   r 4  <<< MSD (most significant digit)
```

Thus the decimal value 1103 is equivalent to 044Fh.

In Pascal, hexadecimal values are preceded by a dollar sign ($), for example $C4.

C.4 Pascal operators

Pascal has a rich set of operators; there are four main types:

- Arithmetic.
- Logical.
- Bitwise.
- Relational.

C.4.1 Arithmetic

Arithmetic operators operate on numerical values. The basic arithmetic operations are add (+), subtract (−), multiply (*), divide (/) and modulus division (mod). Modulus division gives the remainder of an integer division. The following gives the basic syntax of two operands with an arithmetic operator.

---

operand *operator* operand

The assignment operator (:=) is used when a variable 'takes on the value' of an operation. Table C.3 summarizes the arithmetic operators.

Table C.3 Arithmetic operators

Operator	Operation	Example
−	subtraction or minus	5−4→1
+	addition	4+2→6
*	multiplication	4*3→12
/	division	4/2→2
div	integer division	5 div 2 →2
mod	modulus	13%3→1
:=	assignment	x = 1

C.4.2 Relationship

The relationship operators determine whether the result of a comparison is TRUE or FALSE. These operators are greater than (>), greater than or equal to (>=), less than (<), less than or equal to (<=), equal to (=) and not equal to (<>). Table C.4 lists the relationship operators.

Table C.4 Relationship operators

Operator	Function	Example	TRUE Condition
>	greater than	(b>a)	when b is greater than a
>=	greater than or equal	(a>=4)	when a is greater than or equal to 4
<	less than	(c<f)	when c is less than f
<=	less than or equal	(x<=4)	when x is less than or equal to 4
==	equal to	(x==2)	when x is equal to 2
<>	not equal to	(y!=x)	when y is not equal to x

C.4.3 Logical (TRUE or FALSE)

A logical operation is one in which a decision is made as to whether the operation performed is TRUE or FALSE. If required, several relationship operations can be grouped together to give the required functionality. Table C.5 lists the logical operators.

Table C.5 Logical operators

Operator	Example	TRUE condition
and	((x=1) and (y<2))	when x is equal to 1 and y is less than 2
or	((a<>b) or (a>0))	when a is not equal to b or a is greater than 0
not	(not(a>0))	when a is not greater than 0

Logical and operation will only yield a TRUE only if all the operands are TRUE. Table C.6 gives the result of the and operator for the operation Operand1 and Operand2. The logical OR operation yields a TRUE if any one of the operands is TRUE. Table C.6 gives the logical results of the or operator for the statement Operand1 or Operand2.

Table C.6 Logical truth table for and and or

Operand1	Operand2	and	or
FALSE	FALSE	FALSE	FALSE
FALSE	TRUE	FALSE	TRUE
TRUE	FALSE	FALSE	TRUE
TRUE	TRUE	TRUE	TRUE

Table C.7 gives the logical result of the NOT operator for the statement not(Operand).

Table C.7 NOT logical truth table

Operand	Result
FALSE	TRUE
TRUE	FALSE

For example, if a has the value 1 and b is also 1, then the following relationship statements would apply:

Statement	Result
(a=1) and (b=1)	TRUE
(a>1) and (b=1)	FALSE
(a=10) or (b=1)	TRUE
not(a=12)	TRUE

C.4.4 Bitwise

The bitwise operators are similar to the logical operators but they should not be confused as their operation differs. Bitwise operators operate directly on the individual bits of an operand(s), whereas logical operators determine whether a condition is TRUE or FALSE.

The basic bitwise operations are and, or, xor, shl and shr. Table C.8 gives the results of the AND bitwise operation on two bits *Bit1* and *Bit2*. Table C.8 also gives the truth table for the bit operation of the or and xor bitwise operators with two bits *Bit1* and *Bit2*.

Table C.8 Bitwise and, or and xor truth table

Bit1	Bit2	and	or	xor
0	0	0	0	0
0	1	0	1	1
1	0	0	1	1
1	1	1	1	0

Table C.9 gives the truth table for the not bitwise operator on a single bit.

Table C.9 Bitwise not truth table

Bit	Result
0	1
1	0

The bitwise operators operate on each of the individual bits of the operands. For example, if two decimal integers 58 and 41 (assuming eight-bit unsigned binary values) are operated on using the AND, OR and EX-OR bitwise operators, then the following will apply.

	AND	OR	EX-OR
58	00111010	00111010	00111010
41	00101001	00101001	00101001
Result	00101000	00111011	00010011

The results of these bitwise operations are as follows:

```
58 and 41  = 40          (00101000)
58 or 41   = 59          (00111011)
58 xor 41  = 19          (00010011)
```

To perform bit shifts, the shl and shr operators are used. These shift the bits in the operand by a given number defined by a value given on the right-hand side of the operation. The left shift operator (shl) shifts the bits of the operand to the left and zeros fill the result on the right. The right shift operator (shr) shifts the bits of the operand to the right and zeros fill the result if the integer is positive; otherwise it will fill with 1's. The standard format is:

```
operand >> no_of_bit_shift_positions
operand << no_of_bit_shift_positions
```

For example, if y = 59 (00111011), then y shr 3 will equate to 7 (00000111) and y shl 2 to 236 (11101100).

C.4.5 Precedence

The rules of precedence are:

1. An operand between two operators of different precedence is bound to the

operator with higher precedence.

2. An operand between two equal operators is bound to the one on its left.
3. Expressions within parentheses are evaluated before being treated as a single operand.
4. The priority levels for operators are as follows:

HIGHEST PRIORITY

( )	primary
not	unary
* / div mod	arithmetic and multiply
and shl shr	operators
+ - or xor	additive operators
= <> < >	relational
< > <= >=	comparison

LOWEST PRIORITY

For example:

```
23 + 5 mod 3 div 2 shl 1    =>
23 + 2 div 2 shl 1          =>
23 + 1 shl 1                =>
23 + 2                      => 25
```

Delphi Reference

D.1 Standard units

The main Delphi units are:

- **Buttons**. Contains declarations for SpeedButtons and bitmapped buttons.
- **Classes**. Contains declarations for many of the base object classes.
- **ClipBrd**. Contains declaration for the clipboard object and creates an instance of the clipboard.
- **Controls**. Contains declarations for TControl, TWinControl, TGraphic-Control and TCustomControl and their associated routines and types.
- **DB**. Contains declarations for the TDatabase, TDataSource, and TField components and includes their associated routines and types.
- **DBGrids**. The DBGrids unit contains the declarations for the database grid and its associated routines and types.
- **DDEMan**. Contains components and types for dynamic-data exchange (DDE).
- **Dialogs**. Contains declarations for the common dialog boxes which are found on the Dialogs page of the Component palette and routines for displaying message boxes.
- **ExtCtrls**. Contains the declarations for the certain components on the Standard and Additional pages of the Component palette.
- **FileCtrl**. Contains the declarations for the certain components on the System page of the Component palette.
- **Forms**. Contains declarations for TForm and its associated objects, types, and routines.
- **Graphics**. Contains Delphi support for Windows GDI unit.
- **Grids**. Contains the declarations for TDrawGrid, and TStringGrid and their associated types routines.
- **IniFiles**. Contains the declaration for an object which enables you to read and write your own .INI files.
- **Mask**. Contains declarations character masks and picture fields.
- **Menus**. Contains declarations for TMainMenu and TPopupMenu and their associated objects, types, and routines.

- **Mplayer**. Contains declarations for the media player component.
- **Outline**. Contains declarations for TOutline.
- **Printers**. Contains declarations for TPrinter and its associated objects.
- **Report**. Contains declarations for TReport and its associated objects.
- **StdCtrls**. Contains declarations for the components that appear on the Standard page of the Component palette.
- **System**. Contains Delphi run-time library, which implements low-level run-time support routines for all built-in features.
- **SysUtils**. Contains declarations for exception classes, string routines, date and time routines and utility routines.
- **TOCtrl**. Contains declarations for the Ole container for object linking and embedding with other OLE applications.
- **WinProcs**. Defines function and procedure headers for the Windows API.
- **WinTypes**. Defines all the types used by Windows API routines.

D.2 Forms unit

The Forms unit contains declarations for TForm and all its associated objects, types, and routines. The following items are declared in the Forms unit:

Components
    TForm
    TScrollBox

Objects
    TApplication
    TControlScrollBar
    TDesigner
    TScreen
    TScrollingWinControl

Types
    TBorderIcons
    TBorderStyle
    TCloseAction
    TCloseEvent
    TCloseQueryEvent
    TCursorRec
    TExceptionEvent
    TFormBorderStyle
    TFormClass
    TFormState
    TFormStyle
    TIdleEvent
    TMessageEvent
    TModalResult

```
TPosition
TPrintScale
TScrollBarInc
TScrollBarKind
TShowAction
TTileMode
TWindowHook
TWindowState
TWndMethod
```

Variables
```
Application
HintWindow
Screen
```

Constants
```
Ctl3DBtnWndProc
Ctl3DCtlColorEx
Ctl3DDlgFramePaint
```

Routines
```
AllocateHWnd
DeallocateHWnd
DisableTaskWindow
EnableTaskWindow
FreeObjectInstance
GetarentForm
IsAccel
KeyDataToShiftState
KeysToShiftState
MakeObjectInstance
ValidParentForm
```

D.3 WinProcs Unit

The WinProcs unit defines function and procedure headers for the Windows API. These routines provide access to the standard Win32 libraries. They include:

_hread	File read
_hwrite	File write
_lclose	Close a file
_lcreat	File creation
_llseek	Moves file pointer
_lopen	File open
_lread	File read
_lwrite	File write
AbortDoc	Print job termination

AddFontResource	Adds a font to the font table
AdjustWindowRect	Determines the required size of a window rectangle
AllocDiskSpace	Creates a file with some disk space
AllocDStoCSAlias	Translates a data segment to a code segment
AllocFileHandles	Allocates file handles
AllocGDIMem	Allocates all available memory in the GDI heap.
AllocMem	Allocates all available memory.
AllocResource	Allocates memory for a resource
AllocUserMem	Allocates all available memory in the User heap.
AnsiLower	Converts a string to lower case
AnsiLowerBuff	Converts a string buffer to lower case
AnsiNext	Moves to the next character in a string
AnsiPrev	Move to the previous character in a string
AnsiToOem	Translates a Windows string to an OEM string
AnsiUpper	Converts a string to upper case
AnsiUpperBuff	Converts a string buffer to upper case
AnyPopup	Indicates if pop-up or overlapped window exists
AppendMenu	Appends a new item to a menu
Arc	Draws an arc
ArrangeIconicWindows	Arranges minimized child windows
BeginPaint	Prepares a window for painting
BitBlt	Copies a bitmap between device contexts
CallWindowProc	Passes a message to a window procedure
Catch	Captures the current execution environment
ChangeClipboardChain	Removes a window from the clipboard-viewer chain
CheckDlgButton	Changes a check mark by a dialog button
CheckMenuItem	Changes a check mark by a menu item
CheckRadioButton	Places a check mark by a radio button
ChooseColor	Creates a colour-selection dialog box
ChooseFont	Creates a font-selection dialog box
Chord	Draws a chord
ClearCommBreak	Restores character transmission
ClientToScreen	Converts client point to screen coordinates
ClipCursor	Confines the cursor to a specified rectangle
CloseClipboard	Closes the clipboard
CloseComm	Closes a communications device
CloseDriver	Closes an installable driver
CloseMetaFile	Closes metafile dc and gets handle
CloseWindow	Minimizes a window
CombineRgn	Creates a region by combining two regions
CopyCursor	Copies a cursor
CopyIcon	Copies an icon
CopyLZFile	Copies a file and decompresss it if compressed
CopyMetaFile	Copies a metafile
CopyRect	Copies the dimensions of a rectangle
CountClipboardFormats	Returns the number of clipboard formats
CreateBitmap	Creates device-dependent memory bitmap

CreateCursor	Creates a cursor with specified dimensions
CreateDC	Creates a device context
CreateDialog	Creates a modeless dialog box
CreateDIBitmap	Creates bitmap handle from DIB spec
CreateDIBPatternBrush	Creates a pattern brush from a DIB
CreateEllipticRgn	Creates an elliptical region
CreateEllipticRgnIndirect	Creates an elliptical region
CreateFont	Creates a logical font
CreateHatchBrush	Creates a hatched brush
CreateIcon	Creates an icon with the specified dimensions
CreateMenu	Creates a menu
CreateMetaFile	Creates a metafile device context
CreatePalette	Creates a logical colour palette
CreatePatternBrush	Creates a pattern brush from a bitmap
CreatePen	Creates a pen
CreatePolygonRgn	Creates a polygonal region
CreatePolyPolygonRgn	Creates a region consisting of polygons
CreatePopupMenu	Creates a pop-up window
CreateRectRgn	Creates a rectangular region
CreateRoundRectRgn	Creates a rectangular region with round corners
CreateSolidBrush	Creates a solid brush with a specified colour
CreateWindow	Creates a window
DdeAbandonTransaction	Abandons an asynchronous transaction
DdeAccessData	Accesses a DDE global memory object
DdeAddData	Adds data to a DDE global memory object
DdeClientTransaction	Begins a DDE data transaction
DdeCmpStringHandles	Compares two DDE string handles
DdeConnect	Establishes a conversation with a server
DdeConnectList	Establishes multiple DDE conversations
DdeCreateDataHandle	Creates a DDE data handle
DdeCreateStringHandle	Creates a DDE string handle
DdeDisconnect	Terminates a DDE conversation
DdeDisconnectList	Destroys a DDE conversation list
DdeEnableCallback	Enables or disables one or more DDE conversations
DdeFreeDataHandle	Frees a global memory object
DdeFreeStringHandle	Frees a DDE string handle
DdeGetData	Copies data from a global memory object to a buffer
DdeGetLastError	Returns an error code set by a DDEML function
DdeInitialize	Registers an application with the DDEML
DdeKeepStringHandle	Increments the usage count for a string handle
DdeNameService	Registers or unregisters a service name
DdePostAdvise	Prompts a server to send advise data to a client
DdeQueryConvInfo	Gets information about a DDE conversation
DdeQueryNextServer	Obtains the next handle in a conversation list
DdeQueryString	Copies string-handle text to a buffer
DdeReconnect	Reestablishes a conversation with a server
DdeSetUserHandle	Associates a user-defined handle with a transaction

DdeUnaccessData	Frees a DDE global memory object
DdeUninitialize	Frees an application's DDEML resources
DefDriverProc	Calls the default installable-driver procedure
DeferWindowPos	Updates a multiple window position structure
DefFrameProc	Default MDI frame window message processing
DefHookProc	Calls the next function in a hook-function chain
DefMDIChildProc	Default MDI child window message processing
DefScreenSaverProc	Calls default screen-saver window procedure
DefWindowProc	Calls the default window procedure
DeleteDC	Deletes a device context
DeleteMenu	Deletes an item from a menu
DeleteMetaFile	Invalidates a metafile handle
DeleteObject	Deletes an object from memory
DestroyCaret	Destroys the current caret
DestroyCursor	Destroys a cursor
DestroyIcon	Destroys an icon
DestroyMenu	Destroys a menu
DestroyWindow	Destroys a window
DeviceCapabilities	Gets the capabilities of a device
DeviceMode	Displays dialog box for printing modes
DialogBox	Creates a modal dialog box
DialogBoxIndirect	Creates modal dialog box from template in memory
DialogBoxIndirectParam	Creates modal dialog box from template in memory
DialogBoxParam	Creates a modal dialog box
DirectedYield	Forces execution to continue at a specified task
DispatchMessage	Dispatches a message to a window
DlgChangePassword	Changes password for screen saver
DlgDirList	Fills a directory list box
DlgGetPassword	Gets password for screen saver
DlgInvalidPassword	Warns of invalid screen saver password
DOS3Call	Issues a DOS Int 21h function request
DragAcceptFiles	Registers whether a windows accepts dropped files
DragFinish	Releases memory allocated for dropping files
DragQueryFile	Gets filename of dropped file.
DragQueryPoint	Gets mouse position at file drop
DrawFocusRect	Draws a rectangle in the focus style
DrawIcon	Draws an icon in the specified device context
DrawMenuBar	Redraws the menu bar
DrawText	Draws formatted text in a rectangle
Ellipse	Draws an ellipse
EmptyClipboard	Empties the clipboard and frees data handles
EnableCommNotification	Enables/disables WM_COMMNOTIFY posting to window
EnableHardwareInput	Controls mouse and keyboard input queuing
EnableMenuItem	Enabls, disables, or grays a menu item
EnableScrollBar	Enables or disables scroll-bar arrows
EnableWindow	Sets the window-enable state
EndDialog	Hides a modal dialog box

EndDoc	Ends a print job
EndPage	Ends a page
EndPaint	Marks end of painting in the specified window
EqualRect	Determines whether two rectangles are equal
EqualRgn	Compares two regions for equality
Escape	Allows access to device facilities
EscapeCommFunction	Passes an extended function to a device
ExcludeClipRect	Changes clipping region, excluding rectangle
ExcludeUpdateRgn	Excludes an updated region from clipping region
ExitWindows	Restarts or terminates Windows
ExitWindowsExec	Terminates Windows, runs MS-DOS app
ExtDeviceMode	Displays dialog box for printing modes
ExtFloodFill	Fills area with current brush
ExtractIcon	Gets handle of icon from executable file
ExtTextOut	Writes a character string in rectangular region
FatalAppExit	Terminates an application
FatalExit	Displays debug info., causes breakpoint exception
FillRect	Fills a rectangle with the specified brush
FillRgn	Fills a region with a brush
FindExecutable	Gets name and handle of program for a file
FindResource	Locates a resource in a resource file
FindText	Creates a find-text dialog box
FindWindow	Returns window handle for class and window name
FlashWindow	Flashes a window once
FloodFill	Fills area with current brush
FlushComm	Flushes a transmit or receive queue
FrameRect	Draws a window border with a specified brush
FrameRgn	Draws a border around a region
FreeAllGDIMem	Frees memory allocated by AllocGDIMem.
FreeAllMem	Frees memory allocated by AllocMem.
FreeAllUserMem	Frees memory allocated by AllocUserMem.
FreeResource	Unloads a resource instance
FreeSelector	Frees an allocated selector
GetActiveWindow	Gets the handle of the active window
GetAspectRatioFilter	Gets setting of aspect-ratio filter
GetAspectRatioFilterEx	Gets current aspect-ratio filter
GetAsyncKeyState	Determines key state
GetBitmapBits	Copies bitmap bits to a buffer
GetBitmapDimension	Gets width and height of bitmap
GetBitmapDimensionEx	Gets width and height of bitmap
GetBkColor	Gets the current background colour
GetBkMode	Gets the background mode
GetBoundsRect	Returns current accumulated bounding rectangle
GetBrushOrg	Gets the origin of the current brush
GetBrushOrgEx	Gets the origin of the current brush
GetCapture	Returns the handle for the mouse-capture window
GetCaretBlinkTime	Returns the caret blink rate

GetCaretPos	Returns the current caret position
GetCharABCWidths	Gets widths of TrueType characters
GetCharWidth	Gets character widths
GetClassInfo	Returns window class information
GetClassLong	Returns window-class data
GetClassName	Returns window class name
GetClassWord	Returns window class memory word
GetClientRect	Returns window client area coordinates
GetClipboardData	Returns a handle to clipboard data
GetClipboardFormatName	Returns registered clipboard format name
GetClipboardOwner	Returns clipboard owner window handle
GetClipboardViewer	Returns first clipboard viewer window handle
GetClipBox	Gets rectangle for clipping region
GetClipCursor	Returns cursor-confining rectangle coordinates
GetCodeHandle	Determines the location of a function
GetCodeInfo	Gets code-segment information
GetCommError	Returns communications-device status
GetCommEventMask	Gets the device event mask
GetCommState	Reads communications device status
GetCurrentPosition	Gets current position
GetCurrentPositionEx	Gets position in logical units
GetCurrentTask	Returns current task handle
GetCurrentTime	Returns elapsed time since Windows started
GetCursor	Returns current cursor handle
GetCursorPos	Returns current cursor position
GetDC	Returns window device-context handle
GetDCEx	Gets the handle of a device context
GetDCOrg	Gets translation origin for device context
GetDesktopWindow	Returns desktop window handle
GetDeviceCaps	Gets device capabilities
GetDialogBaseUnits	Returns dialog base units
GetDIBits	Copies DIB bits into a buffer
GetDlgCtrlID	Returns child window ID
GetDlgItem	Returns handle of a dialog control
GetDlgItemInt	Translates dialog text into an integer
GetDlgItemText	Gets dialog control text
GetDOSEnvironment	Returns a far pointer to the current environment
GetDoubleClickTime	Returns mouse double click time
GetDriverInfo	Gets installable-driver data
GetDriverModuleHandle	Gets an installable-driver instance handle
GetDriveType	Determines drive type
GetExpandedName	Gets original filename for a compressed file
GetFileResource	Copies a resource into a buffer
GetFileResourceSize	Returns the size of a resource
GetFileTitle	Gets a filename
GetFileVersionInfo	Returns version information about a file
GetFileVersionInfoSize	Returns the size of a file's version information

GetFocus	Returns current focus window handle
GetFontData	Gets font metric data
GetFreeFileHandles	Returns the number of free file handles
GetFreeSpace	Returns number of free bytes in the global heap
GetFreeSystemResources	Returns percentage of free system resource space
GetInputState	Returns mouse, keyboard and timer queue status
GetInstanceData	Copy previous instance data into current instance
GetKBCodePage	Returns the current code page
GetKerningPairs	Gets kerning pairs for current font
GetKeyboardState	Returns virtual-keyboard keys status
GetKeyboardType	Gets keyboard information
GetKeyNameText	Gets string representing the name of a key
GetKeyState	Returns specified virtual key state
GetLastActivePopup	Determines most recently active pop-up window
GetMapMode	Gets mapping mode
GetMenu	Returns menu handle for the specified window
GetMenuItemCount	Returns the number of items in a menu
GetMenuItemID	Returns a menu-item identifier
GetMenuState	Returns status flags for the specified menu item
GetMenuString	Copies a menu-time label into a buffer
GetMessage	Gets a message from the message queue
GetMessageExtraInfo	Gets information about a hardware message
GetMessagePos	Returns cursor position for last message
GetMessageTime	Returns the time for the last message
GetMetaFile	Creates handle to a metafile
GetMetaFileBits	Creates memory block from metafile
GetModuleFileName	Returns the file name for a module handle
GetModuleHandle	Returns a module handle for a named module
GetModuleUsage	Returns the reference count for a module
GetNearestColor	Gets closest available colour
GetNextDlgGroupItem	Returns handle of previous or next group control
GetNextDriver	Enumerates installable-driver instances
GetNextWindow	Returns next or previous window-manager window
GetNumTasks	Returns the current number of tasks
GetObject	Gets information about an object
GetOpenClipboardWindow	
	Returns handle to window that opened clipboard
GetOpenFileName	Creates an open-filename dialog box
GetOutlineTextMetrics	Gets metrics for TrueType fonts
GetPaletteEntries	Gets range of palette entries
GetParent	Returns parent window handle
GetPixel	Gets RGB colour of specified pixel
GetPolyFillMode	Gets the current polygon-filling mode
GetProfileInt	Gets an integer value from WIN.INI
GetProfileString	Gets a string from WIN.INI
GetProp	Returns data handle from a window property list
GetQueueStatus	Determines queued message type

GetRasterizerCaps	Gets status of TrueType on system
GetRgnBox	Gets bounding rectangle for region
GetSaveFileName	Creates a save-filename dialog box
GetScrollPos	Returns current scroll-bar thumb position
GetScrollRange	Returns minimum and maximum scroll-bar positions
GetSelectorBase	Gets the base address of a selector
GetSelectorLimit	Retrieves the limit of a selector
GetStockObject	Gets handle of a stock pen, brush, or font
GetStretchBltMode	Gets the current bitmap-stretching mode
GetSubMenu	Returns pop-up menu handle
GetSysColor	Returns display-element colour
GetSystemDir	Returns the Windows system subdirectory
GetSystemDirectory	Returns the Windows system directory
GetSystemMenu	Provides access to the System menu
GetSystemMetrics	Gets the system metrics
GetSystemPaletteEntries	Gets entries from system palette
GetTempDrive	Returns a disk drive letter for temporary files
GetTempFileName	Creates a temporary filename
GetTextAlign	Gets text-alignment flags
GetTextCharacterExtra	Gets intercharacter spacing
GetTextColor	Gets the current text colour
GetTextExtent	Determines dimensions of a string
GetTextFace	Gets typeface name of the current font
GetTextMetrics	Gets the metrics for the current font
GetTickCount	Returns amount of time Windows has been running
GetTimerResolution	Gets the timer resolution
GetTopWindow	Returns handle for top child of given window
GetUpdateRect	Returns window update region dimensions
GetUpdateRgn	Returns window update region
GetVersion	Returns the current Dos and Windows versions
GetViewportExt	Gets viewport extent
GetViewportOrg	Gets viewport origin
GetWinDebugInfo	Queries current system-debugging information
GetWindow	Returns specified window handle
GetWindowDC	Returns window device context
GetWindowExt	Gets window extents
GetWindowExtEx	Gets window extents
GetWindowLong	Returns long value from extra window memory
GetWindowOrg	Gets window origin
GetWindowPlacement	Returns window show state and min/max position
GetWindowRect	Gets a window's coordinates
GetWindowsDir	Returns the Windows directory
GetWindowsDirectory	Returns the Windows directory
Global32Alloc	Allocates a USE32 memory object
GlobalAlloc	Allocates memory from the global heap
GlobalCompact	Generates free global memory by compacting
GlobalDeleteAtom	Decrements a global atom's reference count

GlobalDosAlloc	Allocates memory available to DOS in real mode
GlobalDosFree	Frees global memory allocated by GlobalDosAlloc
GlobalReAlloc	Changes size/attributes of global memory object
GlobalSize	Returns the size of a global memory object
GrayString	Draws gray text at the specified location
HiliteMenuItem	Changes highlight of top-level menu item
Hmemcpy	Copies bytes
InflateRect	Changes rectangle dimensions
InsertMenu	Inserts a new item in a menu
InterruptRegister	Installs function to handle system interrupts
InterruptUnRegister	Removes function that processed system interrupts
InvertRect	Inverts a rectangular region
InvertRgn	Inverts the colours in a region
IsCharAlpha	Determines if a character is alphabetical
IsCharAlphaNumeric	Determines is a character is alphanumeric
IsCharLower	Determines if a character is lower case
IsCharUpper	Determines if a character is upper case
IsChild	Determines if a window is a child
IsIconic	Determines if a window is minimized
IsMenu	Determines if a menu handle is valid
IsRectEmpty	Determines whether rectangle is empty
IsTask	Determines whether a task handle is valid
IsWindow	Determines if a window handle is valid
IsWindowEnabled	Determines if a window accepts user input
IsWindowVisible	Determines visibility state of a window
IsZoomed	Determines if a window is maximized
KillTimer	Removes a timer
LineTo	Draws a line from the current position
LoadAccelerators	Loads an accelerator table
LoadBitmap	Loads a bitmap resource
LoadCursor	Loads a cursor resource
LoadIcon	Loads an icon resource
LoadLibrary	Returns a handle to a library module
LoadMenu	Loads a menu resource
LoadModule	Loads and executes a program
LoadResource	Returns a handle to a resource
LoadString	Loads a string resource
LocalAlloc	Allocate memory from the local heap
LocalFree	Frees a local memory object
LocalHandle	Returns the handle of a local memory object
LogError	Identifies an error message
LogParamError	Identifies a parameter validation error
LPtoDP	Converts logical points to device points
lstrcat	Appends one string to another
lstrcmp	Compares two character strings
lstrcmpi	Compares two character strings
lstrcpy	Copies a string to a buffer

lstrlen	Returns the number of characters in a string
LZClose	Closes a file
LZCopy	Copies a file and expands it if compressed
LZDone	Frees buffers allocated by LZStart
LZInit	Initializes data structures needed for decompression
LZOpenFile	Opens a file (both compressed and uncompressed)
LZRead	Reads a specified number of bytes from a compressed file
LZSeek	Repositions pointer in file
LZStart	Allocates buffers for CopyLZFile function
MemManInfo	Gets information about the memory manager
MemoryRead	Reads memory from an arbitrary global heap object
MemoryWrite	Writes memory to an arbitrary global heap object
MessageBeep	Generates a beep
MessageBox	Creates a message-box window
ModifyMenu	Changes an existing menu item
ModuleFindHandle	Gets information about a module
ModuleFindName	Gets information about a module
ModuleFirst	Gets information about first module
ModuleNext	Gets information about next module
MoveTo	Moves the current position
MoveToEx	Moves the current position
MoveWindow	Changes the position and dimensions of a window
MulDiv	Multiplies two values and divides the result
NetBIOSCall	Issues a NETBIOS Interrupt 5Ch
OemKeyScan	Maps OEM ASCII to scan codes
OemToAnsi	Translates an OEM string to a Windows string
OffsetClipRgn	Moves a clipping region
OffsetRect	Moves a rectangle by an offset
OffsetRgn	Moves a region by a specified offset
OffsetViewportOrg	Moves viewport origin
OffsetViewportOrgEx	Moves viewport origin
OffsetWindowOrg	Moves window origin
OffsetWindowOrgEx	Moves window origin
OleActivate	Activates an object
OleBlockServer	Queues incoming requests for the server
OleClose	Closes specified object
OleCopyFromLink	Makes an embedded copy of a linked object
OleCopyToClipboard	Puts the specified object on the clipboard
OleCreate	Creates an object of a specified class
OleCreateFromClip	Creates an object from the clipboard
OleCreateFromFile	Creates an object from a file
OleCreateInvisible	Creates an object without displaying it
OleDelete	Deletes an object
OleDraw	Draws an object into a device context
OleEnumFormats	Enumerates data formats for an object
OleEnumObjects	Enumerates objects in a document
OleEqual	Compares two objects for equality

OleExecute	Sends DDE execute commands to a server
OleGetData	Gets data for an object in a specified format
OleReconnect	Reconnects to an open linked object
OleRegisterClientDoc	Registers a document with the library
OleRegisterServer	Registers the specified server
OleRegisterServerDoc	Registers document with server library
OleRelease	Releases an object from memory
OleRename	Informs library an object is renamed
OleRenameClientDoc	Informs library a document is renamed
OleRenameServerDoc	Informs library a document is renamed
OleRequestData	Gets data from a server in a specified format
OleRevertClientDoc	Informs library a doc reverted to saved state
OleRevertServerDoc	Informs library a doc is reset to saved state
OleRevokeClientDoc	Informs library a document is not open
OleRevokeObject	Revokes access to an object
OleRevokeServer	Revokes the specified server
OleRevokeServerDoc	Revokes the specified document
OleSavedClientDoc	Informs library a doc has been saved
OleSavedServerDoc	Informs library a doc has been saved
OleSaveToStream	Saves an object to the stream
OleSetBounds	Sets bounding rectangle for object
OleSetColorScheme	Specifies client's recommended object colours
OleSetData	Sends data in specified format to server
OleSetHostNames	Sets client name and object name for server
OleSetTargetDevice	Sets target device for an object
OleUnblockServer	Processes requests from queue
OleUnlockServer	Releases server locked with OleLockServer
OleUpdate	Updates an object
OpenClipboard	Opens the clipboard
OpenComm	Opens a communications device
OpenDriver	Opens an installable driver
OpenFile	Creates, opens, reopens or deletes a file
OpenIcon	Activates a minimized window
OutputDebugString	Sends a character string to the debugger
PaintRgn	Fills region with brush in device context
PatBlt	Creates a bitmap pattern
PeekMessage	Checks message queue
Pie	Draws a pie-shaped wedge
PlayMetaFile	Plays a metafile
PlayMetaFileRecord	Plays a metafile record
Polygon	Draws a polygon
Polyline	Draws line segments to connect specified points
PolyPolygon	Draws a series of polygons
PostAppMessage	Posts a message to an application
PostMessage	Places a message in a window's message queue
PostQuitMessage	Tells Windows that an application is terminating
PrintDlg	Creates a print-text dialog box

PtInRect	Determines if a point is in a rectangle
PtInRegion	Queries whether a point is in a region
PtVisible	Queries whether point is within clipping region
QueryAbort	Queries whether to terminate a print job
QuerySendMessage	Determines if a message originated within a task
ReadComm	Reads from a communications device
RealizePalette	Maps entries from logical to system palette
Rectangle	Draws a rectangle
RectInRegion	Queries whether rectangle overlaps region
RectVisible	Queries whether rectangle is in clip region
RedrawWindow	Updates a client rectangle or region
RegisterClass	Registers a window class
RegisterClipboardFormat	Registers a new clipboard format
RegisterDialogClasses	Registers dialog classes for screen-savers
RegisterWindowMessage	Defines a new unique window message
RegOpenKey	Opens a key
RegQueryValue	Gets text string for specified key
RegSetValue	Associates a text string with a specified key
ReleaseCapture	Releases mouse capture
ReleaseDC	Frees a device context
RemoveFontResource	Removes font resource
RemoveMenu	Deletes a menu item and pop-up menu
RemoveProp	Removes a property-list entry
ReplaceText	Creates a replace-text dialog box
ReplyMessage	Replies to a SendMessage
ResetDC	Updates a device context
ResizePalette	Changes the size of a logical palette
RestoreDC	Restores device context
RoundRect	Draws a rectangle with rounded corners
SaveDC	Saves current state of device context
ScaleViewportExt	Scales viewport extents
ScaleViewportExtEx	Scales viewport extents
ScaleWindowExt	Scales window extents
ScaleWindowExtEx	Scales window extents
ScreenSaverProc	Processes input to a screen-saver window
ScreenToClient	Converts screen point to client coordinates
ScrollDC	Scrolls a rectangle horizontally and vertically
ScrollWindow	Scrolls a window's client area
ScrollWindowEx	Scrolls a window's client area
SelectClipRgn	Selects clipping region for device context
SelectObject	Selects object into a device context
SelectPalette	Selects a palette into a device context
SendDlgItemMessage	Sends a message to a dialog box control
SendDriverMessage	Sends a message to an installable driver
SendMessage	Sends a message to a window
SetAbortProc	Sets the abort function for a print job
SetActiveWindow	Makes a top-level window active

SetBitmapBits	Sets bitmap bits from array of bytes
SetBitmapDimension	Sets width and height of bitmap
SetBitmapDimensionEx	Sets width and height of bitmap
SetBkColor	Sets the current background colour
SetBkMode	Sets the background mode
SetBoundsRect	Controls bounding-rectangle accumulation
SetBrushOrg	Sets the origin of the current brush
SetCapture	Sets the mouse capture to a window
SetClassLong	Sets a long value in extra class memory
SetClassWord	Sets a word value in extra class memory
SetClipboardData	Sets the data in the clipboard
SetClipboardViewer	Adds a window to the clipboard-viewer chain
SetCommBreak	Suspends character transmission
SetCommEventMask	Enables events in a device event mask
SetCommState	Sets communications-device state
SetCursor	Changes the mouse cursor
SetCursorPos	Sets mouse-cursor position in screen coordinates
SetDIBits	Sets the bits of a bitmap
SetDIBitsToDevice	Sets DIB bits to device
SetDlgItemInt	Converts an integer to a dialog text string
SetDlgItemText	Sets dialog title or item text
SetDoubleClickTime	Sets the mouse double-click time
SetErrorMode	Controls Interrupt 24h Error Handling
SetFocus	Sets the input focus to a window
SetHandleCount	Changes the number of available file handles
SetKeyboardState	Sets the keyboard state table
SetMapMode	Sets mapping mode
SetMapperFlags	Sets font-mapper flag
SetMenu	Sets the menu for a window
SetMenuItemBitmaps	Associates bitmaps with a menu item
SetMessageQueue	Creates a new message queue
SetMetaFileBits	Creates memory block from metafile
SetMetaFileBitsBetter	Creates memory block from metafile
SetPaletteEntries	Sets colours and flags for a colour palette
SetParent	Changes a child's parent window
SetPixel	Sets pixel to specified colour
SetPolyFillMode	Sets the polygon-filling mode
SetProp	Adds or changes a property-list entry
SetRect	Sets a rectangle's dimensions
SetRectEmpty	Creates an empty rectangle
SetRectRgn	Changes a region into specified rectangle
SetResourceHandler	Installs a load-resource callback function
SetScrollPos	Sets scroll-bar thumb position
SetScrollRange	Sets minimum and maximum scroll-bar positions
SetSelectorBase	Sets the base and limit of a selector
SetSelectorLimit	Sets the limit of a selector
SetStretchBltMode	Sets the bitmap-stretching mode

SetSwapAreaSize	Sets the amount of memory used for code segments
SetSysColors	Sets one or more system colours
SetSysModalWindow	Makes a window the system-modal window
SetSystemPaletteUse	Use of system palette static colours
SetTextAlign	Sets text-alignment flags
SetTextColor	Sets the foreground colour of text
SetTextJustification	Sets alignment for text output
SetTimer	Installs a system timer
SetViewportExt	Sets viewport extents
SetViewportOrg	Sets viewport origin
SetWinDebugInfo	Sets current system-debugging information
SetWindowExt	Sets window extents
SetWindowOrg	Sets the window origin
SetWindowPlacement	Sets window show state and min/max position
SetWindowPos	Sets a windows size, position, and order
SetWindowsHook	Installs a hook function
SetWindowText	Sets text in a caption title or control window
SetWindowWord	Sets a word value in extra window memory
ShellExecute	Opens or prints specified file
ShowCursor	Shows or hides the mouse cursor
ShowScrollBar	Shows or hides a scroll bar
ShowWindow	Sets window visibility state
SizeofResource	Returns the size of a resource
SpoolFile	Puts a file in the spooler queue
StartDoc	Starts a print job
StartPage	Prepares printer driver to receive data
StretchBlt	Copies a bitmap, transforming if required
StretchDIBits	Moves DIB from source to destination rectangle
SubtractRect	Creates rect from difference of two rects
SwapMouseButton	Reverses the meaning of the mouse buttons
SwitchStackBack	Restores the current-task stack
SwitchStackTo	Changes the location of the stack
SystemHeapInfo	Gets information about the USER heap
SystemParametersInfo	Queries or sets system wide parameters
TaskFindHandle	Gets information about a task
TaskFirst	Gets information about first task in task queue
TaskGetCSIP	Returns the next CS:IP value of a task.
TaskNext	Gets information about next task in the task queue
TaskSetCSIP	Sets the CS:IP of a sleeping task.
TaskSwitch	Switches to a specific address within a new task
TerminateApp	Terminates an application
TextOut	Writes a character string at specified location
Throw	Restores the execution environment
TimerCount	Gets execution times
ToAscii	Translates virtual-key code to Windows character
TrackPopupMenu	Displays and tracks a pop-up menu
TranslateAccelerator	Processes menu command keyboard accelerators

TranslateMDISysAccel	Processes MDI keyboard accelerators
TranslateMessage	Translates virtual-key messages
TransmitCommChar	Places a character in the transmit queue
UnAllocDiskSpace	Deletes the file created by AllocDiskSpace.
UnAllocFileHandles	Frees file handles allocated by AllocFileHandles.
UngetCommChar	Puts a character back in the receive queue
UnhookWindowsHook	Removes a filter function
UnionRect	Creates the union of two rectangles
UnrealizeObject	Resets brush origins and realizes palettes
UnregisterClass	Removes a window class
UpdateColors	Updates colours in client area
UpdateWindow	Updates a window's client area
ValidateCodeSegments	Test for memory overwrites
ValidateFreeSpaces	Checks free memory for valid contents
ValidateRect	Removes a rectangle from the update region
ValidateRgn	Removes a region from the update region
VerFindFile	Determines where to install a file
VerInstallFile	Installs a file
VerLanguageName	Converts a binary language identifier into a string
VerQueryValue	Returns version information about a block
VkKeyScan	Translates Windows character to virtual-key code
WaitMessage	Suspends an application and yields control
WindowFromPoint	Returns window containing a point
WinExec	Runs a program
WinHelp	Invokes Windows Help
WNetAddConnection	Adds network connections
WNetCancelConnection	Removes network connections
WNetGetConnection	Lists network connections
WriteComm	Writes to a communications device
WriteProfileString	Writes a string to WIN.INI
wvsprintf	Formats a string
Yield	Stops the current task

D.4 System unit

The System unit contains Delphi run-time library, which implements low-level run-time support routines for all built-in features. These include:

Abs	Returns the absolute value of the argument
Addr	Returns the address of a specified object
Append	Opens an existing file for appending
ArcTan	Returns the arctangent of the argument
Assign	Assigns the name of an external file to a file variable
Assigned	Tests to determine if a pointer or procedural variable is nil
BlockRead	Reads one or more records into a variable

BlockWrite	Writes one or more records from a variable
Break	Terminates a for, while, or repeat statement
ChDir	Changes the current directory
Chr	Returns a character with a specified ordinal number
Close	Closes an open file
Concat	Concatenates a sequence of strings
Continue	Continues a for, while, or repeat statement
Copy	Returns a substring of a string
Cos	Returns the cosine of the argument
CSeg	Returns the current value of the CS register
Dec	Decrements a variable
Delete	Deletes a substring from a string
Dispose	Disposes of a dynamic variable
DSeg	Returns the current value of the DS register
Eof	Returns the end-of-file status
Eoln	Returns the end-of-line status of a text file
Erase	Erases an external file
Exit	Exits immediately from the current block
Exclude	Excludes an element from a set
Exp	Returns the exponential of the argument
FilePos	Returns the current file position of a file
FileSize	Returns the current size of a file
FillChar	Fills contiguous bytes with a specified value
Flush	Flushes the buffer of a text file open for output
Frac	Returns the fractional part of the argument
Free	Destroys an object instance
FreeMem	Disposes of a dynamic variable of a given size
GetDir	Returns the current directory of specified drive
GetMem	Creates a dynamic variable of the specified size
Halt	Stops program execution
Hi	Returns the high-order byte of the argument
High	Returns the highest value in the range of the argument
Inc	Increments a variable
Include	Includes an element from a set
Insert	Inserts a substring into a string
Int	Returns the integer part of the argument
IOResult	Returns the status of the last I/O operation performed
Length	Returns the dynamic length of a string
Ln	Returns the natural logarithm of the argument
Lo	Returns the low-order Byte of the argument
Low	Returns the lowest value in the range of the argument
MaxAvail	Returns the size of the largest free block in the heap
MemAvail	Returns the amount of all free memory in the heap
MkDir	Creates a subdirectory
Move	Copies bytes from source to destination
New	Creates a new dynamic variable
Odd	Tests if the argument is an odd number

Ofs	Returns the offset of a specified object
Ord	Returns the ordinal number of an ordinal-type value
ParamCount	Returns the number of parameters passed
ParamStr	Returns a specified command-line parameter
Pi	Returns the value of pi
Pos	Searches for a substring in a string
Pred	Returns the predecessor of the argument
Ptr	Converts a segment base and an offset address to a pointer
Random	Returns a random number
Randomize	Initializes the built-in random number generator
Rcad	Rcads a file component into a variable
Readln	As Read procedure, then skips to the next line of the file
Rename	Renames an external file
Reset	Opens an existing file
Rewrite	Creates and opens a new file
RmDir	Removes an empty subdirectory
Round	Rounds a real-type value to an integer-type value
RunError	Stops program execution
ScrollTo	Scrolls the CRT window to show virtual screen location
Seek	Moves the current position of a file to a specified component
SeekEof	Returns thc cnd-of-filc status of a file
SeekEoln	Returns the end-of-line status of a file
Seg	Returns the segment of a specified object
SetTextBuf	Assigns an I/O buffer to a text file
Sin	Returns the sine of the argument
SizeOf	Returns the number of bytes occupied by the argument
SPtr	Returns the current value of the SP register
Sqr	Returns the square of the argument
Sqrt	Returns the square root of the argument
SSeg	Returns the current value of the SS register
Str	Converts a numeric value to a string
Succ	Returns the successor of the argument
Swap	Swaps the high- and low-order bytes of the argument
Trunc	Truncates a real-type value to an integer-type value
Truncate	Truncates the file at the current file position
TypeOf	Returns a pointer to an object type's virtual method table
UpCase	Converts a character to uppercase
Val	Converts a string value to its numeric representation
Write	Writes a variable into a file component
Writeln	As Write procedure, but outputs an end-of-line marker

D.5 Dialogs unit

The Dialogs unit contains common dialog boxes which are found on the Dialogs page of the Component palette and routines for displaying message boxes. The routines include:

InputBox	Displays an input dialog box for string entry
InputQuery	Displays an input dialog box for string entry
MessageDlg	Displays a message dialog box
ShowMessagePos	Displays a message box with an OK button
ShowMessage	Displays a message box with an OK button

Miscellaneous

E.1 Structure charts

A structure chart is one method used in the design of structured software. Its approach is similar to schematic diagrams used in electronic design where graphical objects represent electronic devices. The structure chart represents each of the functions (or modules) by rectangular boxes, and the relationship between them is represented by connecting arrows. Data flow is also represented by connecting arrows with a circle at their end. If data goes into a module the arrow points into the module, else if it is being returned then the arrow points away from it. Repetition is denoted by a curved arrow and a decision by a diamond. The standard notation for structure charts is given in Figure E.1.

Figure E.2 shows how the flow of data is represented. The main module represents the controlling module (that is, the main program). The diagram shows that `main` initially calls module `mod1` and passes the parameter `val1` to it. This module then returns `val2` back to `main`. This value is then passed into `mod2` which in turn passes back `val3` to `main`. Figure E.3 shows an example of a decision and iteration. The parameter which controls the decision or iteration may also be shown on the chart.

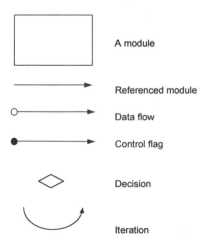

Figure E.1   Structure chart notation

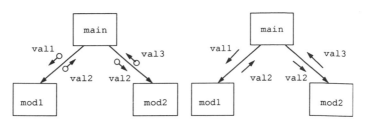

Standard notation   Other possible notation

Figure E.2   Data flow representation

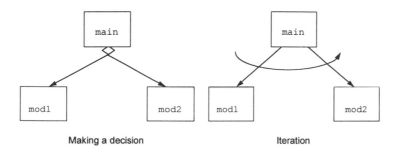

Making a decision   Iteration

Figure E.3   Decisions and iteration

E.2 Programs with errors

The following program have either one or two compiler errors. Locate these
errors and correct the programs.

📋 Program E.1

```
program test(input,output)

(* Three compiler errors *)

var value1,value2,average;

begin
     writeln('Enter value 1 >>');
     readln(value1);
     writeln('Enter value 2 >>');
     readln(value2);

     average:=(value1+value2/2;
     writeln('Average is ',average:8:2);
end.
```

Program E.2

```
program test(input,output);

(* Two compiler errors *)

var value:real;

begin
    writeln('Enter a value >>');
    readln(value);

    result:=sqrt(value);
    writeln('Square root is ',result:8:2);
end;
```

Program E.3

```
program test(input,output);

(* Two compiler errors

var value, result:real;

begin

    writeln('Enter a value  >>');
    readln(value);

    result:=sqr(value);
    writeln('Square is ',result:8:2);
end;
```

Program E.4

```
program test(input,output);

(* Two compiler errors *)

var value:real;

begin

    writeln('Enter a value  >>');
    readln(value);

    if (value<0)
       writeln('Can not calculate square root of a negative')
    else
       writeln('Square root is ',sqrt(val):8:2);

end.
```

Program E.5

```
program test(input,output);

(* Two compiler errors *)

var value1,value2,largest:real;

    writeln('Enter two values  >>');
    readln(value1,value2);

    if (value1>value2) then
        largest:=value1;
    else
        largest:=value2;

    writeln('Largest value is ',largest:8:2);
end.
```

Program E.6

```
program test(input,output);

(* Two compiler errors *)

var value1,value2:real;

begin
    writeln('Enter two values  >>');
    readln(value1,value2);

    if (value2>value1) then
    begin
        (* swap values *)
        temp:=value1;
        value1:=value2;
        value2:=temp;

    writeln('Largest value is ',value1:8:2);
    writeln('Smallest value is ',value2:8:2);
end.
```

Program E.7

```
program test(input,output);

(* Two compiler errors *)

var value1,value2:real;

begin
    writeln('Enter two values  >>');
    readln(value1,value2);
```

```
        if (value2>value1) then
        begin
               (* swap values *)
               temp:=value1;
               value1:=value2;
               value2:=temp;

        writeln('Largest value is ',value1:8:2);
        writeln('Smallest value is ',value2:8:2);
end.
```

Program E.8

```
program test(input,output);

(* Two compiler errors *)

var value:real;

begin

      repeat
             writeln('Enter a positive value >>');
             readln(value);
      until (value>0)

      writeln('Square root is ,sqrt(value));
end.
```

Program E.9

```
program test(input,output);

(* Two compiler errors *)

var value:real;

begin

      repeat
             writeln('Enter a value between 0 and 100>>');
             readln(value);
      until (0<value>100);

      writeln('Square root is ',sqrt(value));
end.
```

Program E.10

```
program test(input,output);

(* Two compiler errors *)

var value,ch:real
```

```
begin

    repeat
         writeln('Enter a value >>');
         readln(value);
         writeln('Square root is ',sqrt(value));
         writeln('Do you wish to continue >>');
         readln(ch);
    until (ch='n');

end.
```

Program E.11
```
program test(input,output);

(* Two compiler errors *)

var i,sqr_value,cube_value:real;

begin

    for i:=1 to 10 do
    begin
         sqr_value:=i*i;
         cude_value:=i*i*i;
         writeln(i:8,sqr_value:8,cube_value:8);
    end;
end.
```

Program E.12
```
program test(input,output);

(* Two compiler errors *)

var i:integer;

begin

    for i=1 to 10 do
    begin
         x:=10*i;
         y:=4*x+1;
         writeln(x:8:2,y:8:2);
    end;
end.
```

Program E.13
```
program test(input,output);

(* Two compiler errors *)

var value1,value2,result:integer;
```

```
function add_values(a,b:integer):integer;
begin
     add:=a+b;
end;

begin
     writeln('Enter two values >> ');
     readln(value1,value2);

     result=add_values(value1,value2);
     writeln('Added the result is ',result);

end.
```

▢ Program E.14

```
program test(input,output);

(* One compiler error *)

var value1,value2,result:integer;

function add_values(a:integer):integer;
begin
     add_values:=a+b;
end;

begin
     writeln('Enter two values >> ');
     readln(value1,value2);

     result:=add_values(value1,value2);
     writeln('Added the result is ',result);
end.
```

▢ Program E.15

```
program test(input,output);

(* Two compiler errors *)

var invalue:real;

function get_real(min,max:real):real;
begin
     repeat
          writeln('Enter a value >> ');
          readln(val);
          if ((val<0) or (val>max)) then
              writeln('INVALID');
     until ((val>min) and (val<max));
end;

begin
     invalue:=get_real(0,100);
     writeln('Input value is ',invalue);
end.
```

⬜ Program E.16

```pascal
program test(input,output);

(* Two compiler errors *)

var invalue:real;

procedure get_real(min,max:real;var val);
begin
    repeat
        writeln('Enter a value >> ');
        readln(val);
        if ((val<0) or (val>max)) then
            writeln('INVALID');
    until ((val>min) and (val<max));
end;

begin
    get_real(0,100,invalue);
    writeln('Input value is 'invalue);
end.
```

Index